INTERDISCIPLINARITY

Second Edition

Joe Moran

Routledge
Taylor & Francis Group

LONDON AND NEW YORK

First edition published 2002
by Routledge
Second edition published 2010
by Routledge
2 Park Square, Milton Park, Abingdon, Oxon OX14 4RN

Simultaneously published in the USA and Canada
by Routledge
270 Madison Avenue, New York, NY 10016

Routledge is an imprint of the Taylor & Francis Group, an informa business

Typeset in Garamond by Taylor and Francis Books
Printed and bound in Great Britain by TJ International Ltd, Padstow, Cornwall

British Library Cataloguing in Publication Data
A catalogue record for this book is available from the British Library

Library of Congress Cataloging-in-Publication Data
Moran, Joe, 1970–
Interdisciplinarity / by Joe Moran.
p.   cm. -- (The new critical idiom)
Includes bibliographical references and index.
1. English literature--History and criticism--Theory, etc.   2. English
literature--Study and teaching.   3. Interdisciplinary approach in
education.   I. Title.
PR21.M67 2010
820.9'0001--dc22
2009030557

ISBN10: 0-415-56006-3 (hbk)
ISBN10: 0-415-56007-8 (pbk)
ISBN10: 0-203-86618-5 (ebk)

ISBN13: 978-0-415-56006-1 (hbk)
ISBN13: 978-0-415-56007-8 (pbk)
ISBN13: 978-0-203-86618-4 (ebk)

Contents

SERIES EDITOR'S PREFACE

The New Critical Idiom is a series of introductory books which seeks to extend the lexicon of literary terms, in order to address the radical changes which have taken place in the study of literature during the last decades of the twentieth century. The aim is to provide clear, well-illustrated accounts of the full range of terminology currently in use, and to evolve histories of its changing usage.

The current state of the discipline of literary studies is one where there is considerable debate concerning basic questions of terminology. This involves, among other things, the boundaries which distinguish the literary from the non-literary; the position of literature within the larger sphere of culture; the relationship between literatures of different cultures; and questions concerning the relation of literary to other cultural forms within the context of interdisciplinary studies.

It is clear that the field of literary criticism and theory is a dynamic and heterogeneous one. The present need is for individual volumes on terms which combine clarity of exposition with an adventurousness of perspective and a breadth of application. Each volume will contain as part of its apparatus some indication of the direction in which the definition of particular terms is likely to move, as well as expanding the disciplinary boundaries within which some of these terms have been traditionally contained. This will involve some re-situation of terms within the larger field of cultural representation, and will introduce examples from the area of film and the modern media in addition to examples from a variety of literary texts.

Preface to the Second Edition

There is a page on Wikipedia that claims to list all the academic disciplines, and arrives at the modest total number of forty-two, which is coincidentally the answer the supercomputer Deep Thought gives to 'The Ultimate Question of Life, the Universe and Everything' in Douglas Adams's *A Hitchhiker's Guide to the Galaxy*. The Internet is sometimes accused of turning the sum of human knowledge into an undisciplined hotchpotch, disseminated by a chaotic babble of contending voices with erratic levels of authority and expertise. So it is rather touching that the world's most celebrated e-encyclopaedia should be so attached to the idea of disciplined, ordered thought.

In fact, Wikipedia is just one example of the resilience of the idea of disciplines in an interdisciplinary age. Interdisciplinarity is even more of a buzzword than it was when I completed the first edition of this book. Almost all academic journals, in their mission statements, now claim to be 'interdisciplinary'; so do many academic departments (particularly English departments) and even entire universities. However, there has also been something of a reaction in literary studies, much of it healthy, against the unreflexive use of the term 'interdisciplinary'.

This second edition attempts to do several things, mainly in a new conclusion on 'interdisciplinarity today' which surveys developments in this area since the book was first published. First, it explores the current state of interdisciplinary literary studies, particularly the efforts to engage with a moment 'post-theory' or 'after theory' through various forms of neo-historicism, and the impact of the expanding area of the digital humanities, with its challenge to conventional notions of what constitutes a text. Second, it aims to introduce students to the institutional politics of interdisciplinarity in a way that I did only briefly at the end of the first edition. Finally, it explores the potential for interdisciplinary work in two contrasting areas: Victorian studies and contemporary literary and cultural studies. It suggests that interdisciplinary developments in English have often been most exciting and innovative when they have taken place within recognized sub-fields with some of the characteristics of disciplines. My conclusion is therefore a return to one of the central arguments of the first edition: that the very idea of interdisciplinarity can only be understood in a disciplinary context.

I have also updated some of the references and examples in the rest of the text, extended the bibliography and included a section on further reading for more advanced discussion of both the problems and potential of interdisciplinarity.

Joe Moran, July 2009

ACKNOWLEDGEMENTS

I am very grateful to the series editor, John Drakakis, for his careful reading of the manuscript and many helpful suggestions; Liz Thompson and Emma Nugent at Routledge for their editorial advice and support; my father, for reading through and commenting on the book in draft form; and my brother, Liam, for helping with scientific queries.

This book has developed over several years of teaching, reading and talking to others about interdisciplinarity, and I have incurred many debts. I have learned most from working with students and colleagues in an interdisciplinary department at Liverpool John Moores University, and I would like to dedicate this book to them.

INTRODUCTION

Before we go any further here, has it ever occurred to any of you that all of this is simply one grand misunderstanding? Since you're not here to learn anything, but to be taught so you can pass these tests, knowledge has to be organized so that it can be taught, and it has to be reduced to information so it can be organized, do you follow that? In other words this leads you to assume that organization is an inherent property of the knowledge itself, and that disorder and chaos are simply irrelevant forces that threaten it from outside. In fact it's exactly the opposite. Order is simply a thin, perilous condition we try to impose on the basic reality of chaos ...

(Gaddis 1976: 20)

This book is about how we organize knowledge into disciplines, and then reorganize it into new configurations and alliances, or forms of 'interdisciplinarity', when these old ways of thinking have come to seem stale, irrelevant, inflexible or exclusory. 'Interdisciplinarity' has become a buzzword across many different academic subjects in recent years, but it is rarely interrogated in any great detail. As Alan Liu puts it, interdisciplinary study is 'the most seriously underthought critical, pedagogical and institutional concept in the modern academy' (Liu 1989: 743). This book aims to examine the ways in which interdisciplinarity has been variously defined, and the debates that have been conducted about its meaning, purpose and practical applications. Within this larger topic, it also has a more specific aim: to introduce students working within the field of literary studies to interdisciplinary perspectives from other fields such as cultural studies, sociology, anthropology, philosophy, psychoanalysis, history, geography and the sciences.

My main argument will be that we cannot understand interdisciplinarity without first examining the existing disciplines, since interdisciplinary approaches are always an engagement with them, and the modes of knowledge that they exclude by virtue of their separation from each other. The term 'discipline' has two principal modern usages: it refers to a particular branch of learning or body of knowledge, and to the maintenance of order and control amongst subordinated groups such as soldiers, prison inmates or school pupils, often through the threat of physical or other forms of punishment. Interestingly, these two usages converged in some of the earlier uses of the term, from the first half of the fifteenth century onwards. 'Discipline' in this context suggested a particular kind of moral training aimed at teaching proper conduct, order and self-control. In fact, the very notion of the term as a recognized mode of learning implies the establishment of hierarchy and the operation of power: it derives from the Latin, *disciplina*, which refers to the instruction of disciples by their elders, and it necessarily alludes to a specialized, valued knowledge which some people possess and others do not. As the *Oxford English Dictionary* points out, one of the earliest uses of the term in English to mean 'a particular course of instruction to disciples' was in relation to the 'Discipline of the Secret', a phrase used after the Protestant Reformation of the sixteenth century to describe the restrictive practices in the early Christian Church which taught the elements of the faith to converts while excluding them from heathens and the uninitiated. From the beginning, the term 'discipline' was caught up in questions about the relationship between knowledge and power.

When we use the word 'interdisciplinary', we are generally suggesting some kind of critical awareness of this relationship. As Roberta Frank argues:

> 'Interdisciplinary' has something to please everyone. Its base, *discipline*, is hoary and antiseptic; its prefix, *inter*, is hairy and friendly. Unlike fields, with their mud, cows, and corn, the Latinate *discipline* comes encased in stainless steel: it suggests something rigorous, aggressive, hazardous to master; *Inter* hints that knowledge is a warm, mutually developing, consultative thing.
>
> (Frank 1988: 100)

According to this sense of the term, 'interdisciplinarity' provides a democratic, dynamic and co-operative alternative to the old-fashioned, inward-looking and cliquish nature of disciplines. And yet this straightforward interpretation begs a number of questions: how exactly does interdisciplinary research aspire to be 'warm, mutually developing, consultative'? Can disciplinary divisions be so easily broken down or transcended? Is it not inevitable that there should be some means of ordering and structuring knowledge? In order to start exploring some of these questions, it might be helpful to begin by looking at the historical development of the academic disciplines.

THE RISE OF THE DISCIPLINES

The idea of shaping knowledge into disciplines can be traced as far back as Greek philosophy. Aristotle, for example, organized different subjects into a hierarchy, according to whether they were theoretical, practical or productive. The theoretical subjects were the highest form of knowledge, and comprised theology, mathematics and physics, in descending order of importance; the practical subjects included ethics and politics; and the productive subjects, which were the lowest in the hierarchy, included the fine arts, poetics and engineering (Aristotle 1947: I, 3–13, 293–9; II, 85–9). By constructing such a schema, Aristotle employed two guiding principles which have also been central to the subsequent development of the disciplines. First, he attempted to establish a clear hierarchy between the different academic subjects. Broadly speaking, the development of disciplines has not merely created self-contained bodies of knowledge, happy in their isolation; it has been accompanied by frequent attempts to assert the superiority of certain fields of learning over others. In particular, there has been a centuries-old debate about the relative merits of 'useful' areas of knowledge that set themselves limited aims but clearly achieve them; and more nebulously defined areas of knowledge that are more ambitious and wide-ranging but not so obviously 'useful'. Aristotle clearly preferred speculative knowledge for its own sake, believing that 'there is a kind of education in which parents should have their sons trained not because it is necessary, or because it is useful, but simply because it is liberal and something good in itself' (Aristotle 1961: 337). Second, he recognized that the ordering of knowledge into disciplines was necessary but regrettable, and so he positioned *philosophy* as the universal field of inquiry which brought together all the different branches of learning, a notion of unity in difference which also influenced the formation of the disciplines within the modern university. As Aristotle's system makes clear, anxieties about the harmful specialization of knowledge are as old as the scholarly disciplines themselves.

The classical divisions of knowledge proved remarkably resilient over the following centuries, but they were eventually transformed by market forces and institutional changes. The development and consolidation of disciplines in the modern era was fundamentally related to both the growth of universities and the increasing complexity of European societies. By the late Middle Ages, as universities in cities like Salerno, Bologna, Paris, Oxford and Cambridge replaced the medieval schools or *studia generalia*, the term 'discipline' was being applied to professions such as medicine, law and theology because of the perceived need to relate education to specific economic, political and ecclesiastical ends (Klein 1990: 20). But there was still a powerful notion that disciplines were not an entirely positive development: until at least the end of the eighteenth century, university students tended to study a core curriculum of the liberal arts, divided into the *trivium* (logic, grammar, rhetoric) and the *quadrivium* (arithmetic, geometry, astronomy and music). They then went on to specialize in the faculties of medicine, law or theology, rather as American students today choose to 'major' in a subject. Disciplinary development was meant to occur within the overall framework of the university as a community of essentially like-minded scholars: indeed, the term 'university' derives from the Latin, *universitas*, meaning 'universal' or 'whole'.

This sense of universality was threatened by the values of the Enlightenment, a European-wide intellectual movement which emerged in the late seventeenth and eighteenth centuries and which sponsored revolutionary changes in art, science, politics and philosophy. Although Enlightenment thought was complex and heterogeneous, it is broadly true that philosophers at this time placed great emphasis on the progress of human knowledge through the powers of reason and rationality. This pursuit of reason was underpinned by the development of clearer procedures and methodologies within disciplines, and greater specialization of learning, changes that were most keenly felt in the sciences and mathematics. In this sense, Enlightenment thought overlapped with and drew on a 'scientific revolution' occurring in the sixteenth and seventeenth centuries, led by scientists such as Copernicus, Kepler, Galileo and Newton, which overturned the view of the natural order established by the ancient Greeks. The scientific revolution was based on two significant new notions: the view of nature as a well-ordered machine, reducible to a relatively small number of universal rules established by humans; and the development of an empirical method which aimed to deal with problems within specific parameters, based on new methods of induction and deduction to test hypotheses and new experimental apparatus, such as the thermometer, microscope and telescope.

The goal of a scientific discipline was therefore necessarily narrow: to establish the laws that explain natural phenomena within its own field, and thus to account for only a small part of reality. The huge advances in knowledge that the new sciences achieved as a result of limiting their concerns in this way represented a powerful argument in favour of disciplinarity, and the scientific model became extremely influential in the subsequent development of all the disciplines. These intellectual realignments can be seen as part of an overall Enlightenment project of ordering and classifying information. This project drew on earlier works that attempted ambitious taxonomies of knowledge, such as Matthias Martini's *Idea methodica* (1606) and Francis Bacon's unfinished *Instauratio magna scientiarum* (*The Great Restoration of Learning*), a multivolume undertaking that aimed 'to commence a total reconstruction of sciences, arts, and all human knowledge, raised upon the proper foundations' (Bacon [1620] 1980: 2). Bacon's desire to reorganize and consolidate the disciplines stemmed from his belief that science should be a collective project based on the orderly exchange of knowledge between scholars undertaking similar research, so that there would be no time-wasting replication of theories and discoveries.

The Enlightenment enterprise of codifying and categorizing knowledge is perhaps most evident in the development of the modern, native language (non-Latin) encyclopaedia in Europe in the eighteenth century. Drawing on the framework established by thinkers such as Martini and Bacon, works such as Ephraim Chambers' *Cyclopaedia* (1728), the first edition of the *Encyclopaedia Britannica* (1768–71) and, most famously, the French *L'Encyclopédie* (1751–80), edited by Denis Diderot, attempted to make sense of the bewildering array of new disciplines. In many ways, encyclopaedias were a typical product of Enlightenment thinking, in that they aimed to encompass the unity and interdependence of knowledge within a few volumes, while also cataloguing and systematizing it. The mathematician Jean d'Alembert's introduction or *Discours préliminaire* to the first volume of *L'Encyclopédie* in 1751, for example, attempted a hugely ambitious survey of the different branches of learning, while also aiming to show how these branches formed part of a coherent overall structure.

The reconfiguration of the disciplines, and in particular the rapid development and success of the sciences, did not go unchallenged. The Italian thinker, Giambattista Vico, claimed that the ascendancy of science and mathematics had led to the neglect of a broad education in favour of specialist knowledge. If students were taught 'the totality of sciences and arts', he argued, 'they would not feel the impulse to step rashly into discussions while they are still in the process of learning; nor would they, with pedestrian slavishness, refuse to accept any viewpoint unless it has been sanctioned by a teacher' (Vico [1709] 1965: 19). In *La Scienza nuova* (*The New Science*, 1725), Vico claimed that knowledge is always constructed by humans rather than simply discovered in nature. He therefore argued that the 'human sciences' such as history, philosophy and law, which concern themselves with humans and society and can achieve knowledge and understanding 'from within', were superior to the 'natural sciences', which can only describe external phenomena in nature. Vico's advocacy of interdisciplinary study connects with many other forms of interdisciplinarity discussed in this book, because it forms part of his critique of the new knowledge hierarchies that asserted the superiority of the sciences over the humanities disciplines. The reason for the success of the former has remained fairly consistent over the past few hundred years: it is that they are able to limit themselves to certain closely defined fields and controlled situations, and thus produce apparently clearer, more rigorous and effective examples of 'useful knowledge'. Interdisciplinary study within the humanities is often an attempt to challenge the pre-eminence of the sciences as a model for disciplinary development, based on the belief that they can obtain neutral, objective forms of knowledge within their own areas of inquiry.

Up until the nineteenth century, however, most scholarly efforts to determine the relationship between the disciplines took the Aristotelian view that philosophy both integrated and transcended more specialized forms of knowledge. As it has developed over the past few thousand years, philosophy has incorporated many different disciplines that have since become autonomous, such as psychology, sociology, science and mathematics. It remains an extremely wide-ranging and amorphous mode of thought which brings together disparate ideas and activities and which, rather than having a specific subject matter of its own, tends to produce a kind of metacommentary on the subject matter of other disciplines. This notion of philosophy as undisciplined knowledge is retained today in the name of the higher degree of Doctor of Philosophy (the Ph.D.), which is gained through the completion of a research dissertation in any subject. Although many thinkers from the seventeenth century onwards engaged in far-reaching attempts to reorganize knowledge, they still tended to base these classifications on a notion of philosophy as the universal science uniting the disciplines. One of the founders of the new scientific method, René Descartes, for example, argued in *The Principles of Philosophy* (1644) that 'philosophy as a whole is like a tree whose roots are metaphysics, whose trunk is physics, and whose branches, which issue from this trunk, are all the other sciences' (Descartes 1955: 211). Writing 200 years later in his *Course in Positive Philosophy* (1830–42), Auguste Comte, who was instrumental in transferring the methods of the natural sciences to the social sciences, claimed that philosophy was still 'that *sapientia humana* [humane wisdom], at which all separate forms of knowledge are ultimately aiming' (Cassirer 1950: 9).

This argument for the centrality of philosophy sees its most sustained justification in the work of the German thinker, Immanuel Kant. Towards the end of the eighteenth century, Kant made a systematic effort to hierarchize the university's disciplines and to show how this hierarchy reflected innate divisions in knowledge and the natural orderings of the human mind. He argued that the disciplines should thus be treated as discrete and self-contained:

> Every science is a system in its own right; ... we must ... set to work architectonically with it as a separate and independent building. We must treat it as a self-subsisting whole, and not as a wing or section of another building – although we may subsequently make a passage to and fro from one part to another.
>
> (Kant [1790] 1928: 31)

However, in his 1798 essay, *The Conflict of the Faculties*, Kant argued that 'reason' functioned as an ultimate value which transcended disciplinary divisions, and that its natural home within the university was in the 'lower' faculty of philosophy. Unlike the three 'higher' faculties of theology, law and medicine, philosophy had no specific content and did not depend for its existence on any higher authority, such as the Bible, legal statutes or medical scholarship. It could therefore 'use its own judgement about what it teaches ... Accordingly, the government reserves the right itself to *sanction* the teachings of the higher faculties, but those of the lower faculty it leaves up to the scholar's reason'. Kant thought it essential that there should be such a faculty that 'having no commands to give, is free to evaluate everything, and concerns itself with the interest of the sciences, that is, with truth' ([1798] 1992: 27–9). This organization of the university into 'lower' and 'higher' faculties, and the privileging of philosophy as a content-less and unconstrained activity, allowed Kant to retain the ideal of unified knowledge within the reality of ever more specialized university faculties.

Kant's ideas on the university influenced a succeeding genera-tion of German philosophers, including Friedrich Schiller, Wilhelm von Humboldt and Johann Fichte. This group of scholars was instrumental in the formation of the secularized, state-controlled, research-oriented university in Prussia in the early nineteenth century, which became the prototype for the modern European and North American university. Schiller, in his inaugural lecture at the University of Jena (1789), laid the groundwork by promoting the notion of *Bildung*, a broad-based education that formed part of the general development of the student, as opposed to *Ausbildung*, which prepared them for a specific vocation. Humboldt, Fichte and others drew on these ideas and related them to the concept of *Wissenschaft*, a not easily translatable term which essentially refers to an all-round, humane education cultivating the whole personality, rather than just the mind, of the individual. The function of universities, according to Humboldt, was thus to 'lay open the whole body of learning and expound both the principles and the foundations of all knowledge' (Lyotard 1984: 33).

However, this ideal of a non-specialist education was almost immediately threatened by the separation of the sciences from other areas of knowledge in a university system that was increas-ingly well organized and professionalized. Up until the first few decades of the nineteenth century, the word 'science' tended to be used interchangeably with 'philosophy', to mean all forms of knowledge rather than particular branches of it. From the 1830s onwards, however, the term 'science' started to refer specifically to the natural sciences and to be distinguished clearly from philosophy in both academic and general usage. The success of the sciences as self-contained bodies of knowledge within the university was demonstrated by the frequent calls for the social sciences, and even some of the humanities disciplines, to fashion themselves according to hard and rigorous scientific models. Comte, the originator of the term 'sociology' in the 1830s, argued that it was necessary to 'complete the vast intellectual operation that was begun by Bacon, Descartes and Galileo' by applying the scientific method to other areas of knowledge ([1830–42] 1974: 39). He noted the problems caused by 'the compartmentalising of intellectual labour', and still held out the possibility of a general philosophy which would have 'the aim of reducing the totality of acquired knowledge to one single body of homogeneous doctrine' (Comte [1830–42] 1974: 51–2, 39). However, he also claimed that the individual sciences developed according to a logic of their own, and that intellectual divisions could be 'extended with impunity as far as is necessary for the development of the various orders of knowledge' (Comte [1830–42] 1974: 30). This belief, that the clearly defined methods and procedures of the sciences needed to be employed in the non-sciences, was a powerful factor in the development of new social-science and humanities disciplines such as politics, economics, sociology, English and the modern languages in the late nineteenth and early twentieth centuries.

The proliferation of academic disciplines around this time raised concerns about over-specialization, particularly amongst philosophers with more speculative and far-reaching interests. The German thinker, Friedrich Nietzsche, was particularly aware of the ways in which these new configurations of knowledge were bound up with issues of power and self-interest. In his essay, 'We Scholars', he attacked the rise of the disciplines, which he saw as a particular product of the German-influenced research university, and which had led to the displacement of the philosopher by the scientific 'scholar': 'The Declaration of Independence of the man of science, his emancipation from philosophy, is one of the more subtle after-effects of the democratic form and formlessness of life: the self-glorification and presumption of the scholar now stands everywhere in full bloom and in its finest springtime' (Nietzsche [1886] 1990: 129).

He was particularly suspicious of the claim that the disciplines achieved disinterested knowledge by limiting the scale of their operations. For Nietzsche, the specialized scholar was concerned less with knowledge for its own sake than with climbing up the career ladder within an increasingly bureaucratized and profession-alized society, with 'that sunshine of a good name, that constant affirmation of his value and his utility with which his inner *distrust*, the dregs at the heart of all dependent men and herd animals, have again and again to be overcome' ([1886] 1990: 133). More specifically, Nietzsche lamented the decline of philosophy as an undisciplined activity. Although the real task of the philosopher was 'to traverse the whole range of human values and value-feelings', he was now becoming just another scientist, who 'will let himself be stopped somewhere and "specialize": so that he will never reach his proper height, the height from which he can survey, look around and *look down*' (Nietzsche [1886] 1990: 142, 131).

The Spanish philosopher, José Ortega y Gasset, writing in 1930, traced a similar narrative about the decline of all-embra-cing knowledge into narrow specialisms. He argued that, while in the past it was easy to distinguish between the learned and the ignorant, there was now a new category of the 'learned ignoramus ... a person who is ignorant, not in the fashion of the ignorant man, but with all the petulance of one who is learned in his own special line' (Ortega [1932] 1957: 112). This new kind of scientist, fully in place by 1890, confined himself to one sub-ject and dismissed any attempt to look beyond his specialized field as dilettantism (Ortega [1932] 1957: 110). Like Nietzsche, Ortega saw the mediocrity and conformity enshrined in the new disciplines as the symptom of a more general phenomenon, the triumph of the masses in increasingly meritocratic Western capi-talist societies. The advantage of philosophy as an undisciplined activity, for Ortega, was that it could not be subsumed into the new bureaucratic systems, and that it 'needs neither protection, attention nor sympathy from the masses. It maintains its character of complete inutility, and thereby frees itself from all subservience to the average man' (Ortega [1932] 1957: 86).

However elitist they now seem, Nietzsche's and Ortega's arguments touch on significant issues about the development of the disciplines. As they point out, this development was not simply an organic consequence of advances in knowledge, but was also the product of institutional and societal factors, particularly the demand for specialists in a complex and technologically sophisticated society. One of the key elements of this new society was the division of labour within an increasingly professionalized bureaucracy. The success of the disciplines depended partly on their external recognition by government and business as a form of accreditation for future careers: two of their chief functions were to prepare people for professions that required particular kinds of expertise, and to give these new professions legitimacy and status by providing them with academic credentials.

Alongside these external influences, the nature of the university as a relatively closed institution contributed to the consolidation of the disciplines. The emergence of a new academic subject has always depended partly on internal factors: on elite universities recognizing it through the creation of separate departments, sufficient students and lecturers being recruited to study and teach it, learned societies and journals forming around it, and recognized career structures developing, usually based on the acquisition of a Ph.D. in that subject. Moreover, since disciplines were influenced by such institutional factors, they tended, like many institutions, to reproduce themselves and become self-perpetuating. By the early 1960s, B.R. Clark was describing the disciplines in anthropological terms, as separate tribes with different cultures and languages:

> Men of the sociological tribe rarely visit the land of the physicists and have little idea what they do over there. If the sociologists were to step into the building occupied by the English department, they would encounter the cold stares if not the slingshots of the hostile natives ... the disciplines exist as separate estates, with distinctive subcultures.

> (Becher 1989: 23)

Clark's complaint remains a commonly voiced one: that once disciplines have established themselves, they develop vested interests, defend their territory and reinforce their exclusivity through particular types of discourse. The term 'discourse', a complex word that has been used in various ways within the humanities and social sciences, will recur in this book and should be preliminarily defined. It emerged in linguistics as a way of pointing to the notion of language as a collective process, constructed and constrained by social patterns or conventions. More generally, it has been used to refer to a mode of thought, cultural practice or institutional framework that makes sense of and structures the world, often from the partial perspective of a particular interest group. In Clark's argument, disciplines are clearly discursive constructions in that their power arrangements permit certain ways of thinking and operating while excluding others.

DEFINING INTERDISCIPLINARITY

As I have suggested here, the critique of the academic disciplines as limited and confining is as long-standing as the disciplines themselves. Historically, this critique has often taken the form of referring back to an older, more unified form of knowledge, usually located in an undisciplined subject such as philosophy. The term 'interdisciplinary' emerged within the context of these anxieties about the decline of general forms of education, being first used in the social sciences in the mid-1920s and becoming common currency across the social sciences and humanities in the period immediately after the Second World War (Frank 1988: 91, 95). However, one of the arguments of this book is that there are competing impulses behind the term. On the one hand, it forms part of this traditional search for a wide-ranging, total knowledge; on the other, it represents a more radical questioning of the nature of knowledge itself and our attempts to organize and communicate it. In this sense, interdisciplinarity interlocks with the concerns of epistemology – the study of knowledge – and tends to be centred around problems and issues that cannot be addressed or solved within the existing disciplines, rather than the quest for an all-inclusive synthesis.

As Geoffrey Bennington points out, 'inter' is an ambiguous prefix, which can mean forming a communication between and joining together, as in 'international' and 'intercourse', or separating and keeping apart, as in 'interval' and 'intercalate' (Bennington 1999: 104). This ambiguity is partly reflected in the slipperiness of the term, 'interdisciplinary'. It can suggest forging connections across the different disciplines; but it can also mean establishing a kind of undisciplined space in the interstices between disciplines, or even attempting to transcend disciplinary boundaries altogether. The ambiguity of the term is partly why some critics have come up with other terms such as 'post-disciplinary', 'anti-disciplinary' and 'trans-disciplinary'. Although these terms are often not defined closely and are sometimes used interchangeably, they all suggest that being interdisciplinary is not quite enough, that there is always another intellectual stage where disciplinary divisions can be more radically subverted or even erased. Rather than flitting between these different terms in this book, though, I want to suggest that the value of the term, 'interdisciplinary', lies in its flexibility and indeterminacy, and that there are potentially as many forms of interdisciplinarity as there are disciplines. In a sense, to suggest otherwise would be to 'discipline' it, to confine it within a set of theoretical and methodological orthodoxies. Within the broadest possible sense of the term, I take interdisciplinarity to mean any form of dialogue or interaction between two or more disciplines: the level, type, purpose and effect of this interaction remain to be examined.

However, it might be helpful to begin by distinguishing 'interdisciplinary' from 'multidisciplinary', words that, again rather confusingly, have sometimes been seen as synonymous. The latter term, though, tends to refer to the simple juxtaposition of two or more disciplines, as one finds on certain joint-honours or combined-arts degrees, or on individual courses that are team-taught by members of staff from different disciplines. Here the relationship between the disciplines is merely one of proximity; there is no real integration between them (Klein 1990: 56). By contrast, I want to suggest, along with Roland Barthes, that

interdisciplinarity is always transformative in some way, producing new forms of knowledge in its engagement with discrete
disciplines:

> Interdisciplinarity is not the calm of an easy security; it begins *effec-*
> *tively* (as opposed to the mere expression of a pious wish) when the
> solidarity of the old disciplines breaks down ... in the interests of a
> new object and a new language neither of which has a place in the
> field of the sciences that were to be brought peacefully together, this
> unease in classification being precisely the point from which it is
> possible to diagnose a certain mutation.
>
> (Barthes 1977: 155)

Barthes suggests that interdisciplinarity has the potential to do
more than simply bring the different disciplines together. It can
form part of a more general critique of academic specialization as
a whole, and of the nature of the university as an institution that
cuts itself off from the outside world in small enclaves of expertise. Interdisciplinary approaches often draw attention, either
implicitly or explicitly, to the fact that what is studied and
taught within universities is always a political question.

As the composite nature of the term itself suggests, 'interdisciplinarity' assumes the existence and relative resilience of disciplines as modes of thought and institutional practices. This
book will therefore be rooted in an awareness of the history,
theory, methodology and subject matter of particular disciplines,
and will aim to explore how exactly these disciplines are brought
together, transformed or transcended in different forms of interdisciplinarity, and what new forms of knowledge are created by
these interactions. In Chapter 1, I examine the history of English
as a discipline in order to show that it has always been driven by
competing impulses: one that seeks to make it more of a 'hard'
science by limiting its area of concern to a recognized phenomenon, 'literature'; and another that aims to establish it as the
interdisciplinary centre of the humanities, in place of older,
humane subjects such as classics and philosophy. Chapter 2 discusses the role of the new paradigm of cultural studies in rede-
fining and expanding the notion of 'culture' as an object of

academic study, and critically reflecting on the nature of disciplinary and interdisciplinary knowledge. Chapter 3 examines 'theory' as undisciplined knowledge, and the productive engagement between literature, philosophy and psychoanalysis which has opened up interdisciplinary questions about language, subjectivity, gender, sexuality and the body. Chapter 4 analyses recent developments at the intersection between literary studies and history as part of a longer narrative of the problematic relationship between the two disciplines. Chapter 5 explores the attempts to establish links between science, geography and cultural criticism in relation to issues about the body, technology, space, mapping, genetics and the environment. Finally, the Conclusion discusses some of the problems and limitations of interdisciplinarity and outlines the most recent developments in interdisciplinary study in the humanities.

The topics considered in these individual chapters are not meant to be mutually exclusive: the intellectually promiscuous and interlocking nature of interdisciplinarity means that it can never finally be separated out and cordoned off. By organizing the discussion in this way, however, the book aims to provide an introduction to a range of approaches that will highlight the scope and potential for interdisciplinary study. If a university student today chose to sample a range of courses across the humanities and social sciences, they would probably be surprised at the amount of overlap between them, and the duplication of theories, conceptual frameworks, terminologies and texts. As the anthropologist Clifford Geertz has written, we are living in an age of 'blurred genres', a 'jumbling of varieties of discourse', within which disciplinary distinctions are increasingly hard to call (1983: 20). This book is an attempt to cut through some of the confusion that this blurring of genres has inevitably engendered, while also valuing the necessarily diverse and complex nature of interdisciplinarity.

1

INTERDISCIPLINARY ENGLISH

More than any other subject, English has been at the centre of academic debates about the shaping and division of knowledge. As a relative latecomer to disciplinary consolidation, it has often been torn between the institutional imperative to stake out its own territory, define its activities and justify its autonomy from other areas of study, and its reliance on the approaches and subject matter of other disciplines. Indeed, it is possible to argue that all the major critical developments and controversies within English since its inception as a university subject have been related in some sense to the difficulty of containing its concerns within a single discipline and to its interdisciplinary possibilities. As Harold Rosen puts it, English is

> the least subject-like of subjects, the least susceptible to definition by reference to the accumulation of wisdom within a single academic discipline. No single set of informing ideas dominate its heartland. No one can confidently map its frontiers: it colonizes and is colonized. When we inspect the practices which cluster together

uncomfortably under its banner, they appear so diverse, contradictory, arbitrary and random as to defy analysis and explanation.

(Rosen 1981: 5)

From its earliest origins in British colleges and universities, English's weak institutional base, its newness and insecurity as a discipline, meant that it was more likely than the established disciplines to interrogate its own assumptions and practices. Critics from D.J. Palmer onwards have traced the roots of English as the 'poor man's classics' in Mechanics' Institutes, evening classes and non-Oxbridge colleges and universities, where it was sometimes taught alongside other 'national' subjects such as history and geography (Palmer 1965: vii, 18). Since the birth of a new discipline is always partly dependent on the accumulation of intellectual prestige – and particularly on whether or not influential institutions and scholars recognize it as a separate entity – it was not until the late nineteenth and early twentieth centuries that English was fully accepted as a reputable area of study, largely as a result of being established within the elite universities of Oxford and Cambridge. Even then, it was looked down upon by the more traditional disciplines as what would nowadays be called a 'Mickey Mouse' subject, an easy option for the less able students. William Sanday, Professor of Theology, supported the introduction of a School of English at Oxford at the end of the nineteenth century, for example, because 'there were the women to be considered, and the third rate men who would go on to become schoolmasters' (Bergonzi 1990: 41).

This comment points to a further problem which still vexes the subject: unlike many other academic disciplines, English does not make a strong connection between education and training for future careers. Science and professional subjects, which partly developed as a response to the demand for specialists in capitalist societies, tend to be targeted at specific areas of the graduate marketplace, and service the economy with 'human capital' in concrete ways. Most English students will be familiar with the ribbing by students in subjects such as law, engineering and medicine along these lines, as in the graffiti underneath the toilet-roll holder, 'English degrees, please take one', or the equally hilarious: 'What do you say to an English graduate? Big Mac and Fries, please.'

This is part of a wider question about the non-specialized nature of English and the fact that its object of study – literature – is generally accessible to those working outside the discipline in a way that, say, particle physics or differential equations are not. And this is still the case: even with the huge boom in popular science and history writing over the last few years, these kinds of books are still greatly outnumbered by fiction, poetry and drama in bookshops and libraries. One of the reasons for this is that literature is about everything – love, sex, friendship, family relationships, ageing, death, social and historical change, religious faith, intellectual ideas, and so on. In short, it is about life in all its diversity, and this is hard to accommodate within the narrow parameters of a discipline. As Leslie Fiedler says, 'literary criticism is always becoming "something else," for the simple reason that literature is always "something else"' (Klein 1996: 137). Unless we are solely concerned with the mechanical and formal properties of language, sooner or later we have to start dealing with the relationship between words and their referents, or between literature and 'the outside world'. Mark Schoenfield and Valerie Traub thus suggest that the study of literature necessarily contains a contextual element: 'To the extent that literary criticism has concerned itself with reference, it has had an interdisciplinary object ... The assumption that words *mean* is itself interdisciplinary' ('Forum: Defining Interdisciplinarity' 1996: 280).

The theory and practice of interpreting texts – hermeneutics – which has formed the main activity of literary studies since at least the end of the First World War, also derives from two much older disciplines, theology and law. Holy scripture was the primary object of early textual study and interpretation. Medieval bibles were often extensively annotated, for example, so that the textual commentaries merged with and sometimes overwhelmed the words of the Bible itself. The Protestant Reformation of the sixteenth century greatly increased the opportunities for such interpretation by taking the responsibility for biblical exegesis away from the Catholic Church in Rome and dispersing it amongst individual theological scholars. Martin Luther's dictum was *sola Scriptura* ('scripture alone'): only by interpreting the Bible itself, rather than by accepting the authority of the established Church, could the will of God be known. Biblical scholars today practise skills of close textual analysis and background research which are also employed by literary critics, and they ask many of the same questions: about authorship, the status of supporting sources, translation and even canonicity, since the term 'canon' derives from attempts within the Christian Church to separate authoritative from apocryphal biblical texts. In the field of law, the interpretation of a relatively fixed canon of legal texts, which is subtly modified by new statutes and judicial rulings, has always required a large element of textual study; it involves deciphering the ambiguities and nuances of written language in relation to specific, real-life situations and an abstract notion of 'justice'. In fact, the awareness of this relationship has given rise in recent years to the burgeoning area of critical legal studies, which treats the law as a text to be deconstructed by the critic. Although literary critics have often sought to claim textual interpretation as an activity that marks out the discrete disciplinarity of their subject, this claim is clearly questionable.

THE BIRTH OF ENGLISH

The academic subject of English properly emerged with the birth of the modern, professionalized, research university towards the end of the nineteenth century, at a time when new subjects in the sciences and social sciences were also proliferating and con-solidating themselves. When set against the clearly defined aims and quantifiable achievements of these new disciplines, however, English seemed rather woolly and ill-focused. For some, the prob-lem was its reliance on an activity that every educated gentleman was supposed to be doing, or indeed to have done, anyway: becoming acquainted with the great works of literature. In 1887, E.A. Freeman, the Regius Professor of History at Oxford, opposed the establishment of an English school there on the grounds that 'English literature is only chatter about Shelley', and that 'we do not want ... subjects which are merely light, elegant, interesting.

As subjects for examination, we must have subjects in which it is possible to examine' (Graff 1989: 123; Milner 1996: 4). Precisely the same objections were made against the development of the new subject in America: one college dean, for example, said that he failed to see why a new discipline needed to be created in order to study the books he read on the train to work (Graff 1996: 12). Broadly speaking, English has responded to this impugning of its disciplinary credentials in two ways. First, some professional literary critics have sought to follow the rigid model of other, more established subjects by developing 'scientific' approaches with clear procedures and measurable effects. Second, others have made a virtue of the subject's weak disciplinary base, its fluidity, open-endedness and lack of overall coherence.

Philosophers of science such as Karl Popper and Stephen Toulmin have proposed a distinction between 'hard' disciplines in the sciences and 'soft' disciplines in the humanities and social sciences, which are perceived as being at an early stage of evolutionary development, not yet having attained the status of a fully fledged academic subject. Toulmin, for example, differentiates between 'compact', 'diffuse' and 'would-be' disciplines, which are at various levels of progression towards a state of rigour and internal consistency (1972: 378–95). The English School at Oxford, which was established in 1893, seemed to accept that it lagged behind the more traditional disciplines in this regard. From the beginning, Oxford English tried to make itself 'compact', emphasizing linguistic and historical scholarship rather than literary criticism or appreciation, and forging strong links with philology.

Philology is a subject that originated in the classical world but emerged as a modern discipline towards the end of the eighteenth century, particularly in Germany. It involved the close examination of the textual (usually written) sources of past cultures and societies, and could be applied to a wide range of material such as classical, legal, philosophical or historical texts. It was often engaged in establishing the authenticity of archaic or esoteric texts or reconstructing and annotating them from fragmented sources, and was seen as a way of bringing the precision of the new scientific disciplines to bear on textual materials. As the subject developed throughout the nineteenth century, it became more concerned with the science of language in relation to its historical development and established a close relationship with the new discipline of linguistics, although this latter subject tended to emphasize spoken over written texts and examine linguistic structures independent of their historical context. The Oxford English course, along with other English degrees throughout the country, still contains a detailed study of Old English and the history and use of the English language, which is partly a hangover from these earlier efforts to impose the scientific rigour of philology on the new discipline.

Another, ultimately more influential attempt to make English more systematic and methodical was made in the 1920s by I.A. Richards, who succeeded in placing the activity of literary criticism at the centre of the new subject. Richards set his students an 'unseen' exercise in which they were asked to evaluate individual poems without knowing the author or the title of the work; the huge range of wildly speculative answers he received convinced him of the need for a new science of interpretation, 'Practical Criticism'. From the very first sentences of his classic work, *Principles of Literary Criticism*, which assert that 'a book is a machine to think with' and that this particular study is 'a loom on which it is proposed to re-weave some ravelled parts of our civilisation' (Richards 1926: 1), Richards makes clear his dual aim: to turn the practice of textual interpretation into an activity every bit as precise and painstaking as a laboratory experiment, and to use this newly acquired methodology to challenge the dominance of scientific rationality in society. Surveying the current 'chaos of critical theories', Richards concludes that literary criticism has no clear theoretical underpinning or *modus operandi*:

> A few conjectures, a supply of admonitions, many acute isolated observations, some brilliant guesses, much oratory and applied poetry, inexhaustible confusion, a sufficiency of dogma, no small stock of prejudices, whimsies and crotchets, a profusion of mysticism, a little genuine speculation, sundry stray inspirations, pregnant hints and *aperçus*; of such as these, it may be said without exaggeration, is extant critical theory composed.
>
> (Richards 1926: 5–6)

In a later book, *Science and Poetry*, Richards tries to position literary criticism as a more intellectually demanding alternative to organized religion in an age of the *'Neutralization of Nature*, the transference from the Magical View of the world to the scientific' (Richards 1935: 52). Science, while greatly improving the material conditions of our lives, provides 'indifferent and emotionally neutral knowledge' which 'can tell us nothing about the nature of things in any ultimate sense' (Richards 1935: 58). The problem is that other kinds of intellectual inquiry have not kept up with the sciences in structuring and codifying their theories and practices. If the humanities were to achieve this scientificity, then 'practical consequences might be expected even more remarkable than any that the engineer can contrive' (Richards 1935: 12). Richards' counter-response to the ascendancy of the natural sciences in contemporary society, then, is to institute literary studies as a scientific, disciplinary activity.

LITERATURE, LIFE AND THOUGHT

Despite this emphasis on close reading, the study of English at Cambridge, which became massively influential throughout the world through its central figure, F.R. Leavis, was always more interdisciplinary than English at Oxford. When the English School was first established at Cambridge in 1917, the lecturers appointed had been trained in other subjects such as classics, philosophy, history and, in the case of Richards himself, psycho-analysis. As the initial name of its degree, 'Literature, Life and Thought', suggests, Cambridge English had an expansiveness and openness to new approaches which were sharply opposed to Oxford's scholasticism. Sir Arthur Quiller-Couch was made the first Professor of English in 1912 (in a chair significantly funded by the press baron Sir Harold Harmsworth, founder of the *Daily Mail*), and 'Q', as he was known, was a jobbing author and newspaper man who had published in a variety of forms: essays, novels, poems and anthologies. Up until the 1920s, the rather quirky Cambridge examination papers reflected his influence, being aimed more at impressionistic and allusive literary appreciation than detailed analysis and requiring students to pitch their work somewhere between scholarly writing and belletristic journalism (MacKillop 1997: 54–7).

F.R. Leavis was radically opposed to Quiller-Couch's idea of literary studies as a training for *belles-lettres*, but he retained the notion that it should not be narrowly academic. It is worth reminding ourselves of this, because Leavis is sometimes seen as being a purely textual critic, committed solely to dealing with the 'words on the page'. While this was certainly an important aspect of his work, he was always interested in context: he had initially embarked on a degree in history, and his 1924 Ph.D. dissertation on 'the relationship of journalism to literature' could be said to be a protean version of what later became 'cultural studies', in that it dealt with the divide between high- and low-brow culture produced by the entanglement of different modes of writing in the emerging capitalist marketplace.

Leavis disapproved of what he saw as the deadening academicism of the Oxford English School, which 'expresses itself in compulsory Anglo-Saxon and the naive associated notions of "language" and "discipline"' (1969: 11–12). Although he certainly drew on Richards' work to formulate his own techniques of close textual analysis, he also criticized 'the implication ... that "Practical Criticism" was a specialized kind of gymnastic skill to be cultivated and practised as something apart' (Leavis 1975: 19). In the schools, in particular, as his classroom primer, *Culture and Environment* (1933), demonstrates, Leavis favoured extending the techniques of practical criticism to such phenomena as advertising, popular newspapers, pulp fiction, book clubs and the literary-heritage industry. His hugely influential journal, *Scrutiny*, which became one of the prime means for the dissemination of Leavisite views, was also a model of interdisciplinary scholarship, including essays and reviews on the cinema, music, advertising and other forms of popular culture alongside its more conventional literary criticism. Leavis saw literary criticism as a clearly defined but relatively permeable enterprise, peripherally concerned with many other areas of cultural activity, since 'a real literary interest is an interest in man, society and civilization, and its boundaries cannot be drawn; the adjective is not a circumscribing one' (Leavis 1972: 200).

Leavis's 'Sketch for an English School', written in 1940 and aimed at redesigning the Cambridge English course, reflected this overall view in its proposal that English students should study a foreign language, comparative literature and political, economic, social and intellectual history alongside the established literary canon (Leavis 1948: 54). In the name of greater inter-disciplinarity, Leavis's hypothetical English degree also included a special subject – the seventeenth century – in which the rela-tionship between literature and society could be studied in more depth. This subject would draw on the fields of sociology, econ-omics, politics and history as well as literature, covering such themes as the civil war, the rise of capitalism, the new sciences and the shifting relations between sophisticated and popular culture (Leavis 1948: 52–4).

These curricular concerns need to be understood in relation to Leavis's general ideas about the university as an institution. The development of these ideas can be traced at least as far back as the third issue of *Scrutiny* in 1932, in which he reviews Alexander Meiklejohn's *The Experimental College*. Leavis draws on Meikle-john's work, which reports on the foundation of a wide-ranging liberal arts course at the University of Wisconsin, to argue that the central problem with the modern university is one that afflicts society as a whole: the division of labour into self-contained units in 'technologico-Benthamite civilisation' (Leavis 1969: 24). This term, which recurs in a pejorative context throughout Leavis's writings, is worth explaining. It refers to the philosophy of 'uti-litarianism' proposed by Jeremy Bentham who, in *An Introduction to the Principles of Morals and Legislation* (1789), argued that the purpose of life is happiness, that any moral philosophy should be based on achieving 'the greatest happiness for the greatest number', and that degrees of happiness could be determined through a 'felicific calculus'. To these ends, Bentham also argued that education should be based on the 'chrestomathic' principle, meaning that it should be devoted to useful knowledge rather than learning for its own sake (Bentham [1789] 1982: 1–41). For Leavis, the ascendancy of Benthamite principles in capitalist society has helped to sponsor a relentless process of rationalization and standardization, and an uncritical belief in the power of science and technology to improve people's lives. While the formation of armies of dedicated specialists is increasingly seen as 'the supreme end of the university, its *raison d'être*' (Leavis 1948: 25), Leavis argues instead for the survival of the notion of a civilizing, all-round, humane education which formed the basis for the foundation of the modern, liberal university in Europe at the beginning of the nineteenth century.

Leavis, though, recognizes that there can be no unproblematic return to the ideal of an all-encompassing system of knowledge. Instead, the universities need to adapt this ideal to the complex demands of the modern world, fostering the 'co-presence of the specialist studies ... with a strong humane centre' (Leavis 1969: 3). Within the obdurate reality of increasing specialization, one subject has to serve as the fulcrum for Leavis's interdisciplinary ideal. Perhaps unsurprisingly for an English don, he suggests that English should be repositioned as this pivotal subject, forming a centre of attraction and point of liaison for all the other disciplines within the university. His own subject is particularly able to perform such an integrative function because

> it is a humane school, and the non-specialist intelligence in which the various studies are to find their centre is to be one that gets its own special training in literature. Its special – but not specialist – discipline is to be the literary-critical, a discipline of sensibility, judgment and thought which, of its essential nature, is concerned with training of a non-specialist intelligence.
>
> (Leavis 1948: 43)

Above all, Leavis regards English as necessarily interdisciplinary, since the work of the great writers which forms its syllabus inevitably encompasses a much broader interest in life, society, civilization and thought: 'One of the virtues of literary studies is that they lead constantly outside themselves, and ... while it is necessary that they should be controlled by a concern for the essential discipline, such a concern, if it is adequate, counts on associated work in other fields' (Leavis 1948: 35).

There is clearly a tension here between fortifying English as a discipline and encouraging its productive cross-fertilization with other subjects. Alongside the concern with its range of reference and receptiveness to other subjects, Leavis is also 'very much preoccupied with vindicating literary criticism as a specific discipline – a discipline of intelligence, with its own field, and its own approaches within that field' (Leavis 1969: 45). The word 'discipline' occurs frequently within his writings, both as a way of defining English as a discrete entity and of referring to the use of a demanding critical intelligence which he sees as one of its main activities. In fact, it is hard to understand his model of English as the 'humane centre' of his ideal university without acknowledging the immense difficulty with which Leavis and others established English as a recognized and reputable subject at Cambridge, and his often bitter arguments with colleagues, both within the English faculty and outside it, about the status and direction of the discipline. In this context, his 'Sketch for an English School' seems not so much interdisciplinary as imperialistic, the aim being to focus all academic study around the English faculty and strengthen the power base of his own subject, a project that is made all the more significant for his unwillingness to acknowledge it as an influence on his thinking.

This attempt to establish the pre-eminence of literary studies over other disciplines took two principal forms. First, Leavis was engaged in a struggle to consolidate the new dominance of English in relation to classics and philosophy, its immediate forebears as embodiments of the humane ideal – although he magnanimously declined to banish them from his ideal university (Leavis 1948: 39). F.L. Lucas, the Cambridge classics don and nemesis of the English School, dismissed literary criticism as 'a charming parasite' engaged in 'training reviewers', and upheld his own subject as the supreme training for cultivated gentlemen (Mulhern 1981: 31). Leavis responded by criticizing classics for being unconcerned with the tasks of literary evaluation and discrimination which were crucial to the critic's role in society, so that 'persons of undisturbed classical training' could assign greatness to the work of such insignificant authors as P.G. Wodehouse and A.E. Housman (Leavis 1948: 39). Leavis's aversion to philosophy is clearly evident in his discussion with the critic René Wellek about the role of theory in literary studies, in which he calls for the separation of literature from philosophy to prevent the 'blunting of edge, blurring of focus and muddled misdirection of attention: consequences of queering one discipline with the habits of another' (Leavis 1972: 213). But it is perhaps most neatly encapsulated in the title of a posthumously collected book of essays: *The Critic as Anti-Philosopher* (Leavis 1982).

Second, Leavis's model of a broad-based education was implacably hostile to the sciences, as his coruscating attack on C.P. Snow's 'The Two Cultures and the Scientific Revolution' in the early 1960s demonstrates. Snow, a well-known novelist who had trained as a scientist, gave a lecture in which he lamented the inability of the science and humanities disciplines to be able to communicate with one another on a common plane. Responding to Snow's contention that an educated person should be equally well acquainted with the Second Law of Thermodynamics as with the work of Shakespeare, Leavis makes a clear distinction between the two cultures, arguing that 'equations between orders so disparate are meaningless'. He attributes his argument with Snow to their contrasting views of academia, for although they both look to the university as an archetype for their ideal society, Leavis is concerned 'unlike Snow ... to make it really a university, something [that is] more than a collocation of specialist departments – to make it a centre of human consciousness: perception, knowledge, judgment and responsibility' (Leavis 1962: 27, 29). This seems unfair, given that Snow's lecture, despite a pronounced scientific bias, is actually about bridging the chasm between the sciences and the humanities. Leavis's response does make clear, though, that his notion of an interdisciplinary, liberal-arts education, with English as its centrepiece, was based on the systematic exclusion of the sciences as representative of the technocratic, utilitarian society he deplored.

Leavis's programme for literary studies was also based on other prohibitions, since his form of criticism was strongly evaluative and involved policing admission to a 'great tradition' of English literature. The attention that Leavis paid to popular culture was therefore extremely grudging: while its pervasive influence demanded that it be studied, this was only so that it could be dismissed for pandering to a taste for 'substitute-living' and rendering the masses open to 'the cheapest emotional appeals' (Leavis and Thompson 1933: 99; Leavis 1948: 149), allowing them to confuse the mediocre and undemanding with serious art. If disciplines are defined fundamentally by what they exclude from their remit, then Leavis's project was thoroughly disciplinary, since it involved limiting its area of concern to a small canon of recognized texts and studying other forms of culture only insofar as they failed to live up to its standards.

LEAVIS AND THE UNIVERSITY

I have suggested already that any discussion of interdisciplinarity needs to be related to institutional developments in academia, and Leavis's ideas are no exception. His writing career spanned a period of enormous change in British universities, extending from the early 1930s, when a tiny proportion of the population attended a small number of elite universities or university colleges, to the 1970s, by which time the formation of the 'white-tile' campus universities, the polytechnics and the Open University had completely transformed British higher education. Many of his ideas about English and the university were formulated in response to these developments, since Leavis was a self-confessed elitist, maintaining all along that 'Oxford and Cambridge cream the country' (Leavis 1982: 161), and fiercely arguing for the preservation of the independence and ascendancy of the ancient universities.

In Leavis's ideal university, this autonomy was to be reinforced by the still more autonomous and elite citadel of his proposed English school, based on Part II of the Cambridge degree. This was designed to be academically challenging and rigorous, and would be aimed at attracting only the select members of an already exclusive institution, reconciling itself to modest student numbers but providing 'a standard, a centre and a source of stimulus and suggestion' (Leavis 1948: 42) for the rest of the university. Similarly, the university as a whole was imagined as 'a centre of consciousness and human responsibility for the civilized world' (Leavis 1969: 3), which meant that it was clearly positioned as both separate from society and crucially connected to it: its enlightened qualities were supposed to filter through to the wider culture by osmosis, functioning as an important symbol of tradition and peerless excellence within an otherwise debased culture. How exactly the university and the English school were supposed to infiltrate the sensibilities of those outside the academy when they remained such closed institutions was not always made clear.

At the same time as Leavis looked to the university as an important disseminator of redemptive values within a generally philistine society, he also regarded it with a passionate ambivalence, acknowledging the often tenuous relationship between his notion of academia as the centre of humane, disinterested scholarship and the nature of the institution itself. His proposal for an English school was partly a recognition that the university rarely lives up to its ideals, in that it attempted to set up an uncorrupted space within an already fallen institution. Since the 'English Research Society', an ad hoc and unhierarchical organization of undergraduates, graduate students and faculty which had met at his house in the 1930s, Leavis had envisaged a kind of self-contained stronghold within the university. This was exemplified by the journal *Scrutiny*, which he referred to as 'the essential Cambridge in spite of Cambridge' (Leavis 1982: 175), owing its existence to the university but often marginalized by its most powerful elements. It was precisely because of Leavis's ambivalence about academia that he envisaged the English School as the vibrant centre of the university, representing its best elements while also rising above the rigidity and introspection of the Ivory Tower.

This partly explains the apparently contradictory positioning of English within his criticism as both disciplinary and interdisciplinary. Leavis takes the uncertain disciplinary basis of English – its opposition to the abstractions of philosophical theory and the utilitarianism of science, and its ability to overlap with the concerns of other humanities disciplines – and makes it an indicator of its centrality within the university. He presents literary criticism as simultaneously a discipline of extreme intellectual rigour and one of emotional responsiveness and creativity, 'a training of intelligence that is at the same time a training of sensibility; a discipline of thought that is at the same time a discipline in scrupulous sensitiveness of response to delicate organizations of feeling, sensation and imagery' (Leavis 1948: 38). The same process can be seen at work in the notoriously vague terms of approbation that are repeated throughout his writings on literature, such as 'reverent openness before life', 'vigour', 'wit', 'experience', 'moral intensity' and 'cerebral muscle'. These terms gesture beyond the text to life as a whole, and suggest that the concerns of English cannot be articulated through an abstract scientific language, but they could also be said to form part of what the philosopher Richard Rorty refers to as a 'final vocabulary'. For Rorty, a vocabulary is 'final' when, 'if doubt is cast on the worth of these words, their user has no noncircular argumentative recourse. Those words are as far as he can go with language; beyond them there is only helpless passivity or resort to force' (Rorty 1989: 73). In this sense, Leavis's largely unexplained terms are not very different from the kind of technical vocabulary associated with any discipline: they are an unanswerable, closed language which is meant to be accepted by all those working within the field and which brooks no argument. The same kind of disciplinary project is evident in his definition of textual analysis, which he describes as

the process by which we seek to attain a complete reading of the poem – a reading that approaches as nearly as possible to the perfect reading. There is about it nothing in the nature of 'murdering to dissect', and suggestions that it can be anything in the nature of laboratory-method misrepresent it entirely. We can have the poem only by an inner kind of possession; it is 'there' for analysis only in so far as we are responding appropriately to the words on the page.

(Leavis 1948: 70)

There is a Wordsworthian celebration of spontaneity and naturalness here which presents itself as antithetical to the conventional scholarly activities of argument and analysis. However, the poem is still 'there' to be got at and studied, and requires the learning of skills that will enable us to do this.

It is worth questioning this belief in the ability of literary studies to be both within the university and outside it, and to function as a discipline without being quite a discipline, which again owes much to the problematic origins of the subject and Leavis's own sense of alienation from the Cambridge English faculty. His idea of an untouchable English school overlooks the nature of universities, and of *all* the disciplines within them, as institutions organized by the hierarchical distribution of privileges, and inextricably connected to the broader power networks of government, society and culture. In this respect, his proposal for an English school that transcends the corrupting influence of the academy is similar to Kant's organization of the university in *The Conflict of the Faculties*, which I discussed in the introduction. In this essay, Kant looks to philosophy as a subject that remains free of the influence of government and other material concerns, and that is thus able to function as a kind of overseer of all the other disciplines, guided only by the disinterested exercise of 'reason'. As Jacques Derrida argues convincingly, Kant's essay is based around a misguided search for origins, because 'there can be no pure concept of the university ... due very simply to the fact that the university is *founded*. An event of foundation can never be comprehended merely within the logic that it founds' (Derrida 1992b: 30). In other words, Kant sets up an area of study that somehow wipes its hands clean of the internal power structures of the university and its accountability to society and the state. Similarly, while much of Leavis's work is based around an opposition to the progressive division of labour in capitalist society, which he blames for producing the 'functionless purity' of 'pure specialisms' (Leavis 1948: 62), he excludes his own subject from this historical process by marking it out as 'special' rather than 'specialist'. Leavis establishes parameters and protocols for English which position it clearly as a discipline, while also commending its unique status as an inclusive and interdisciplinary field.

THE CULTURAL PROJECT OF ENGLISH

Leavis's interdisciplinarity thus has a limit: it is based on the notion that a sense of cultural unity has been lost, and that an elite group, working within a discipline, needs to be formed to ensure that this unity is recaptured. In this sense, it draws on a rich vein of cultural criticism stretching at least as far back as Samuel Taylor Coleridge and Matthew Arnold, which itself relies on a post-Romantic idea of the aesthetic as 'the heart of a heartless world' (Easthope 1991: 13). In *On the Constitution of the Church and State* (1830), Coleridge proposed the formation of a kind of 'clerisy' of writers and artists, an alternative 'National Church' which would be positioned

> at the fountainhead of the humanities, in cultivating and enlarging the knowledge already possessed, and in watching over the interests of physical and moral science ... the objects and final intention of the whole order being these – to preserve the stores and to guard the treasures of past civilization, and thus to bind the present with the past.
>
> (Williams [1958] 1961: 78)

Matthew Arnold suggested a similar antidote to the philistinism of the middle classes and the discontent of the working classes in the Victorian era: the 'anarchy' of society was to be saved by the liberatory power of 'culture' as a repository for 'the best that has been thought and said' and a source of 'sweetness and light'. Arnold seems to have been actively opposed to the limiting of culture to a professional coterie, since the great men of culture were those 'who have laboured to divest knowledge of all that was harsh, uncouth, difficult, abstract, professional, exclusive; to humanise it, to make it efficient outside the clique of the cultivated and the learned' (Arnold [1869] 1993: 79). But he did accept that a concentrated effort was needed if culture was to achieve the aim of societal transformation, and that this effort could only be conducted by a group of disinterested 'aliens' who would be able to step back from the degradations and corruptions of society and keep aloof from 'the practical view of things' (Arnold [1869] 1993: 110, 37).

Although Arnold was not directly concerned with professional literary criticism, and indeed was against its development as an autonomous discipline, English professors of the late nineteenth and early twentieth centuries, such as David Masson, Henry

Morley, George Gordon and Quiller-Couch, adopted some of these ideals of cultural enlightenment as a justification for the new discipline of English. The Arnoldian enterprise was further consolidated in a 1921 government-sponsored report on 'The Teaching of English in England', produced by a committee chaired by Sir Henry Newbolt and including both Quiller-Couch and Richards. Written in a patriotic spirit soon after the First World War, the Newbolt report sets up English literature as the prime purveyor of national culture, argues that it should take the place of classics as the central humane discipline, and even expresses the hope that it will assume the sacralizing role of religion in a primarily secular society. This cultural mission, which affirms the inseparability of literature and life, means that English cannot be positioned as a straightforwardly disciplinary mode of inquiry, concerned solely with the technical aspects of literature such as 'whether a poem is a lyric or an epic, whether it is in trochees or iambics' (Board of Education 1921: 273):

> English is not merely the medium of our thought, it is the very stuff and process of it ... the element in which we live and work. In its full sense it connotes not merely an acquaintance with a certain number of terms, or the power of spelling these terms without gross mistakes. It connotes the discovery of the world by the first and most direct way open to us, and the discovery of ourselves in our native environment.
>
> (Board of Education 1921: 20)

Significantly, the report is also suspicious of the conveyor-belt mentality encouraged by the professionalization of the discipline in American research universities:

> Many of the elaborate theses on English Literature produced by American students for their Doctorate, and afterwards published, were monuments of misdirected effort; in short, a true sense of literature as a living thing was lost, and in its place was substituted an investigation after the worst pattern of German 'research', deadening alike to those who wrote and those who read it.
>
> (Board of Education 1921: 236–7)

The Newbolt report thus makes the case for humanistic generalism over what it sees as dry-as-dust Germanic 'scholarship', an emphasis that was again partly a product of anti-German sentiment in the aftermath of the First World War. But the report is clearly torn between positioning English as a broad church and defining it as a discipline: it stresses the usefulness of historical contexts and philosophical arguments to literary study, for example, but warns against the 'grave mistake' of supposing that literature is merely an offshoot of history, sociology or philosophy (Board of Education 1921: 205–6). English is seen as sufficiently expansive to incorporate a whole range of material, but it still has to have the clear terms of reference of a conventional discipline, and should not use literature 'to cultivate a shallow impressionism and an insincere fluency' (Board of Education 1921: 126). From the beginning, then, academic literary study saw itself as part of a broad project of moral regeneration, class harmonization and the promotion of a specifically national identity, and this project existed alongside, and sometimes sat uneasily with, the perceived need to establish English as a discipline.

Leavis inherits from his predecessors an interdisciplinarity which is founded on a nostalgic belief that the task of criticism is to restore a lost sense of wholeness in society and culture. In this respect, though, Leavis is just as strongly influenced by one of his contemporaries, T.S. Eliot. Like Leavis, Eliot proposes an inclusive notion of culture as 'all the characteristic activities and interests of a people', while also placing his ultimate faith in elite culture, and the minority who can preserve a sense of cultural continuity with the great writers of the past (Eliot 1948: 31, 16). In his essay, 'The Metaphysical Poets', Eliot refers to a 'dissociation of sensibility' originating in the seventeenth century from which all subsequent literature has suffered. Whereas the metaphysical poets 'feel their thought as immediately as the odour of a rose', writers since then have tragically separated thought from feeling, intellect from emotion (Eliot 1951: 287). Leavis's work is heavily influenced by this notion of a catastrophic moment of schism, and he extends it into a broader critique about the loss of an organic community in the division of culture from society; indeed, he recommends the seventeenth century as a special subject in his proposed English degree precisely because it is when the dissociation of sensibility begins.

The purpose of literary criticism, according to Leavis, is to heal this tragic division which has blighted the past few centuries, and in this sense his criticism is retrospectively interdisciplinary: culture and society have become separated from one another, and the rift needs to be mended through the integrated study possible within a university discipline. The paradox, that this discipline is practised by a minority which is itself separate from the rest of society, is partly concealed by Leavis's insistence that English is a discipline like no other.

The role that Leavis envisages for literary criticism thus develops out of his more general argument, first formulated in an early essay, 'Mass Civilization and Minority Culture', that 'civilization' and 'culture' have become detached from one another and that 'in any period it is upon a very small minority that the discerning appreciation of art and literature depends' (Leavis 1948: 143–4). In his works on the university and the future of English, it is clear that Leavis sees the discipline of literary study as the safeguard of this minority culture. The literary critic's task is to make a kind of strategic retreat from society in order to form an academic discipline which will eventually achieve an interdisciplinary synthesis and a transformation of society. Aiming to steer a middle course between paralysed nostalgia and capitulation to the forces of modernization, Leavis proposes a rearguard action by consolidating the 'special' discipline of English. His model for English remained the dominant one within the discipline until the past few decades: its interdisciplinarity was inspired by its broader project of cultural renewal, but this was accompanied by an insistence that the study of English should involve a scrupulously 'neutral' textual reading, the skills for which could only be acquired within the discipline. Within this emphasis on the close reading of a canon of works, the redemptive mission of English was meant to speak for itself: the critic's own institutional investment in the discipline, and the politics of its relationship to other disciplines and society as a whole, were rarely acknowledged.

ENGLISH IN AMERICA

I now want to turn briefly to the situation in the USA, where professional literary studies was born at around the same time as in Britain, with the transformation of the old liberal arts colleges into the new research universities in the last quarter of the nineteenth century. From the beginning, American literary criticism was dogged by the same controversies about the relationship between the scientific status of English as a discipline and its interdisciplinary ambitions. The impetus for the initial professionalization of literary studies in the USA was largely provided by German-trained philological scholars, whose incontestable rigour essentially enabled literary studies to call itself a discipline within the modern, departmentally organized university. This original link with linguistic scholarship is still evident in the name of the professional body for English in America: the Modern Language Association, founded in 1883. For these language specialists, literature was often simply something to be raided for examples, so that purists like James Bright of Johns Hopkins University could say that 'describing a philologist as a professor of literature would be as absurd as describing a biologist as a professor of vegetables' (Graff 1989: 68). However, there were traditional humanist generalists, proponents of Arnold's notion of literary criticism as cultural crusade, who strongly opposed this model for the discipline. As with the British universities, there was a clear link between these early versions of interdisciplinarity and a persistent strain of anti-academicism. The humanists supported the philologists in establishing English as a discipline because they thought it might serve their own Arnoldian ends, but they were also highly sceptical about subordinating these ends to professional imperatives. As Arthur N. Applebee puts it, 'the prestige of philology served to *justify* English studies without necessarily *limiting* them' (Graff 1989: 56).

The situation was further complicated by the growth in importance of English composition, a subject that developed from rhetoric and oratory classes in the old colleges and that responded to the increased demand in both government and industry for good standards of technical writing. English departments in the

USA financed much of the rest of their research and teaching by offering composition classes to students in other university departments, and indeed, many of them still do. As Richard Ohmann argues, echoing Applebee's comments, 'literature is the subject that the profession chose, but composition is the subject that created the profession' (Ohmann 1976: 94). 'Freshman English' or 'English 101' threatened to push the subject in a different kind of disciplinary direction, one founded more on the notion of specialist professional training than the broad-based, interdisciplinary ideals held by many literary critics. These courses, although often influenced by the progressive beliefs of their teachers, were essentially framed by the demands of industry and government for 'rhetoric for the meritocracy' (Ohmann 1976: 97). However, although it financed many of the other activities undertaken by English departments, composition did not seriously interfere with the rise to ascendancy of literary criticism as their central activity.

As in Britain, literary criticism became fully professionalized in America from about the 1920s onwards, and it did so by dispensing with the notion of literary study as merely the appreciation and celebration of genteel taste, and establishing the primacy of textual interpretation. This move coincided with the rise to prominence of the 'New Critics', figures such as John Crowe Ransom, Allen Tate, Yvor Winters and Cleanth Brooks. Compared to their British peers, the New Critics were arguably more locked into the professional disciplinary contexts of the university, and the training of aspiring academic critics, partly because American universities have historically been geared more towards graduate research than undergraduate teaching. The British critic who exerted most influence over the New Critics was not Leavis, who belonged to a more specifically British strain of cultural criticism, but Richards. Adapting Richards's practical criticism to their own purposes, the New Critics tended to see the literary text as sufficient unto itself, clearly distinguishing it from other kinds of text, and discouraging psychological, biographical or socio-historical readings.

In his essay, 'Criticism, Inc.', Ransom argues that the discipline of English needs to develop a clear professional footing, based on 'the erection of intelligent standards of criticism', developed not by amateurs but by 'the collective and sustained effort of learned persons' (Ransom 1938: 328–9). According to Ransom, the English department also needs to separate itself off from neighbouring disciplines and define clearly what it does:

> It is really atrocious policy for a department to abdicate its own self-respecting identity. The department of English is charged with the understanding and the communication of literature, an art, yet it has usually forgotten to inquire into the peculiar constitution and structure of its product. English might almost as well announce that it does not regard itself as entirely autonomous, but as a branch of the department of history, with the option of declaring itself occasionally a branch of the department of ethics.

> (Ransom 1938: 335)

The New Critics' work as a whole was distinguished by this attempt to stand guard over the frontiers of the discipline. In two much-cited essays, for example, W.K. Wimsatt Jr. and Monroe C. Beardsley refer to 'the intentional fallacy', which involves the reading of literary works in relation to the intentions of the author, and 'the affective fallacy', which involves the intervention of subjective, emotional responses into the critical act, as common ways of misreading texts (Wimsatt [1954] 1970: 3–39). The use of the word 'fallacy' in both cases is a common New Critical strategy: it implies that there is a literary critical norm which needs to be defended, and that there are certain kinds of critical activity that are straightforwardly 'wrong'. These approaches are usually ones that draw on extraneous material from other disciplines, such as philosophy, psychology or history.

As in Britain, however, this disciplinary impetus did not go uncontested nor escape its own internal inconsistencies. Many of the New Critics were committed to a Leavisite project of using poetry and criticism to counter the 'technocratic' and dehumanizing tendencies of modern society, often championing the rural Old South against the industrial North of the USA, and as a whole they were far more concerned with historical and philosophical questions than is sometimes acknowledged. For example,

René Wellek and Austin Warren's *Theory of Literature*, first published in 1949, is often seen as a New Critical bible, and it is indeed very concerned with the nature of 'literariness', its argument being that the work of art is 'an object of knowledge *sui generis* [of its own kind]' and that 'the natural and sensible starting-point for work in literary scholarship is the interpretation and analysis of the works of literature themselves' (Wellek and Warren 1949: 157, 139). But Wellek and Warren are careful to make room for both 'intrinsic' readings and the kinds of 'extrinsic' readings that rely on biographical background, psychology, sociology, philosophy and the other arts, even if they regard the latter as ultimately flawed. The final chapter of the first edition, 'The Study of Literature in the Graduate School', also maintains that disciplinary specialization and professionalization need to be combined with a 'general intellectual and literary distinction', including a knowledge of foreign languages, comparative literature and philosophy (Wellek and Warren 1949: 291–5). Their conclusion does not seem overly prescriptive in its disciplinary aims, arguing that 'concentration seems a necessary antidote to the expansionist movement through which literary history has passed in the last decades', but that 'the individual may elect to combine several methods' (Wellek and Warren 1949: 282).

Even at the height of the New Criticism's influence there were also dissenting voices, propounding what Gerald Graff calls the 'new humanism' and keeping faith with the idea of a generalist, non-disciplinary education (Graff 1989: 149). The so-called Chicago School of critics also had a slightly different agenda: they shared the New Critical concern to develop a more structured and scientific critical practice around literary study, but they argued that literary critics should be 'pluralist' in approach. One of the Chicago School's leading critics, R.S. Crane, criticized the 'unexamined confidence' with which critics like Richards worked, arguing that the times required 'an enlargement rather than a further restriction of the resources of criticism' (Crane 1957: iv–v). Another member of the school, Elder Olson, similarly claimed that:

> Criticism in our time is almost a sort of Tower of Babel ... it is well to remember that at Babel men did not begin to talk nonsense; they

merely began to talk what *seemed* like nonsense to their fellows ... The extreme diversity of contemporary criticism is no more alarming than – and, indeed, it is connected with – the similar diversity of contemporary philosophy; and the chief import of both is of the need for some critique which shall examine radically how such diversity arises, by considering what aspects of a given subject are amenable to treatment, what problems they pose, and how these may be diversely formulated.

(Olson 1952: 546–7)

Olson's project was thus quite different from Ransom's in 'Criticism, Inc.' Although he believed that the diverse critical schools should work towards critical consensus, he accepted that this project would always be incomplete. In practice, this meant that the Chicago critics were more likely than their New Critical counterparts to draw on historical analysis, philosophy and, above all, the history of literary criticism. It is clear that literary studies in America, although perhaps more openly implicated in the professional contexts of the university than its British counterpart, was still riven with the same tensions about its ambiguous status as a discipline.

THE FALL OF ENGLISH

As I have sought to demonstrate in this chapter, interdisciplinarity in literary studies is nothing new: it has never been a 'pure' discipline but a hotchpotch of contending aesthetic, theoretical and scientific discourses. One might say that it has been particularly aware of its own 'problematic': in other words, it has speculated continually about the intellectual foundations within which its key questions are framed and which make it possible, and how things might be otherwise. At the same time, literary studies has been driven by a competing impulse to define itself more clearly and precisely as a discipline in its own right.

This tension was explored by Graham Hough in an article on the future of literary studies in a 1964 edited collection, *The Crisis in the Humanities*. While making only passing reference to Leavis, Hough's article is clearly concerned with the ways in which Leavis's interdisciplinary ideals have been dissipated by the emergence of English as an autonomous discipline, a development that Leavis also promoted. Hough suggests that at one time it was believed that literature would be the core subject in the humanities, replacing classics as 'the unifying, central study for everyone who did not want a scientific or purely professional training', but in practice 'it has turned out to be just a "subject" like any other' (Hough 1964: 98–9). For Hough, this is a direct consequence of the development of a separate honours degree in English: students who choose to do this degree tend to read only English literature, without having to study a foreign language or become acquainted with social and intellectual history, while those who do not opt for English honours can avoid the subject altogether. He argues that there are two problems with the notion of training literary critics in the same way as scientists or doctors: first, 'it is a severe contraction of the generous aims of humanist education', and second, 'it involves a large element of falsity and humbug' (Hough 1964: 102). Far from emerging as the humane centre of the university, English now teaches 'a set of special tricks' (Hough 1964: 99) in which students and critics are encouraged to adopt a specific terminology to express critical opinions that they do not really share. Hough concludes:

> I do not believe that anyone should have their higher education in literature alone. What is disgustingly called 'English' in universities should never have grown into a separate and isolated 'subject' as it has. It needs to be closely integrated with the study of other languages, with history and the history of ideas.
>
> (Hough 1964: 108)

Hough makes the important point that, for all its generalist aspirations, the shaping of English into a discipline was necessarily limiting. First, it was limiting in terms of methodology: the Leavisite and New Critical projects, as he suggests, were based on establishing a series of methods and procedures that were peculiar to English and that could only be applied within that discipline. Second, it was limiting in terms of subject matter: when faced with the possibility that the broadness of its concerns might make it too amorphous and ill defined, English gained disciplinary coherence by focusing on certain clearly defined works. However, this has often meant that its sole justification as a subject has been an extremely unstable conception of what constitutes 'literature', based around value judgements and particular cultural agendas. As Franco Moretti argues: 'If everyone behaved like literary critics who only study what they "like", doctors might restrict themselves to studying only healthy bodies and economists the standard of living of the "well-off"' (Moretti 1988: 14).

Hough's article was written on the cusp of huge changes in higher education, and to some extent anticipated these changes. The problem with the notion of a fixed canon was one of cultural authority: who decided which texts should be studied and why. This problem was a surmountable one when a university education was limited to a favoured few, and members of this elite class shared similar assumptions about which forms of culture were worth knowing and preserving. But the transformation of higher education since the 1960s has undermined the notion of 'the common pursuit of true judgment' (Leavis 1948: 70–1) on which Leavis's criticism, and that of many of his contemporaries, depended. In Britain, for example, the coming of age of the post-war baby-boom generation led to an expansion in British universities from the early 1960s onwards, and there has been an even bigger increase in student numbers since the early 1990s. There are more women, mature and working-class entrants, and more students from ethnic minorities, and their teachers are also less exclusively white, male and middle-class. These changes have been mirrored internationally, in countries such as the USA, Australia and Canada. The increasing diversity of the student and lecturing body has thrown into question the value-laden assumptions about literature on which the discipline of literary studies has traditionally been based. This climate of intellectual uncertainty has been echoed across the humanities and social-science disciplines, as notions of scientific objectivity and disciplinary coherence have been seen to rest on exclusions that sit uneasily within an increasingly pluralist university.

These developments have not only meant that the academic content of literary studies has been greatly expanded in the intervening years to include many different kinds of text but, more generally, that the status and future of the discipline has been questioned. Many of the examples of interdisciplinarity I have examined so far represent a kind of nostalgia for the lost unity of knowledge, and they see the discipline of English as the best way of restoring this. The interdisciplinary developments of the post-Leavis era may have been motivated partly by these synthesizing aims, but they have also been informed by a profound intellectual scepticism and uncertainty. They have interrogated both the status of 'the literary' as a distinct and studiable category, and the whole nature of disciplines as the purveyors of progressively more enlightened knowledge and understanding.

2

LITERATURE INTO CULTURE

There is a sense in which the contemporary field of 'cultural studies' could be said to be synonymous with interdisciplinarity itself, given that it draws variously on sociology, anthropology, history, linguistics, philosophy, textual criticism, visual culture, the philosophy of science, geography, politics, economics and psychology, among other areas. In this chapter, though, I am going to be more specifically concerned with the positioning of cultural studies at the intersection between the social sciences, particularly sociology and anthropology, and the humanities. One of the effects of this has been to challenge the disciplinary identity of literary studies by dissolving the category of 'literature' into the more inclusive notion of 'culture'. More broadly, it has meant that cultural studies has been characterized by its critical reflection on the confining nature of disciplines and the possibilities for interdisciplinary knowledge.

It is worth pointing out, first of all, that cultural studies is about far more than challenging the divisions between individual disciplines. Rooted in socialist politics and new social movements such as feminism, anti-racism and gay activism, its commitment to integrative study and to expanding the definition of 'culture' has been linked to questions about the cultural construction of identity and meaning, particularly in relation to the broader operations of power in society. Cultural studies therefore tends to be suspicious of those interdisciplinary programmes that merely adopt an inclusive approach to the study of culture without engaging with these concerns about the politics of knowledge and representation. In this context, Patrick Brantlinger criticizes American studies, which emerged as an interdisciplinary collaboration between literature and history departments after the Second World War, in reaction to what was perceived as the narrowly textual approach of academic literary criticism. Brantlinger argues that the apolitical interdisciplinarity of American studies meant that it ended up propounding 'an academic cultural chauvinism' in which American exceptionalism was crudely celebrated (Brantlinger 1990: 27).

While many contemporary American studies scholars would baulk at this description of their work, it is certainly true that American studies departments rose rapidly to institutional consolidation and respectability in America, Europe and elsewhere in the post-war period, often supported by funding from the US government and government-sponsored bodies like the Fulbright Commission. This contrasted sharply with the early existence of cultural studies at the very margins of the university. It is this institutional marginality, along with the explicitly political agenda of cultural studies, that has made it so sceptical of the traditional disciplines, and the way that they enclose scholars within academic enclaves, separate from the concerns of the outside world. Richard Johnson argues that cultural studies has been perennially anxious about the possibility that it might be institutionalized and disciplined and so lose its ability to plunder the more established disciplines while remaining separate from them:

A codification of methods or knowledges ... runs against some main features of cultural studies as a tradition: its openness and theoretical versatility, its reflexive even self-conscious mood, and, especially, the importance of critique. I mean critique in the fullest sense: not criticism merely, nor even polemic, but procedures by which other traditions are approached both for what they may yield and for what they inhibit. Critique involves stealing away the more useful elements and rejecting the rest. From this point of view cultural studies is a process, a kind of alchemy for producing useful knowledge; codify it and you might halt its reactions.

(Johnson 1996: 75)

As cultural studies has developed as a fashionable area of study, the future of this critical relationship to the more traditional disciplines has become a fierce point of contention, which I will discuss towards the end of this chapter. Since cultural studies is a much-contested and heterogeneous field, I will not attempt to provide a comprehensive survey of its interdisciplinary possibilities. Instead, I want to discuss the work of six key figures: Richard Hoggart, Raymond Williams, Stuart Hall, Michel de Certeau, Pierre Bourdieu and John Frow. In their diverse ways, these critics have particularly explored questions about the nature of disciplines and interdisciplinarity, and their work provides a useful means of opening up a more general discussion of these issues within cultural studies.

FOUNDING DOCUMENTS

The rise of cultural studies to a position of institutional respectability within the university has been a long and occasionally painful process. The early work of Richard Hoggart and Raymond Williams, two of the central figures in its early development, grew not out of university teaching but out of their initial posts at centres for continuing education, and was probably also influenced by their own personal feelings of exclusion as working-class scholarship boys who made it to university. The question of origins, though, is a problematic one for a subject that makes much of its scepticism about disciplines: both Hoggart and Williams dismissed their roles as 'founding fathers', and the term does indeed have a disciplinary, patriarchal slant: it implies a body of wisdom, a discrete series of concepts and methodologies handed down from privileged knowers.

According to Tom Steele, there is also a common misconception that cultural studies in Britain simply emerged as the⸺

'bastard offspring' of English studies, a radical offshoot of Leavi-sism (Steele 1997: 49, 3). In fact, although English may have acted as a 'midwife', cultural studies really developed out of the political and interdisciplinary commitments of adult-education programmes between the 1930s and the 1950s (Steele 1997: 9). There were extensive debates amongst adult educators at this time about the relationship between literature and sociology, and between politics and culture (Steele 1997: 3–4). The context of teaching workers with particular life experiences also meant that the agenda had to be set through a dialogue between tutors and students. As one tutor for the Workers' Educational Association put it in 1939:

> Whatever the purpose of study elsewhere, it seems to me that in the WEA the study of one subject should not only give an understanding of that subject but be a gateway through which a vista should be glimpsed of the importance of other subjects. A subject encased within the high walls of specialisation, whether of subject matter or of theory – economic, scientific, aesthetic – leads, I believe, up a blind alley.
>
> (Steele 1997: 18)

The institutionalization of cultural studies within higher educa-tion was partly aided by changes in the structure of British universities from the 1960s onwards, which allowed for more flexibility and co-operation between the disciplines. For example, some of the new campus universities, like Sussex (opened in 1961) and East Anglia (1963), were based on interdisciplinary 'schools of study' rather than departments, which brought to-gether common work from specialists in many different fields and which required students to study subjects other than their major discipline. More importantly, the formation of the Open Uni-versity (an open-access institution which teaches part-time students through correspondence, television and summer schools) and the polytechnics (higher-education institutions evolving out of the old technical colleges, often teaching subjects with a voca-tional base) in 1969 and 1970 respectively, provided a significant impetus for interdisciplinary study. When English was studied in polytechnics, for example, it was likely to be situated within a broader humanities department and to be taught as part of a combined honours degree, because of resource constraints as well as the interdisciplinary commitments of the lecturers. The Open University, meanwhile, pioneered the development of inter-disciplinary courses in the humanities on the subject of 'culture'. It was in these institutions that cultural studies approaches really began to gain ground from the early 1970s onwards.

However, the first institutional foothold for cultural studies had already been established at Birmingham University in 1964, with the founding of the Centre for Contemporary Cultural Studies (CCCS) under Hoggart's directorship. His *The Uses of Literacy* (1957), which is often seen as inaugurating the field, opens up whole new areas of working-class culture to critical scrutiny: allotment-keeping and gardening, brass bands, whist drives, charabanc trips to the seaside, dancing, gambling, working-men's clubs, pigeon-fancying and pub-singing. This is an undisciplined text not only in its choice of subject matter but in its methodol-ogy, since it combines social history, anthropology and cultural criticism with a series of autobiographical reflections on the author's working-class Yorkshire childhood. As Hoggart wrote later, his own discipline of literary studies was somewhat snob-bish about this inclusiveness: 'Many people I knew in ... depart-ments of English kept fairly quiet about it, as though a shabby cat from the council house next door had brought an odd – even a smelly – object into the house' (Hoggart 1991: 143). These atti-tudes emerged again during the difficult birth of cultural studies at Birmingham. Although the Centre began as an adjunct to the English department, funding had to be raised from external sources, and one of Hoggart's erstwhile colleagues referred to the new subject as his 'nice line in cheap hats' (Steele 1997: 119).

Hoggart's text has an ambivalent attitude to popular culture, though, which is suggested by the division of the book into two halves. The first section, 'An "Older" Order', describes a traditional working-class culture organized around family and neighbourhood rituals, and is largely sympathetic and celebratory. The second section, 'Yielding Place to New', laments the dan-gerous influence of a new form of Americanized popular culture on working-class life, a 'candy-floss world' of popular songs, 'spicy' magazines and titillating novels (Hoggart [1957] 1958: 223, 250). Hoggart particularly condemns the emerging youth culture of 1950s Britain, the 'jukebox boys' who dress in drape jackets and hang around in milk bars, producing 'a sort of spiritual dry-rot amid the odour of boiled milk' (Hoggart [1957] 1958: 248). While Hoggart suggests that we need to open up literary studies to other forms of inquiry, he seems to retain the traditionally evaluative aims of the discipline, and in particular the old Leavisite distinction between 'good' and 'bad' folk culture.

In his writings produced after the founding of the CCCS, Hoggart develops some of these themes into a discussion of the role of English and its relation to other disciplines. He acknowledges, first of all, that there is no intrinsic reason why it should exist as a discrete subject:

> Sometimes I think there is no recognisable discipline of 'English', no genuine whole, but only a set of contrived frontiers and selected approaches which, for complicated historical and cultural reasons, have come to be known as 'a subject'. Thousands are living within this frame of reference: it is part of the self-justifying, self-perpetuating, closed world of 'English studies'; and it has its counterparts among the other humanities.
>
> (Hoggart 1982: 125)

Hoggart aims to correct this anomaly through the new field of contemporary cultural studies, which he divides up into three parts: the historical–philosophical; the sociological; and the literary-critical, the latter being 'the most important' (Hoggart 1970: 255). This formulation recognizes the importance of interdisciplinarity, but there is still a sense that the different disciplines remain separate even as they are brought together productively, with one subject being regarded as central. Hoggart's justification for privileging the literary in this way is that it offers unique insights into the nature of society which are not provided by other cultural forms or intellectual frameworks, because 'literature is uniquely concerned with the total human response, with

"the quality of life," in the fullest sense we are able to imagine'
(Hoggart 1982: 136). He warns against the 'hard-nosed unim-
aginativeness' of a social science that claims to be 'value-free', and
argues that if we fail to recognize the unique value of certain kinds
of text 'we will sooner or later stop talking about literature and
find ourselves talking about history or sociology or philosophy –
and probably about bad history and bad sociology and bad philosophy' (Hoggart 1970: 274, 259). Although Hoggart is in favour of
reinvigorating the discipline of English with the insights of
sociology and history, he ultimately seems to remain loyal to his
home discipline.

The work of Raymond Williams represents a more sustained
critique of the conventionally narrow definition of 'literature'
which has been central to the formulation of English as a discipline, and which he sees as a suppression of 'the actual multiplicity of writing' (Williams 1977: 149). As Williams points out,
the original meaning of 'literature' was interdisciplinary, since up
until the end of the eighteenth century it referred to all types of
writing: scientific, autobiographical and historical as well as fictional. The notion of literature as a specialized, highly valued
kind of writing which deals with the imaginative or creative as
opposed to the factual or practical, is largely an invention of the
post-Romantic period (Williams [1976] 1988: 183–8). In fact,
there was still a residue of the earlier, expansive notion of literature in early courses in language and rhetoric at universities in
the nineteenth century, which tended to group together all kinds
of text – fiction, poetry, speeches, memoirs, history and philosophy – as exemplary pieces of 'good writing'. Williams makes a
similar argument about an even more complicated term, 'culture',
which was also broadly defined until, from the eighteenth century
onwards, it acquired associations with class, gentility and value
(Williams [1976] 1988: 87–93).

Williams's work is thus centrally concerned with tracing the
changing use of significant 'keywords' and the way that these
meanings have been used to reify the divisions between potentially integrated concepts. This project has some affinities with
the Leavisite one of idealizing a lost age of cultural unity but is
far more historically specific. Indeed, Williams's first major work,

Culture and Society, describes Leavis's evocation of an organic past as 'a surrender to a characteristically industrialist, or urban, nostalgia' (Williams [1958] 1961: 252–3). He also criticizes Leavis's school primer, *Culture and Environment*, for deriving its notion of lived experience solely from literary sources, and argues that a truly comprehensive study of culture needs to take account of all sorts of material, including the scientific and philosophical discourses that Leavis so readily excludes:

> The ways in which we can draw on other experience are more various than literature alone. For experience that is formally recorded we go, not only to the rich source of literature, but also to history, building, painting, music, philosophy, theology, political and social theory, the physical and natural sciences, anthropology, and indeed the whole body of learning.
>
> (Williams [1958] 1961: 248)

In his next book, *The Long Revolution*, Williams extends this argument, claiming that the ultimate aim of cultural analysis is to 'reveal unexpected identities in hitherto separately considered activities' (Williams [1961] 1965: 63). He identifies three ways of defining culture: the 'ideal', which represents the Arnoldian notion of a 'selective tradition' of high art and literature; the 'documentary', which means the different ways in which human experience and intellectual life are recorded through various media; and the 'social', which refers to a 'particular way of life' expressed through institutions and everyday practices (Williams [1961] 1965: 57). A thorough analysis of culture needs to bring together all of these different elements: high culture, mass entertainments, historical records, fashions, lifestyles and attitudes. The aim is to locate what Williams defines as the 'structure of feeling' of a particular period, a term that refers to 'the most delicate and least tangible parts of our activity ... the particular living result of all the elements in the general organization' ([1961] 1965: 64). This notion suggests that Williams's interdisciplinarity, despite his opposition to Leavis's nostalgic evocation of an organic society, is still based on the idea of a 'common culture', a social totality which can be discovered and analysed by criticism. However, he does stress that this is 'in no sense the idea of a simply consenting, and certainly not of a merely conforming, society', but refers to a 'free, contributive and common *process* of participation in the creation of meanings and values' (Williams 1989: 37–8).

Given this inclusive definition of culture, it is not surprising that Williams was one of the first British critics to turn his attention to new forms of mass media in works such as *Communications* (1962) and *Television, Technology and Cultural Form* (1974). Like Hoggart, though, Williams remained critical of some aspects of the mass media because he saw them as saturated with economic interests and detached from the real experience of working-class life. In *The Long Revolution*, he criticizes 'a popular form of demagogy' that ignores 'the problem of bad culture':

> Can we agree ... that football is indeed a wonderful game, that jazz is a real musical form and that gardening and homemaking are indeed important? Can we also agree, though, that the horror-film, the rape-novel, the Sunday strip-paper and the latest Tin-Pan drool are not exactly in the same world, and that the nice magazine romance, the manly adventure story (straight to the point of the jaw) and the pretty, clever television advertisement are not in it either?
>
> (Williams [1961] 1965: 364)

Williams finds common cause with Leavis here, arguing that the methodicalness of his practical criticism of popular texts functions as a necessary counter to the equally organized efforts of powerful institutions to threaten traditional forms of community, and that in the face of these institutions 'the magnificent contrasting vitality of literature is an essential control and corollary' (Williams [1961] 1965: 250). When Williams uses the term 'common culture', he thus partly means that culture is the whole 'way of life of a people', but he is also 'using the idea of the common element of the culture – its community – as a way of criticising that divided and fragmented culture we actually have' (1989: 35). He argues that these divisions can be healed by making the mass media more collective and publicly owned and by democratizing and popular-izing high culture so that it can be appreciated by the working classes. In this sense, Williams's interdisciplinarity is informed partly by a 'left-Leavisite' preference for certain cultural forms that, it is claimed, are better able to bring about a common culture. Despite his attempts to deconstruct and broaden the categories of 'literature' and 'culture', the traditionally evaluative and disciplinary aims of literary studies seem to remain in some of Williams's work in muted form.

THE SOCIOLOGICAL TURN

Under the directorship of Stuart Hall between 1968 and 1979, the CCCS started to draw more extensively on sociological notions of culture. Sociology is a branch of the social sciences that deals with the study of human society and social relations, and its advantage from a cultural studies perspective is that it is necessarily extremely wide ranging and, perhaps more than any other social science, is receptive to the theories and methods of other disciplines such as philosophy, history and politics. However, the engagement of Hall and his colleagues with sociology was not an uncritical one: in particular, they were sceptical of sociology's traditional definition of itself as a science, which can be traced back to its nineteenth-century origins in the work of Auguste Comte and Émile Durkheim.

Comte coined the term 'sociology' in 1830 as part of his advocacy of 'positivism', which proposed that all real knowledge was gained through empirical methods and that the procedures of the natural sciences could thus be transferred to the social sciences. Indeed, he defined sociology, which he envisaged as a comprehensive study of society incorporating all the social sciences, as 'social physics'. Now that 'the human mind has created celestial and terrestrial physics, mechanics and chemistry', Comte argued, sociology would 'complete the system of the observational sciences' ([1830–42] 1974: 27). Durkheim, the central figure in the founding of sociology as a university subject at the end of the nineteenth century, also envisaged society as having a kind of objective reality independent of individual agency and urged sociologists to *consider social facts as things*' (Durkheim [1895] 1964: 14). In fact, many of the subsequent debates within sociology have turned on the validity of its scientific status, since there are clearly problems with importing the methods of the natural sciences into purely sociological concerns: the huge complexity and number of variables in social life, for example, and the fact that social experiments can never simply reproduce natural conditions.

Hall has written that when he began his academic career in the 1950s, sociology was heavily reliant on American theories and methodologies which were 'militantly empiricist and quantitative' because of their origins in this positivist tradition (Hall 1980a: 21). While this may be an oversimplification of a complex field, it is true that, as sociology was being professionalized in the USA, it tended to eschew an interest in political commitment and policy prescription in favour of an abstract theorizing of social relations, or a number-crunching and model-building similar to that undertaken in economics. The birth of cultural studies at Birmingham did actually produce some disciplinary skirmishes with 'hard' social scientists along these lines: the opening of the Centre provoked a letter from two sociologists who warned the subject off their own territory, suggesting that if it attempted to move beyond textual analysis to the study of contemporary society, there would be 'reprisals'. Early applications from the Centre for research grants were also only approved with the proviso that the research would be supplemented by the work of 'proper' social scientists who would back up the theoretical speculations of the Centre with empirical evidence (Hall 1980a: 21–2).

The work of the Centre under Hall thus steered clear of statistical, quantitative methods in favour of fieldwork-based research, interviews and *ethnography*: the direct observation of a social group over an extended period. Although the ethnographic method had already been used in sociology – particularly within a British tradition that produced detailed community studies of family, kinship and work cultures (Dennis *et al.* 1956; Young and Wilmott 1957; Kerr 1958) – it was more closely associated with social and cultural anthropology, a related subject that deals with the structure and culture of human societies. Until the early twentieth century, anthropology and sociology were often situated in the same university department, the former being distinguished by its focus on 'primitive' cultures, often small tribes, and the latter by its focus on 'complex' Western cultures. This traditional distinction has meant that anthropology has sometimes been accused of emphasizing the uncivilized 'other-ness' of developing cultures and thus reproducing colonialist attitudes. The CCCS, though, used ethnographic methods to examine cultures closer to home, employing them as a counter-point to the more empirical work undertaken by traditional social scientists. Its ethnographic studies, such as Paul Willis's *Learning to Labour* (1977), were more methodical and rigorous than Hoggart's quasi-ethnographic *The Uses of Literacy*, which relied primarily on personal memories rather than prolonged observation. For his project, Willis spent three years with a group of twelve boys from a Midlands comprehensive – talking to them, attending their classes and following them through their first few months at work, while also interviewing their parents, teachers, careers officers, shop stewards and employers – in order to show how the boys developed a powerful subculture of cynicism and rebellion at school which ensured that they entered jobs with limited prospects.

These ethnographic methods were also an implicit rebuke to textual criticism, since rather than stepping back from culture and discussing it at one remove, the CCCS researchers were prepared to get their hands dirty with participant observation. However, their work still demonstrated a concern with language, textuality and meaning which was in part a product of the CCCS's origins within an English department, and which moved it beyond the concerns of mainstream sociology. Hall and his colleagues summarize this dual notion of culture as the distinctive arrangements of social life and the means by which social groups give expression to those arrangements: 'A culture includes the "maps of meaning" which make things intelligible to its members ... Culture is the way the social relations of a group are structured and shaped: but it is also the way those shapes are experienced, understood and interpreted' (Clarke *et al.* 1976: 10–11).

The CCCS defined the cultural 'text' extremely broadly, to incorporate everyday practices, rituals, social groups, genres and different forms of media, thus thoroughly dismantling the moral-evaluative distinction between different kinds of culture that lay at the heart of the literary-critical enterprise. Significantly, the most influential aspects of the Centre's work look at the symbolic resources of youth sub-cultures, those groups that Hoggart had specifically criticized. Several projects analyse the ways in which groups of working-class youths such as skinheads, mods, rockers, punks and rastas engage in a kind of 'resistance through rituals'. Others explore the role of the dominant culture, particularly the media and the education system, in representing these young people. In *Policing the Crisis* (1978), for example, Hall and his collaborators discuss the media panic around mugging in the 1970s and its implicit associations with the 'threat' represented by young black men. While being fundamentally involved with the deciphering of cultural meaning, the concerns of the CCCS thus tended to mirror broader debates within sociology about the relationship between social structure and individual agency. In sociological terms, this might be defined as the tension between functionalism (which argues that the social world constrains and limits individuals) and interactionism (which argues that individuals can interact productively with the social world).

Hall argues that the Centre did not want to position cultural studies as 'yet another academic sub-discipline' and worked hard to prevent 'its easy absorption and naturalization into the social division of knowledge' by refusing to map out the field prescriptively (Hall 1980a: 18). It thus tended to sponsor collaborative, multi-authored projects or working papers, which aimed to subvert the usual context of disciplinary work: the rise to tenure, promotion and professional status of individual scholars through the development of a reputation amongst peers and fellow specialists. Most importantly, the Centre's interdisciplinarity was more than simply a matter of pluralism or inclusiveness; it was underpinned by explicitly political commitments, which partly explains its almost-exclusive focus on contemporary society and culture. As Hall puts it, the contemporary refuses to provide the 'benefit of that scholarly detachment or distance which the passage of time alone sometimes confers on other fields of study. The "contemporary" ... [is] by definition, hot to handle' (Hall 1980a: 17). In other words, the contemporary is necessarily an unmapped, provisional field, because its disparate elements are only just becoming part of public discussion and record; it has not yet been 'disciplined'.

Perhaps the most significant exclusion from the interdisciplinary work of the CCCS was the literary; if written texts were discussed at all within the CCCS, they tended to be popular cultural forms such as teen magazines or women's weeklies. This emphasis on 'lived' as opposed to written culture was partly corrective, since cultural studies emerged as a way of challenging the positioning of literature at the core of the humanities disciplines. This has been carried over into contemporary cultural studies, much of which cites the work of the CCCS as an important influence, and which tends to focus on relatively modern media such as film, television and digital technologies, or on cultural practices and social forms. Indeed, it is probably fair to say that, since this 'ethnographic turn', contemporary cultural studies has had more in common with its social-scientific than with its literary descendants. Pertti Alasuutari even suggests that cultural studies is simply 'another generation of sociology', one that recognizes that the complexity of post-industrial culture and society requires more than statistical, quantitative methods to make sense of it (Alasuutari 1995: 24).

But this is to be too prescriptive: cultural studies has never seen itself as the logical development of a particular discipline, but as creating a space between disciplines to examine all forms of culture in relation to questions of power. Although the case studies that the CCCS produced in the 1970s tended to be based around sociological concerns such as social inequality and class, race and gender divisions, much of their work involved a process of theoretical ground-clearing which has proved fruitful for other kinds of analysis. Hall's notion of 'encoding and decoding', although specifically addressed to television, is a good example of how cultural studies readings can be applied to a wide range of texts. Briefly, encoding refers to the production of media texts, and decoding refers to their consumption by audiences, and texts are unstable social phenomena precisely because these two processes are never entirely identical. In the complex negotiation between media institutions, social and political structures, the rules of language and the various decipherings of different audiences, texts become multifaceted and 'polysemic' (Hall 1980b: 134).

This sort of cultural studies approach can usefully remind us that books are media texts as well: in fact, the book was really the first form of mass media, widely circulated after the invention of the printing press and fully implicated in the rise of entrepreneurial capitalism and the development of new technologies and commodity forms. Like other mass media, books are produced by up-to-date forms of technology and are sold through sophisticated packaging, marketing and distribution techniques. Indeed, it is fair to say that every major technological development in the media in the past two centuries – the invention of the rotary press, photography, radio, the cathode-ray tube, the computer and the Internet – has affected the production of literary texts, either in the way that they are written, published, marketed or distributed. Literary works are also interesting ideologically precisely because they often fulfil several functions which coexist or conflict with each other. While they can be used to disseminate official ideologies or to make a profit for their authors and publishers, they also feed into the wider circulation of meanings and signification in the culture as a whole. The process by which a writer's words are transferred onto paper and into the hands, eyes and mind of a reader is not a neutral, unmediated one, and is just as complicated for literary texts as it is for other kinds of media texts. In this sense, the engagement of cultural studies with a sociology of the mass media might allow us to see literature as part of a wider series of economic and cultural practices.

THE CULTURE OF EVERYDAY LIFE

In his most influential work, *The Practice of Everyday Life*, Michel de Certeau further expands the interdisciplinary possibilities of cultural studies by aiming to 'bring scientific practices and languages back toward their native land, everyday life' (de Certeau 1984: 6). This book explores the ways in which everyday cultural practices, such as walking, playing games, reading, shopping and cooking, slip through the extensive power and surveillance networks in contemporary culture, precisely because of their perceived triviality and banality. These activities can then be used as a way of subtly resisting the dominant culture from within, appropriating it for subversive purposes (de Certeau 1984: xii–xiii). De Certeau's work has been most commonly employed in cultural studies, notably in the work of John Fiske, to argue that the consumption of popular-culture texts can be used to challenge the apparently all-powerful constructions of capitalism, racism and patriarchy (Fiske 1989: 35).

More broadly, though, de Certeau's discussion of everyday cultural practices is related to his concern with the institutional politics of knowledge: the compartmentalizing of academic life, the fossilization of disciplines and the modern triumph of the 'expert' over the 'philosopher' (de Certeau 1984: 7). For de Certeau, academic disciplines are always defined by 'what they have taken care to exclude from their field in order to constitute it' (1984: 61). Most significantly, they ignore the practices of everyday life, by dividing modern life up into 'scientific and dominant islands set off against the background of practical "resistances" and symbolizations that cannot be reduced to thought' (de Certeau 1984: 6). This allows the disciplines to step back from the object or experience they are analysing and to academicize it, discarding what they deem to be irrelevant and preserving the remainder as the basis for a 'science'. Every discipline thus 'grants itself a priori the conditions that allow it to encounter things only in its own limited field where it can "verbalize" them', and its intellectual rigour is 'measured by the strict definition of its own limits' (de Certeau 1984: 61, 6).

De Certeau makes an important distinction between 'strategies' and 'tactics' which further links his theories of the everyday to the academic disciplining of knowledge. A 'strategy' is 'the calculus of force-relationships which becomes possible when a subject of will and power ... can be isolated from an "environment"' (de Certeau 1984: xix). In other words, it is the activity, which occurs within academic disciplines and other powerful institutions with vested interests, by which dominant groups position undesirable elements as the excluded 'other'. A tactic, by contrast, is a form of 'anti-discipline' practised by these undesirable elements from a position of relative powerlessness, 'a calculated action determined by the absence of a proper locus' which must 'play on and with a terrain imposed on it and organized by the law of a foreign power' (de Certeau 1984: 37). Tactics are practices of everyday life which function as a kind of micropolitics for those whose power in society is limited, and it is these practices that need to be the object of interdisciplinary work, because they have been so systematically excluded from the traditional disciplines. It is worth noting that de Certeau defines a 'tactic' in quite limited terms, arguing that it is not capable of overthrowing the system, because 'people have to make do with what they have', taking pleasure in 'getting around the rules of constraining space' (de Certeau 1984: 18). Similarly, we can never wholly discard disciplines as ways of organizing and constraining knowledge, but we can use subversive 'tactics' to imagine disciplines that are more aware of what they have had to exclude to come into being (de Certeau 1984: 61).

In this approach, de Certeau is influenced by the pioneering work of Henri Lefebvre who, in his *Critique of Everyday Life* (1947), experiences a similar frustration with the readiness of the established disciplines to dismiss this sort of culture as banal and unworthy of our attention:

> Everyday life, in a sense residual, defined by 'what is left over' after all distinct, superior, specialized, structured activities have been singled out by analysis, must be defined as a totality. Considered in their specialization and their technicality, superior activities leave a 'technical vacuum' between one another which is filled by everyday life. Everyday life is profoundly related to *all* activities, and encompasses them with all their differences and their conflicts; it is their meeting place, their bond, their common ground.
>
> (Lefebvre 1991a: 97)

For Lefebvre, the study of everyday life is thus interdisciplinary not simply because it encompasses material overlooked by the existing disciplines but because it forms a kind of connecting glue which shows how these established systems of thought are ultimately related to each other, even as they attempt to deny this relationship.

It is important to stress, though, that the work of both Lefebvre and de Certeau is microcosmic in focus and directly opposed to the kind of interdisciplinary work that assumes the possibility of an all-encompassing synthesis of knowledge. De Certeau succinctly states his scepticism towards totalizing modes of thought that aim to see 'the big picture' when, in a chapter titled 'Walking in the City', he recalls surveying Manhattan from the 110th floor of the World Trade Center, and wonders 'what is the source of this pleasure of "seeing the whole", of looking down on, totalizing the most immoderate of human texts' (de Certeau 1984: 92). Lefebvre and de Certeau are both critical of the ways in which disciplines seek to appropriate and master their subject matter, and they propose the study of everyday life as a more provisional and tentative relationship with less directly tangible phenomena. Some of de Certeau's examples of everyday 'tactics' are relatively concrete, such as *la perruque*, which literally means 'wigging' and which he identifies as the practice by which employees get one over on their employers by doing fun activities (such as phoning friends, or booking holidays on the Internet) on the company's time (de Certeau 1984: 25–6). Other examples, such as gestures, habits, dreams and memories, which challenge 'the modern mutation of time into a quantifiable and regulatable space' (de Certeau 1984: 89), are less easily categorized. In this sense, de Certeau's work focuses specifically on 'undisciplined' material, the momentary, fleeting aspects of experience that are difficult to represent or analyse. Ultimately, though, even the most insubstantial, elusive experiences of everyday life are mediated through discourse because, like all 'tactics', they have to work within existing power structures.

For de Certeau, the inevitable narrativization of everyday practices makes *reading* 'the "exorbitant" focus of contemporary culture and its consumption' (de Certeau 1984: xxi). As I have already suggested, there has been a tendency within cultural studies to de-emphasize the literary text as an object of study, because of its associations with outdated and class-specific notions of cultural value, and because the concern with the contemporary in cultural studies tends to steer it towards those forms of mass media produced by modern technologies: television, cinema, popular music and the Internet. De Certeau, instead, proposes the activity of reading as a foundational one in contemporary culture, the basis for all kinds of other cultural practices in a society that is 'increasingly written, organized by the power of modifying things and of reforming structures on the basis of scriptural models (whether scientific, economic, or political)' (de Certeau 1984: 167–8). In this context, de Certeau sees the activity of reading a book, in which the reader can transform and create meanings never intended by the author, as a paradigm for many other subversive 'tactics' within contemporary culture.

Like the practices of everyday life, the established academic disciplines are also immersed in narrative, but they try to conceal their narrativity beneath a veneer of scientificity. For de Certeau, the value of literary forms such as the novel is that, unlike the established disciplines, they foreground their narrativity and are open to all kinds of undisciplined material, becoming 'the zoo of everyday practices since the establishment of modern science' (1984: 78). In other words, the novel is such a capacious, hetero-geneous form, which brings together many different modes of writing and types of human experience, that it contains much that is excluded from the traditional disciplines, particularly those shadowy and barely perceptible customs and practices that de Certeau defines as the 'everyday'. For de Certeau, literary texts are worthy of study because they provide the basis for a transforma-tive practice of reading, and because they are able to mop up the 'leftover', undisciplined elements of experience. His work could thus be said to be interdisciplinary for two reasons: it opens up the study of culture to previously neglected material, and it connects this material to more traditional concerns within literary studies such as language, reading and narrative.

CLASS AND CULTURAL CAPITAL

The theories of the French sociologist, Pierre Bourdieu, have been influential in recent years in negotiating the boundaries between the social sciences and humanities, particularly between sociology and literary criticism. Although it ranges over many different subjects, Bourdieu's work is fundamentally concerned with the relationship between cultural value and class differentiation. He argues that this question permeates all forms of culture, so that a similar reinforcement of social distinctions is going on when we choose to buy particular types of food (organic tofu or tinned spaghetti), book holidays (the Algarve or Magaluf), go to the theatre (Samuel Beckett or Andrew Lloyd-Webber) or read a novel (Ian McEwan or Dan Brown). Bourdieu's work thus represents a sustained critique of the supposed autonomy of art and literature from broader social formations, and discusses many different kinds of cultural activity in relation to the sociological concerns of class and inequality.

Bourdieu's most important concept is the 'field', which he sees as a basic organizing element in social life. The field is a structured system with its own internal logic and hierarchical relationships created by the struggle for different forms of 'capital': economic, cultural, social and so on. The field of cultural production, according to Bourdieu, is specifically concerned with the market for cultural capital within 'the cultural value stock exchange' (1993: 137). Cultural capital is gained through the accumulation of status or prestige within the cultural sphere, and is only obtained when directly economic interests are either absent or concealed, because they threaten the field's claim to a monopoly of power within its own sphere of influence. Cultural producers are thus relatively autonomous, gaining power within their own field by virtue of their separation from other fields and other forms of capital. But this should not blind us to the self-interest inherent in all cultural production, for cultural capital is simply a 'misrecognizable, transfigured and legitimated form' of the most basic form of capital, the economic (Bourdieu 1991: 170).

Bourdieu's notion of the 'habitus', another important concept in his work, explains the process by which individuals within each field have a 'feel for the game', a socially constituted disposition to behave in a certain way depending on their struggle for capital and their corresponding position within a particular field (1990: 11). Moreover, according to Bourdieu, an author's work will reflect or refract these power struggles and position-takings (1971: 161). In this context, the work of a contemporary author such as Martin Amis might be seen as the product of a competitive celebrity culture of literary prizes, huge publishers' advances, aggressive forms of book marketing and media interest in authors. Novels such as *Money* (1984), *London Fields* (1989) and *The Information* (1995), for example, are frequently concerned with metropolitan and transatlantic literary culture and articulate anxieties about the complex relationship between commerce and cultural value in multinational capitalism. The market for cultural capital also affects how readers and audiences relate to literary texts, since Bourdieu argues that cultural consumption is motivated by our desire to display taste and discrimination, which is in turn inspired by our need to place ourselves within social hierarchies. Readers choose between and consume texts in a variety of ways according to their different class positions and what kinds of cultural capital they have accumulated or aspire to obtain. As Bourdieu puts it, there is simply 'no way out of the game of culture' (1984: 12).

Bourdieu's work is unusual in contemporary cultural studies in being significantly concerned with the production and consumption of literature, if only to point to its close relationship to other forms of culture and its 'social function of legitimating social differences' (1984: 7). A Bourdieu-influenced study of avant-garde modernist poetry, for example, might look at how its attempts to define itself explicitly against a philistine, market-driven culture of 'kitsch', are aimed at fetishizing the work of art as wholly disconnected from the sphere of exchange or profit, and producing a kind of 'charismatic illusion' around the figure of the poet as a repository of cultural rather than economic capital (Bourdieu 1996b: 319). The readers and critics of such poetry, meanwhile, might be seen as attempting to accumulate particular forms of intellectual kudos associated with elite as opposed to popular forms.

It is possible to argue that, rather than being interdisciplinary, Bourdieu's work is sociologically reductionist, in that it makes literature solely the object of sociology, and therefore tends to regard complex works of art as mere functions of self-promoting, strategic moves within society as a whole. To be fair, Bourdieu does propose what he calls a 'genetic structuralism' which

recognizes the importance of individual agency in structured systems, and he uses the deliberately imprecise term, 'field', in order
to suggest something fluid and porous, open to negotiation,
conflict and change (1990: 14). Moreover, because a field is constituted through signifying practices, individual agents (such as
authors, critics, publishers and readers within the field of cultural
production) have the ability to transform it through their own
responses, interpretations and writings. Amis's critique of literary
celebrity in his novels, for example, itself becomes a part of how
celebrity is produced and received in contemporary culture. This
clearly opens up possibilities for an interdisciplinary preoccupation with the relationship between material practices and literary
and cultural texts.

In practice, though, Bourdieu's field of cultural production
seems quite systemic, being envisaged as an all-encompassing
structure in which writers and artists of varying degrees of
notoriety, editors, critics, publishers, readers and consumers are
all implicated in the same struggle for cultural capital. Bourdieu's
work makes use of a mass of quantitative sociological data, produced by a large team of researchers, to demonstrate the significance and inevitability of this struggle. In *Distinction*, his
encyclopaedic work about the cultural tastes of the French, for
example, he produces a series of elaborate graphs and tables to
point to the statistical relationship between an individual's class
position and her cultural preferences. For all his stated desire to
produce a 'reflexive' sociology which recognizes its own involve-
ment in the cultural phenomena it analyses, Bourdieu also tends
to employ a dispassionate, dense prose style which draws on the
traditional authority of sociology as a 'science'.

Bourdieu's concern with the relationship between cultural
production and consumption and the acquisition of power and
privilege extends to an interest in the politics of education and
the institutional practices of academic life. This is partly because
schools, colleges and universities are crucial in the propagation
of elite culture and the concomitant dissemination of cultural
capital. 'Literature', as Bourdieu understands it, is simply what
gets taught in the academic discipline of literary criticism,
allowing the favoured few who attend the elite institutions to

build up social competences and knowledges which can then be used to perpetuate class differences. On top of this, however, these institutions themselves create power divisions which are generated by the struggle for cultural capital. In this respect, a discipline is, like any other 'field', an enclosed space with its own hierarchies determined by the struggle for academic capital appropriate to that discipline. Disciplines tend to conceal this fact, however, by communicating their findings in a specialist language which has the dual function of warding off non-specialists and concealing the personal investments of its practitioners (Bourdieu 1988: 25). The problem with this is that academia then serves simply to 'inspire aspirations and assign them limits', creating 'a world without surprises' (Bourdieu 1988: 153). Like de Certeau's work, Bourdieu's theory of disciplines as closed, inert institutions emerges out of a broader project: that of questioning the apparently disinterested nature of cultural production, by pointing to its role in reproducing wider social inequalities.

In fact, some of Bourdieu's more recent work reveals a significant change of emphasis in that it criticizes the 'doxosophes', the media intellectuals who seek to manoeuvre their way into the academic field and challenge its traditional autonomy and independence (1996b: 343–7). Writing within a French context in which writers and intellectuals frequently become celebrities by appearing on late-night talk shows, Bourdieu argues that 'television rewards a certain number of *fast-thinkers* who offer cultural "fast food" – predigested and prethought culture ... Supported by external forces, these agents are accorded an authority they cannot get from their peers' (1996a: 29, 59). These comments on the usurpation of intellectual life by the field of journalism seem to uphold the value of traditional academic and disciplinary expertise. They form part of Bourdieu's overall criticisms of any kind of culture that attempts to bridge the distinction between high and mass culture, what he calls the 'partial revolutions in the hierarchies' created by 'the new cultural intermediaries' who 'have invented a whole series of genres half-way between legitimate culture and mass production' (Bourdieu 1984: 325–6). As David Swartz suggests, there is a tension in Bourdieu's work between an unmasking of the provisional nature of cultural distinctions and hierarchies in his 'field' theory, which seems to open the way to an interdisciplinary preoccupation with the relationship between cultural forms that are conventionally discussed separately; and a much more prescriptive view of how intellectuals and authors should critically engage with society and culture, which arguably involves a reinforcement of these distinctions and hierarchies (Swartz 1997: 222).

CULTURAL VALUE AND THE KNOWLEDGE CLASS

The Australian cultural critic, John Frow, has more recently interrogated the relationship between literature and other forms of culture by returning to these questions of cultural value. Frow argues that cultural studies has often fudged the question of cultural value by adopting a sweeping definition of culture as a 'whole way of life', or by uncritically celebrating popular culture and dismissing high culture as elitist. While stressing that he has no wish to return to a purely aesthetic notion of value which sees it as separate from broader institutional, economic or social factors, and which was so central to traditional disciplinary notions of literary studies, Frow does suggest that value judgements are inescapable (1995: 1). His concern with cultural value is aimed at questioning an emptily inclusive interdisciplinarity which embraces an undifferentiated and homogeneous notion of 'culture'. If we are going to study culture in its entirety, he argues, we need to distinguish more adequately between its disparate elements and recognize the different investments in cultural value attendant upon distinctions between 'highbrow', 'lowbrow' and 'middlebrow' culture.

Frow argues that cultural studies has appropriated an inclusive notion of culture from disciplines such as anthropology and sociology, without similarly making use of theories from these disciplines that might help it to recognize how complex and differentiated 'culture' actually is. He criticizes Williams's notion of culture as an 'all-embracing totality', for example, arguing that he remains tied to narrowly national concerns and fails to recognize the hybrid nature of all forms of culture (Frow 1995: 8–10). Frow also questions the emphasis in the work of John Fiske and others on the resistant politics of popular culture. While claiming to be inclusive, this emphasis is still unavoidably saturated with questions of value. This means that certain forms of the popular, such as gangsta rap, club culture, punk, fashion and the Internet are regarded as worthy of study, while others, such as easy-listening music, boy bands and bingo, are not (Frow 1995: 82). Frow is not criticizing the attempt within cultural studies to reach out to different disciplines and to incorporate new material, but he argues that we should continually reflect on our aims and motives in doing this, because 'if the concept of culture says everything then it says nothing' (1995: 10).

Unlike Bourdieu, Frow also believes that cultural value has many other functions than merely to differentiate social status, particularly in advanced capitalist societies where both cultural and class distinctions have diversified and fragmented. In particular, he suggests that the division between high and low culture is breaking down because of two factors: the commodification of high culture and the democratization of low culture. Both high and low culture are now fully part of the marketplace, and the former is no longer the 'dominant culture', as Bourdieu suggests, but is instead 'a *pocket* within commodity culture': a 'niche' market, certainly, but not a particularly unique or authoritative one (Frow 1995: 86, 23). This commodification of high culture can be seen, for example, in the mass-marketing of highbrow authors by major publishers and their repositioning as media celebrities, and the branding of classic authors such as Shakespeare, Dickens and Jane Austen through television and film adaptations, the heritage industry and tie-in editions of novels and plays. Inclusive mass audiences have also developed for texts such as soap operas, mainstream films and popular fiction by authors such as Stephen King and John Grisham, which often appeal to people of different classes and levels of education. Frow suggests that, although cultural studies has become fixated on the popular as a representation of the political potential of repressed cultures, high and low culture should *both* be studied in order to explore the complex relationship between cultural value and commodity forms in capitalist societies. Since no cultural product can escape the market for cultural value, he suggests, we can neither bracket off high culture nor essentialize the popular as a privileged space. As with Bourdieu's work, this opens up the possibility for a re-engagement with the literary in cultural studies.

As part of this reconsideration of cultural value, however, Frow formulates a notion of intellectuals and their relationship to the disciplines that specifically opposes Bourdieu's arguments. Since Bourdieu sees a direct correlation between the consumption of high culture and social class, he argues that intellectuals form part of the dominant class of the bourgeoisie, albeit in a slightly displaced relationship which makes them the 'dominated fraction' of that class (Bourdieu 1993: 198). For Frow, this argument is undermined by the existence of a rapidly growing, mediating class of intellectuals whose interests cannot simply be reduced to those of a dominant class. He adopts Antonio Gramsci's notion of 'organic intellectuals', defining them as 'all of those whose work is socially defined as being based upon the possession and exercise of knowledge, whether that knowledge be prestigious or routine, technical or speculative' (Frow 1995: 90). This broadly defined 'knowledge class' incorporates not only academics but writers, critics, editors, advertising copywriters and people who work in television, film and other media.

Frow's aim in identifying a knowledge class in this way is to raise the same sorts of issues about the vested interests of intellectuals that are typically raised in cultural studies, without reverting to the 'self-hatred and self-idealization' that he sees as the inevitable by-product of a more narrowly academic conception of the intellectual (1995: 90). He suggests that the claim which is often made within cultural studies to speak up for subordinated and marginalized cultures outside academia is based on a false belief that it is possible to transcend the conditions of intellectual production, and is thus dependent on a self-serving distinction 'between "real" intellectuals and "pseudo-" intellectuals (the treacherous clerks within the disciplines, the bureaucrats and journalists without)' (Frow 1995: 168). While recognizing that intellectuals must be self-critical about their work and aware of their own struggles for 'cultural capital' within academia or elsewhere, Frow is sceptical of what he sees as the knee-jerk anti-academicism of cultural studies as a field. He suggests that, rather than claiming to speak for anyone else, intellectuals should speak as intellectuals and address their readers as such (Frow 1995: 131).

This attempt to reconceive the role of the intellectual as a kind of public knowledge-worker is clearly relevant to any discussion of disciplines and the potential of cultural studies as an inter-disciplinary field. Frow does not attempt to defend disciplines as neutral or organically developing knowledge structures, but he does suggest that there is no such thing as non-disciplinary knowledge: we cannot just dispense with disciplines altogether in the hope of discovering a higher or purer form of truth, because the institutionalization of knowledge is inevitable and necessary. The limiting nature of disciplines is thus

> not the repression of a spontaneously developing knowledge but is precisely productive of knowledge ... [T]here can be no knowledge whatsoever that is not enabled by some such structure, however informal, however embedded in everyday life it may be. The question is not, therefore, whether or not there should be disciplines and disciplinary relations, but can only be about their form, their relative flexibility, their productiveness, and so on.
>
> (Frow 1988: 307, 320)

In other words, there is no mode of thought that comes before and exists independently of our attempts to structure and limit it: interdisciplinary study must start from a recognition that disciplinarity is inescapable, and that all we can hope to do is produce more open-ended and critically aware procedures for organizing knowledge.

Frow's comments tap into broader concerns about the scope and limits of cultural studies as an interdisciplinary field and whether or not it should aspire to be a discipline in its own right. These controversies have been given added impetus by the growing strength of cultural studies within universities. Stuart Hall, among others, has warned against the dangers of the institutionalization of the field, particularly in the context of its rapid rise to respectability and prominence in the USA. He regards the professionalization and 'Americanization' of cultural studies as 'a moment of profound danger', because this is bound to threaten its role as an interdisciplinary field which draws strength from its marginality within the academy (Hall 1992: 285). This issue is not simply confined to the USA, however: cultural studies is now a burgeoning field internationally, developing its own, well-funded departments and research centres and attracting students and scholars with its popular and readily available material.

Tony Bennett's response to these changed circumstances is the opposite of Hall's and amounts to a critique of what he calls the 'disciplinary bashfulness' of cultural studies. Like Frow, he suggests that institutionalization is not a looming threat from outside the field which needs to be repelled, because cultural studies is already disciplined by virtue of being a named and identifiable field of knowledge organized by academic professionals within universities. Rather than subscribing to the heroic notion of 'a knowledge forged-in-opposition' that is common to much cultural studies work, Bennett argues that we *should* think about 'disciplining' cultural studies if this means articulating its distinctive aims and methods and considering its practical applications (1998: 9). We should not, however, dispense with the specific forms of training and expertise available to cultural studies from discrete disciplines in the social sciences and humanities, since these 'need to be both defended and promoted instead of being "white-anted" [sabotaged or undermined from within] by misplaced and overgeneralising assessments of the value of interdisciplinariness' (Bennett 1998: 19). He argues that cultural studies should perform a kind of 'clearinghouse function' in which it co-ordinates the activities of other disciplines to the extent that they deal with the relationship between culture and power, and should not strive to be 'a putative intellectual synthesis in which existing disciplinary specialisms would be overcome or rendered redundant' (Bennett 1998: 28).

In similar vein, Bill Readings has expressed scepticism about the rise of cultural studies as what he sees as the dominant paradigm of an ill-defined and undiscriminating interdisciplinarity within the humanities. As a form of interdisciplinarity, he argues, cultural studies is 'characterized above all by resistance to all attempts to limit its field of reference', and has become a kind of 'quasi-discipline' which aims either to unify the humanities disciplines or supersede them (Readings 1996: 98, 91). Readings is suspicious of this notion of cultural studies as 'the discipline that will save the university by giving it back its lost truth', because for him it represents a backward-looking search for total knowledge (1996: 18). Despite its apparently radical questioning of the traditional academic disciplines, he fears that cultural studies may ultimately turn out to be 'animated by Kantian nostalgia' for an all-inclusive, humane education, a desire that has characterized the human sciences since their inception (Readings 1996: 122).

There is some validity in these arguments. The virtues of interdisciplinarity have often been touted in cultural studies with quite a vague sense of what the term means and how disciplines are actually supposed to be challenged or transcended. It is worth reminding ourselves that academic fields, even ones that are hostile to disciplinary consolidation like cultural studies, are always inevitably the product of institutional pragmatics, power relationships and attempts to organize knowledge. However, there are different degrees and types of institutionalization, and Hall is surely right that cultural studies has recently undergone a rapid transformation which affects how the field conceives itself and its relationship to the established disciplines. As will be evident from the discussion in this chapter, though, these are debates that have animated cultural studies from the beginning. Readings, Frow and Bennett suggest that cultural studies is characterized principally by its expansiveness, its attempt to transcend the limiting and elitist exclusions of more traditional humanities subjects; but it is possible to argue that it is equally as concerned with the way in which knowledge itself is produced and articulated, and that their own work forms part of this concern. Indeed, the modes of interdisciplinarity discussed in this chapter are characterized not so much by their longing for the authoritativeness of inclusive knowledge as by their uncertainty about how knowledge is formulated and how disciplines fit together. It is this kind of intellectual scepticism within cultural studies, rather than its mere 'inclusiveness', that has been so productive in developing interdisciplinary perspectives across the humanities disciplines.

3

THEORY AND THE DISCIPLINES

'Theory' is a notoriously nebulous and ill-defined term, which has been applied to many different modes of thought across the humanities disciplines. But it is still possible to identify a moment of 'theory', which emerged from a reconfiguration of the humanities disciplines from the late 1960s onwards, and which brought together diverse intellectual movements with at least one thing in common: their critical relationship to the traditional disciplines. In this context, theory means almost the exact opposite of what it means in the sciences. A scientific theory aims to advance knowledge within its particular discipline in an ordered, systematic way by proposing a law about the natural world which can then be empirically verified. If numerous experiments under diverse conditions have upheld the theory, it is accepted as true by the scientific community, at least until a better theory comes along. Theory within the humanities disciplines, however, is not so easily related to practice, since it is not simply concerned with developing analytical procedures for the interpretation of primary material, such as literary texts or historical documents. More broadly, it encompasses ways of thinking that cannot be easily pigeonholed within any of the established academic disciplines, and that attempt to question the basic assumptions of those disciplines. As Terry Eagleton puts it, 'theory' emerges at the point at which 'routine social or intellectual practices have come unstuck, run into trouble, and urgently need to rethink themselves' (1996: 207).

Theory is sometimes unpopular with students precisely because its relationship to its home discipline can seem tangential ('What has *this* got to do with English? I came here to read literature!'). It has also been regarded with suspicion by more traditional scholars because, as Jonathan Culler points out, it refuses to be judged by the conventional models of disciplinary expertise and authority. When being 'theoretical', for example, we might read Sigmund Freud without being aware of the latest research within psychoanalysis or psychiatry, Karl Marx without being a political economist, or Jacques Derrida without being a trained philosopher (Culler 1983: 9). Theory is concerned with big questions about the nature of reality, language, power, gender, sexuality, the body and the self, and it offers a framework within which students and sch-olars can debate about these broad-ranging issues without getting too extensively mired in detailed arguments within disciplines.

One of the principal aims of theory is the questioning of interpretations of the world that are usually taken for granted. For example, it is regarded as common sense that language is always secondary: that it neutrally describes phenomena, and that as independent, autonomous individuals, we can use language as a way of expressing ourselves and our relationship to others and the world. This belief, which has been disputed by certain kinds of theory, allows most people to get up in the morning and live their everyday lives without constantly questioning the nature of individual identity or external reality. Within academia, disciplines are a similar form of common sense, allowing us to keep doing what we do without continually speculating about its purpose, limits and ultimate worth. They enable us to locate manageable objects of inquiry, set limits to our study and present our findings to a community that understands the intellectual framework within which we are working. By questioning the pragmatism of this approach, theory is inherently interdisciplinary. In this chapter, I want to consider a number of critical interventions – structuralism, deconstruction, psychoanalysis, feminism and queer theory – in relation to how they feed into these questions about the nature of disciplines.

LINGUISTICS AND LITERARINESS

Structuralism, a movement that gathered momentum amongst French literary and cultural theorists in the 1950s and 1960s, has its roots in the discipline of linguistics, and specifically Ferdinand de Saussure's *Course in General Linguistics*. In this text, de Saussure proposes a science of sign systems, which he calls 'semiology' and defines as '*a science that studies the life of signs within society*' (de Saussure [1916] 1966: 16). He argues that language does not have a direct relationship to reality but functions as a system of differences: words (signifiers) have no inherent relation to the concrete things that they describe (signifieds), but generate meaning as a result of their differential relationship with other signifiers. The derivation of structuralism in linguistics, and in particular this notion of language as a relational system of signs, opens up a number of interdisciplinary possibilities for literary studies. In particular, it challenges two of the determining categories of English as a discipline: the author and the canonical literary text. Structuralist approaches tend to emphasize 'intertextuality', the notion that texts are formulated not through acts of originality by individual authors but through interaction and dialogue with other texts, and so they question the attempt within literary studies to regard certain kinds of authors or texts as more valuable or worthy of study than others. In structuralist analyses, literary texts tend to be positioned as part of the overall sphere of language and discourse, and thus as one type of text among many, including non-linguistic forms such as cinema, photography, music and fashion. These texts are then analysed 'structurally', emphasizing the form that they share with other texts rather than their specific content.

The early work of Roland Barthes demonstrates some of this interdisciplinary potential. Barthes's *Mythologies* (1957) is a key work of early structuralism and also a founding text of cultural studies in its pioneering discussion of popular culture. It deconstructs a whole range of cultural phenomena from 1950s France, such as wrestling matches, margarine advertisements, Blue

Guides, soap powders, children's toys and Citroën cars. Barthes shows how these phenomena generate a kind of 'metalanguage' (1973: 124), a series of secondary connotations alongside their more obvious meanings. The frequently circulated image of Einstein's brain as 'an object for anthologies, a true museum exhibit', for example, conveys the idea that scientific innovation and discovery are propelled by individual genius rather than social, cultural or institutional factors (Barthes 1973: 75–7). This broadly defined notion of the cultural 'text' allows Barthes to propose a model of interdisciplinarity that does not simply bring different disciplines together but allows them to converge around a completely new object of study:

> *Interdisciplinary studies* ... do not merely confront already constituted disciplines ... it is not enough to take a "subject" (a theme) and to arrange two or three sciences around it. Interdisciplinary study consists in creating a new object, which belongs to no one. The Text is, I believe, one such object.
>
> (Barthes 1986: 72)

Structuralism is interdisciplinary because all kinds of artefacts and phenomena can be interpreted as 'texts': for Barthes, a text is simply a vehicle for the production and dissemination of cultural meanings, 'a tissue of quotations drawn from the innumerable centres of culture' (1977: 146).

One area of structuralist criticism that has provided a particularly fruitful area of interdisciplinary textual study has been narratology. Critics such as Gérard Genette and A.J. Greimas, for example, have taken narratives apart and shown how they work in extraordinary detail, by examining such elements as temporal order, duration, frequency, perspective and point of view. Narratologists specifically focus on narrative *as narrative*, independent of its content and of the medium in which it is produced; a narrative, for them, is simply any structured series of events that occurs in chronological time. This emphasis on form over content has been partly corrective, a challenge to the traditional emphasis within literary studies on the text as a discrete entity. As Genette puts it, 'literature had long enough been regarded as a message without a code for it to become necessary to regard it for a time as a code without a message' (1982: 7).

Narratologists thus have little respect for the kinds of evaluative distinctions that formed the disciplinary basis of literary studies, and they apply narrative codes not only to canonical texts but also to popular culture genres such as fairytales, detective novels, spy thrillers and Mills and Boon romances. Indeed, this kind of formulaic fiction has provided a highly fruitful source for structuralist analyses, perhaps because its narrative mechanisms are more transparent than in other kinds of texts. Narratology can also be applied to film, television and other forms of mass media, as well as aspects of everyday life: when we tell a joke, gossip or follow some daily routine, we are narrating our own and other people's lives. In this context, narrative is as broadly defined as Barthes's notion of the 'text'; it is a way of ordering human experience, communicating ideas and knowledge about the world to ourselves and others.

It should be added that, although the general impetus within structuralist theory is towards texts and narratives rather than more narrowly literary formulations, other elements have been specifically concerned to distinguish between the literary and the non-literary. In the first decades of the twentieth century, for example, Russian formalist critics such as Viktor Shklovskii, Iurii Tynianov and Roman Jakobson attempted to define the formal elements of 'literariness' (*literaturnost*), defining it as a product of the 'defamiliarization' or making strange (*ostranenie*) of normative language. As Tony Bennett points out, many of the formalists came to the eventual conclusion that 'literariness' was always a social effect determined by historical and cultural forces, and therefore not an unchanging constant (1979: 34–5). However, this concern with the specific nature of the literary distinguishes Russian formalism from the interdisciplinary concern with text and narrative in other schools of structuralism. Jakobson, for example, made it clear that the objective of formalism was to create a science with its own specific areas of inquiry and to exclude interdisciplinary practices:

> The object of study in literary science is not literature but literariness – that is, that which makes a given work a work of literature. Until now

literary historians have preferred to act like the policeman who, intending to arrest a certain person, would, at any opportunity, seize any and all persons who chanced into the apartment, as well as those who passed along the street. The literary historians used everything – anthropology, psychology, politics, philosophy. Instead of a science of literature, they created a conglomeration of home-spun disciplines.

(Eichenbaum 1965: 107)

More generally, there might be said to be a disciplinary impetus that connects Russian formalism with other examples of structuralism, in that they all seek to offer a scientific basis for the study of texts by focusing on their structure rather than their content. In this sense, the structuralist concern with narrative codes and systems can be seen as part of an ongoing attempt within literary studies to view texts as the products of a decipherable system, an aspiration to scientificity that runs through the history of the discipline, from its origins in departments of philology to the later work of I.A. Richards and the New Critics. As Barthes argues, the aim of structuralism, when 'confronted by the heterogeneity of language' and 'the infinity of narratives' is 'to extract a principle of classification and a central focus for description from the apparent confusion of the individual messages' (1977: 80). He renounced this project in his later work, criticizing structuralism's desire to reduce texts to an all-inclusive typology, 'equalizing them under the scrutiny of an in-different science' (Barthes 1975: 3). Although structuralism challenges disciplinary divisions through its broad definition of the cultural 'text', it still supposes a fairly narrow definition of theory as the foundation for a scientific textual practice. In structuralist analyses, the meanings within texts tend to be seen as complex but relatively stable, ultimately capable of being brought under disciplinary control by the textual critic.

DECONSTRUCTING PHILOSOPHY

In one of his first books, *Writing and Difference* (1967), Jacques Derrida criticizes structuralism for just this reason: its assumption of disciplinary mastery, its attempt to produce a kind of 'meta-linguistic', quasi-scientific discourse which presumes to pass judgement on its area of study from a position of unquestioned authority (1978: 278–93). Derrida suggests that, although structuralism shows that the relationship between signifier and signified is provisional and unstable, it still believes in the possibility of a fixed origin or stable meaning, what he calls a 'transcendental signified': a thing that has an existence independent of the word that describes it (1981: 19). For Derrida, meaning can never be wholly closed off in this way because it is purely an effect of language, produced by chains of free-floating signifiers with no secure point of reference. Deconstruction, the intellectual strategy with which Derrida has been closely associated, thus aims to question the 'hermeneutical or exegetical method which would seek out a finished signified beneath a textual surface' (Derrida 1981: 63), and which falsely assumes that meaning can be ultimately mastered.

This notion of meaning and knowledge as the products of language clearly has implications for any understanding of the nature and role of academic disciplines. As Jonathan Culler puts it in a discussion of Derrida's work:

> Any discipline must suppose the possibility of solving a problem, finding the truth, and thus writing the last words on a topic. The idea of a discipline is the idea of an investigation in which writing might be brought to an end. Literary critics ... frequently attempt to imagine ways of bringing writing to an end by reformulating the goals of literary criticism to make it a true discipline ... They invoke the hope of saying the last word, arresting the process of commentary.
>
> (Culler 1983: 90)

This is exactly Derrida's point: a discipline forms part of this mistaken search for stability of meaning or a single, organizing structure which his own work aims to critique. Every discipline supposes an ultimate point, albeit an only hypothetically achievable one, at which its aims are realized and its project completed. For Derrida, however, writing will always generate more writing, or as he puts it, *'there is no outside-the-text* ... nothing that completely escapes the general properties of textuality' (Derrida 1992a: 102).

Derrida, though, does not simply seek to undermine the disciplinary enterprise of structuralism, but criticizes similar assumptions of authority that have pervaded the whole history of Western philosophy. Derrida's intellectual background is primarily a philosophical one, but he attempts to use other frames of reference to question philosophy's claims to be a privileged form of knowledge. Indeed, one of the main aims of his work is to deconstruct the traditional hierarchy that subordinates literature to philosophy, and to point to their common immersion in the complexities and instabilities of language. This aim is first formulated in another early work, *Of Grammatology* (1967), as part of a more general attempt to challenge the conventional notion that speech is more truthful than writing. Derrida claims that this notion can be traced as far back as Plato who, in works such as the *Republic* and *Phaedrus*, criticizes poets for their dubious commitment to truth and argues that writing is the poor, impure relation of speech, prejudices that are reiterated throughout the history of Western philosophy. Since philosophy aims to be guided solely by 'reason', Derrida suggests, it often tends to be suspicious of writing as an activity that obstructs the purity of thought and spoken language. His discussion of Jean-Jacques Rousseau, for example, shows how the French philosopher positions writing as 'that dangerous supplement' to thought and speech, that which 'wrenches language from its condition of origin' (Derrida 1976: 141, 243).

Derrida also argues that this privileging of speech over writing formed the basis for the institution of linguistics as a scientific discipline. In opposition to this, he proposes the counter-discipline of grammatology, a 'science of writing' that, instead of fetishizing its scientificity, permanently brings its own assumptions into question (Derrida 1976: 4, 28). Derrida's grammatology also aims to subvert the emphasis on linguistic transparency that pervades the academic disciplines: scholarly writing is traditionally praised for being straightforward and 'lucid' (a word that literally means transparent), and for not letting language get in the way of the transfer of knowledge from author to reader. Derrida's own writing, in contrast, is playful and open-ended, full of puns, neologisms, deliberate ambiguities and typographical innovations. This reinforces and enacts his overall argument that thought can never exist in a 'pure' form prior to language, and that 'beyond the philosophical text there is not a blank, virgin, empty margin, but another text, a weave of differences of forces without any present center of reference' (Derrida 1982: xxiii).

Derrida's work thus fundamentally questions the traditional separation of philosophy from more interpretative and textually oriented humanities disciplines, and it is largely the resistance to this aspect of his work that has made him such a controversial figure within academia. During the controversy over Cambridge University's decision to award him an honorary degree in 1992, for example, an international group of academic philosophers wrote a protest letter to *The Times*, in which they explicitly questioned his disciplinary credentials:

> M. Derrida describes himself as a philosopher, and his writings do indeed bear some of the marks of writing in that discipline. Their influence, however, has been to a striking degree almost entirely in fields outside philosophy – in departments of film studies, for example, or of French and English Literature ... We submit that, if the works of a physicist [say] were similarly taken to be of merit primarily by those working in other disciplines, this would in itself be sufficient grounds for casting doubt upon the idea that the physicist in question was a suitable candidate for an honorary degree.
>
> (Derrida 1995: 419–20)

In an interview that discusses this controversy, Derrida rejects this assumption that those working within recognized fields are the ultimate arbiters of intellectual worth, arguing instead that 'philosophy, in its best tradition, has never allowed itself to be put under house arrest within the limits of its own discipline, to say nothing of the limits of its profession' (1995: 404). He suggests that this potential for openness and reflexivity within philosophy needs to be distinguished from the attempt by academics within philosophy *departments*, working within the constraints of cross-disciplinary rivalries, to distinguish themselves competitively from other faculties within the university, since these people 'confuse philosophy with what they have been taught to *reproduce* in the tradition and style of a particular institution, within a more or less well protected ... social and professional environment' (Derrida 1995: 411).

Like Nietzsche in 'We Scholars', which I discussed in the introduction, Derrida makes the case against a philosophy that sees itself as a professionalized, positivist science with narrowly defined aims and methodologies. The context for this argument with his fellow philosophers is the rise of analytical philosophy as the dominant paradigm within academic philosophy in the second half of the twentieth century. Analytical philosophy tends to eschew the more broadly speculative aims of philosophy in favour of refashioning it as a scientific activity defined by intellectual rigour and clarity; it can be traced back to the school of 'logical positivism' which emerged in Vienna in the 1920s, and which largely analysed the structure of sentences in terms of their empirical verifiability or logical form. Logical positivists evaluated propositions according to a 'verification principle' and determined whether they were true, false or meaningless. This meant that they rejected the wider concerns of metaphysics, aesthetics, theology and ethics and engaged with narrower debates about, for example, the existence or non-existence of objects. The development of these analytical schools of thought is championed in works such as Hans Reichenbach's *The Rise of Scientific Philosophy*, which argues that 'philosophic speculation is a passing stage, occurring when philosophic problems are raised at a time which does not possess the logical means to solve them ... philosophy has proceeded from speculation to science' (1951: vii). Derrida would agree with Richard Rorty that this represents a mistaken quest for an unachievable certainty, and that we should not worry 'about whether what we, or somebody else, is doing is "really philosophy". We should let a hundred flowers bloom, admire them while they last, and leave botanizing to the intellectual historians of the next century' (Rorty 1991: 219).

Derrida's arguments about philosophy are connected to his concerns about the nature of the university as an institution. He suggests that the problem with both academic disciplines and universities as a whole is that they set themselves up as sites of disinterested knowledge by virtue of the axiom that 'scholars alone can judge other scholars' (Derrida 1992b: 5), which disconnects the disciplines from each other and from the world outside academia. Derrida's undermining of the intellectual certainties of the disciplines thus has the explicitly political purpose of questioning the traditional separation of scholars from the broader social sphere, which in turn only tends to call on them when their disciplinary expertise is required.

Critics of deconstruction often argue that, in practice, it has assumed the form of an intricate and highly sophisticated close textual analysis which actually reinforces the distinctions between literary studies and other disciplines. Frank Lentricchia, for example, claims that it is really just a more theoretically sophisticated form of the New Criticism, 'an activity of textual privatization' which produces 'something like an ultimate mode of interior decoration' (1980: 186). Lentricchia is particularly referring to the American form of deconstruction, associated with the so-called 'Yale School' of critics, which includes figures such as J. Hillis Miller, Geoffrey Hartman and Paul de Man. In this form, deconstruction (or 'post-structuralism', a word that is sometimes used interchangeably with deconstruction but that is also an umbrella term incorporating a range of similar approaches) has generally been limited to the study of literature, and particularly to the canonical texts of Romantic poetry and the nineteenth-century novel. It could certainly be defined as a form of close reading, in that its emphasis on the instability of language and meaning leads to a notion that the text contains within itself the means for its own critique: the critic's task is to tease out the gaps and contradictions within it, often by concentrating on apparently insignificant elements.

This form of textual reading is particularly associated with the work of Paul de Man, a central figure in the application of Derridean thought to literary studies. De Man understands theory quite narrowly, not as the questioning of disciplinary common sense but as 'the rooting of literary exegesis and of critical evaluation in a system of some conceptual generality' (de Man 1986: 5). For de Man, theory and literature go hand in hand, because theory is fundamentally concerned with 'the rhetorical or tropological dimension of language' (1986: 17), and this dimension is more explicitly foregrounded in literature than in other forms of language. This emphasis on the linguistic elements of literary texts, at the expense of their interpretative or contextual aspects, positions his work as part of the scientific project of literary criticism, which stretches back to its origins in philology. Indeed, de Man describes literary theory as a 'return to philology ... an examination of the structure of language prior to the meaning it produces', and suggests that textual analysis can still be done on the basis of the *trivium*, that part of the traditional liberal arts education which comprises grammar, rhetoric and logic (1986: 24, 13). It could be argued, in fact, that he turns Derridean deconstruction on its head: rather than using it to question the status of discrete disciplines and the nature of knowledge, he seeks to establish literary studies as 'an autonomous discipline of critical investigation', which 'separates the sheep from the goats, the consumers from the professors of literature, the chit-chat of evaluation from actual perception' (1986: 7, 24). While sharing Derrida's concern to question philosophy's claims to ultimate truth, he seems to set up literary study in its place, suggesting that 'philosophy is nothing more than an endless reflection on its own destruction at the hands of literature' (de Man 1979: 115).

PSYCHOANALYSIS, LANGUAGE AND CULTURE

The potential for interdisciplinarity within psychoanalysis lies in its ambivalent relationship to science, and particularly clinical medicine, and its progressive willingness to move away from straightforwardly scientific models towards a more speculative and theoretical consideration of the relationship between the self, language and culture. Just as Derrida's work engaged specifically with what philosophy had excluded from its terms of reference, Freudian psychoanalysis was founded on a desire to challenge the disciplinary exclusions of medicine, and to investigate the sorts of illnesses and phenomena that it failed to consider. The subject of medicine could be seen as an exemplary case of disciplinary development, in that it has largely developed by shoring up its boundaries and rigorously excluding certain kinds of 'illegitimate' knowledge. Practices that were once seen as part of reputable medicine, such as herbal remedies, faith-healing, bloodletting and purging, were ruthlessly proscribed in the eighteenth and nineteenth centuries as the profession gained institutional power and increasingly used the university as a form of accreditation. While this was obviously partly to do with developments in research and advances in knowledge, it was also the product of emerging power relationships, as strict hierarchies developed, with physicians at the top and surgeons and apothecaries at the bottom, and other healers dismissed as quacks (Porter 1997: 11).

Indeed, as Roy Porter argues, the medical profession gained power and prestige almost independently of its ability to save patients' lives; it was not until the invention of sulphur drugs and antibiotics in the early twentieth century that medicine started to have a really positive effect in this regard (Porter 1997: 11). As he points out, the Western medical tradition has been distinguished by its explanation of sickness not in terms of the relation between the individual and the world but in terms of the body itself (Porter 1997: 7). When the medical profession took on new objects of knowledge, such as the human mind, it tended to do so on a purely clinical basis: academic psychiatry, for example, has traditionally relied on neurology and neuropathology, which emphasize organic explanations for brain disorders (Porter 1997: 509). Freud, who trained as a doctor but who became frustrated with attempts to find narrowly somatic causes for hysteria, mounted the first significant challenge to this sort of scientific materialism. From the beginning, he saw psychoanalysis as a way of breaking out of the disciplinary strictures of orthodox medical knowledge.

One way in which he sought to achieve this was to claim psychoanalysis as a coherent discipline and scientific activity in its own right: hence the hard second term, 'analysis'. Freud begins his introductory lectures by conceding that psychoanalysis is distinct from conventional medicine because, in the mere exchange of words between analyst and patient, it cannot obtain direct contact with its object of inquiry; the unconscious (Freud [1915] 1973: 41). Despite the absence of hard data and the often unpredictable results of the analytical process, however, Freud insists that psychoanalysis is a science, and that 'like every other natural science, it is based on a patient and tireless elaboration of facts from the world of perception' (Freud [1925] 1986: 268). The scientific claims of psychoanalysis are implicit in its development as a profession, with rules of operation, a specialized vocabulary, hierarchical structures and clear patterns of career development. For example, there is a central accrediting and regulating organization, the International Psychoanalytical Association, made up of many national component organizations which in turn accredit training institutes and impose restrictions on membership. The internal politics of psychoanalysis, as exemplified in the acrimonious debates amongst different schools, the expulsion of heretics from the rival organizations and the competing claims to be the true heirs of Freud, certainly suggest that it regards itself as a discipline.

Although Freud saw himself primarily as a scientist, his work has been vastly more influential in the non-scientific disciplines. Freud's theories, and those of his psychoanalytic successors, have often been criticized by 'hard' scientists for their uncertain empirical basis, and their extrapolation of theories from metaphors, analogies and untested assumptions. Unlike the scientific disciplines, psychoanalysis also finds it difficult to limit its terms of reference. Clinical medicine has a clear object of study, defined as the cure and prevention of disease in the human body through the intervention of drugs, technology or surgery. Psychoanalysis can never be confined within such clear boundaries: it is concerned with everything that the unconscious produces, and the way it influences all forms of human thought, feeling and behaviour. Psychoanalysis inevitably encompasses an interest in literature, art and culture because, as Freud puts it, our basic instinctual impulses 'make contributions that must not be underestimated to the highest cultural, artistic and social creations of the human spirit' (Freud [1915] 1973: 47). Freud himself was immensely well read, and many of the key terms of psychoanalysis, such as the Oedipus complex, narcissism, sadism and masochism, derive from literature and mythology. Moreover, psychoanalysis is, like literary criticism, a fundamentally hermeneutic activity: because the unconscious is repressed, it cannot be clinically discovered but only *interpreted* through its partial manifestation in conscious and subconscious statements and behaviour, such as dreams, slips of the tongue and free association.

However, Freud's many essays of literary criticism, and those of early Freudian critics such as Ernest Jones and Otto Rank, tend to use literature simply as the raw material for psychoanalytical case studies. Most commonly, early psychoanalytic criticism treats the text as a sublimation of the author's unconscious desires, instinctual needs or neuroses. Since the text is always seen as secondary to the psychic processes that are revealed through it, this form of criticism amounts to an appropriation of literary criticism by the new discipline of psychoanalysis rather than a genuine interchange between the two. As Shoshana Felman puts it, early psychoanalytic criticism represents

> not so much a relation of coordination as one of *subordination*, a relation in which literature is submitted to the authority, to the prestige of psychoanalysis. While literature is considered as a body of *language* – to be *interpreted* – psychoanalysis is considered as a body of *knowledge*, whose competence is called upon to *interpret*.
>
> (Felman 1982: 5)

In this convergence of psychoanalysis and literature, in other words, the first term is favoured: psychoanalysis is seen as a mature science which makes sense of and appropriates other, less developed, 'non-scientific' forms of knowledge.

While classical Freudian psychoanalysis tries to open up the natural sciences to new areas of study, psychoanalytic *theory* tends to be more sceptical of the scientific, medical pretensions of psychoanalysis. This is most evident in the work of the French psychoanalyst, Jacques Lacan, who proposes a 'return to the work of Freud' which will focus on 'the poetics of the Freudian corpus' at the expense of its more straightforwardly clinical ambitions (1977a: 57, 102). In fact, Lacan's relationship to science, like Freud's, is an ambivalent one, since at times he does suggest that his aim is to provide psychoanalysis with a scientific basis (1977a: 77). His concept of the mirror phase, during which the young child is provided with a satisfying (although illusory) sense of identity by recognizing its image in a mirror, is based on the scientific experiments of the child psychologist Henri Wallon who, in *Les Origines du caractère chez l'enfant* (*The Origins of the Child's Character*, 1934), examined the ways in which young children respond to their mirror image in a way that other primates, such as chimpanzees, do not. Lacan's writings also make prolific use of mathematical concepts such as equations, algorithms, graphs and diagrams in order to explain psychoanalytic ideas. However, the scientific status of these critical interventions is not always clear: Lacan seems to refer not to an actual mirror but to a general process of self-recognition which cannot be confirmed by 'objective data' (1977a: 5), and he principally uses mathematics as a source of metaphors rather than empirical proofs.

The principal way in which Lacan questions the clinical basis of psychoanalysis is by reasserting the importance of Freud's notion that the individual subject is essentially divided, confronted by a constant struggle between the competing elements of the human psyche forged in early childhood, and driven by contradictory drives towards sexual fulfilment and death. Lacan is particularly hostile to the field of ego psychology, an application of Freud's work that deals with the adaptation of the individual to the environment and that he sees as a corruption of Freud's legacy, because it suggests a stable subject and an ego that the individual can know and control. If we ignore 'the self's radical ex-centricity to itself', according to Lacan, we shall make psychoanalysis 'nothing more than the compromise operation that it has, in effect, become, namely, just what the letter as well as the spirit of Freud's work most repudiates' (1977a: 171).

Like Derrida, Lacan questions the common-sense idea of language as a neutral medium through which we communicate our individual identities and our relationship to the world. In the conventional notion of the psychotherapeutic process, the patient comes to terms with his oro her unconscious desires and becomes a 'whole' subject through the acquisition of self-knowledge. Lacan instead draws attention to the narrative structure of the 'talking cure', the way in which the psychoanalytic act creates a gap 'between the subject's ego (*moi*) and the "I" (*je*) of his discourse'

(1977a: 90) – in other words, between the subject who is talking and the subject being talked about. More generally, Lacan sees the individual subject as divided by his or her entry into the realm of language, because what he calls the 'symbolic order' is based on hierarchy and division, and this produces an unresolvable feeling of absence or lack in the subject. So Lacan replaces the Freudian notion that human behaviour is motivated by the need to satisfy basic human instincts (such as the sex and death drives) with the much more amorphous and unsatisfiable notion of desire, which is mediated through, although never fully contained by, language.

This means that the traditional object of psychoanalytic study, the unconscious, is no longer seen as a private area inside each individual mind, but as a 'transindividual' space which is 'not at the disposal of the subject' (Lacan 1977a: 49). The unconscious is *structured like a language*, because it comes into being when the child enters the symbolic order, and it works through and is mediated by signifying processes: 'Before any experience, before any individual deduction ... something organizes this field, inscribes its initial lines of force ... Nature provides ... signifiers, and these signifiers organize human relations in a creative way, providing them with structures and shaping them' (Lacan 1977b: 20). The unconscious is thus only detectable through linguistic forms, being the 'censored chapter' of our personal histories which can only be rediscovered because 'it has already been written down elsewhere' in the form of childhood memories, stories, rituals and private vocabularies (Lacan 1977a: 50). As Julie Thompson Klein puts it, this new understanding of the unconscious clearly offers potential for interdisciplinary study because it moves psychoanalysis away from the workings of the individual psyche and towards larger issues about language, texts, culture and subjectivity (Klein 1996: 158).

As in Derrida's work, this questioning of the status of 'scientific' knowledge by stressing the complex relationships between language, identity and culture extends into a concern with the nature of intellectual institutions. One of the problems with psychoanalysis, for Lacan, is that its clinical aspirations have created a kind of closed and hierarchical knowledge system. As with all disciplines that develop their own institutional momentum, the procedures of psychoanalysis have been 'deadened by routine use' and 'reduced to mere recipes, rob[bing] the analytic experience of any status as knowledge and even any criterion of reality' (Lacan 1977a: 33). Lacan refused to submit to many of the rules of the profession: his psychoanalytic sessions, for example, were of variable lengths, often much shorter than the standard fifty minutes. This and other issues led to his resignation in 1953 from the Société Psychanalytique de Paris to form a breakaway organization which was never recognized by the International Psychoanalytical Association (IPA). Above all, Lacan criticizes the fact that the establishment of psychoanalysis as a professionalized discipline relies on the belief in an ultimate and unquestioned source of authority and knowledge:

> What does an organization of psychoanalysts mean when it confers certificates of ability, if not that it indicates to whom one may apply to represent the subject who is supposed to know? ... [N]o psychoanalyst can claim to represent, in however slight a way, a corpus of absolute knowledge. That is why, in a sense, it can be said that if there is someone to whom one can apply there can be only one such person. This *one* was Freud, while he was alive ... The function, and by the same token, the consequence, the prestige, I would say, of Freud are on the horizon of every position of the analyst.
>
> (Lacan 1977b: 232)

Lacan here seems to compare the discipline of Freudian psychoanalysis with a religious cult, in which the various members profess their loyalty to a founding father, and indeed, he likens his treatment at the hands of the IPA to an excommunication (1977b: 3–4).

For Lacan, the value of psychoanalysis does not lie in its disciplinary ambitions but in the fact that it is situated somewhere between philosophy and science, on the 'frontier between truth and knowledge'. What he seems to mean by this distinction is that truth is what is excluded from knowledge in order for the latter to become organized and disciplined: 'truth is in a state of constant re-absorption in its own disturbing element, being in itself no more than that which is lacking for the realization of knowledge ... truth is nothing other than that which knowledge can apprehend as knowledge only by setting its ignorance to work' (Lacan 1977a: 296). Scientific knowledge, in particular, is always incomplete because it assumes that it is objective and detached, whereas in fact people are always implicated in any knowledge they produce. When it learns to recognize this, psychoanalysis will represent 'the re-entry of truth into the field of science', and a redrawing of 'the distorting map of clinical medicine' (Lacan 1977a: 297). In other words, when it succeeds in being thoroughly interdisciplinary, psychoanalysis will be able to offer a sustained critique of the disciplinary aspirations of science.

FEMINISM AND THE BODY

Feminism brings together the disparate interests of literary and cultural criticism, the social sciences, philosophy, psychology and psychoanalysis in its concern with the ways in which women have been represented and represent themselves, and with their oppression and emancipation. But feminist theory, as Diane Elam puts it, is 'not just another interdisciplinary handshake' (1994: 12): it is about challenging the values and priorities of the existing disciplines rather than merely integrating them. Above all, feminist theory's critique of the disciplines has been founded on an impatience with the power arrangements of the university as an institution, and the way that the experience of women is devalued or excluded. The agenda of feminist theory often reflects this deep ambivalence not only about the disciplines but about academic work and writing as a whole.

Feminist theory emerged out of the so-called 'second wave' of feminism, a movement beginning in the late 1960s that extended its remit beyond the achievement of political and social equality and towards a consideration of the cultural and psychological contexts of patriarchal power. Given this context, the founding texts of this new kind of feminism were necessarily interdisciplinary in focus. Simone de Beauvoir's *The Second Sex* (1949), for example, ranges widely across the disciplines in its effort to show how women are culturally constituted and represented. Part

One, 'Destiny', explores the ways in which patriarchal ideas are embedded in the discourses of biology, Freudian psychoanalysis and Marxism. De Beauvoir argues that these discourses imagine that individual identities are determined by the anatomy, the unconscious or economic forces, when in fact they are produced by the broader operations of society and culture:

> One is not born, but rather becomes a woman. No biological, psychological, or economic fate determines the figure that the human female presents in society; it is civilization as a whole that produces this creature, intermediate between male and eunuch, which is described as feminine.
>
> (de Beauvoir [1953] 1997: 297)

The remainder of the book uses a variety of sources, such as literary texts, visual art, historical documents, biographies and everyday objects like dolls and dresses, to show how women's identities are created and constrained by social attitudes and cultural forms. De Beauvoir's book is therefore interdisciplinary in two senses: it draws on several of the established disciplines to reveal their inadequacies in dealing with the experience of women, and it brings together a variety of sources from different fields to demonstrate the pervasiveness of patriarchal power. Betty Friedan's classic *The Feminine Mystique* (1963) follows a similar two-handed approach: it questions the 'functionalism' of psychoanalysis, sociology, anthropology and the other behavioural sciences, arguing that their self-professed scientificity is founded on a denial of the real experience of women; and it discusses a range of texts, such as sex surveys, women's magazines, advertisements and fictional representations of 'the happy housewife heroine', in order to reveal the power of the 'feminine mystique', the belief that women are most fulfilled within the family and home.

In the work of French feminist theorists such as Hélène Cixous, Luce Irigaray and Julia Kristeva, these wide-ranging, interdisciplinary concerns are extended into a productive but prickly engagement with psychoanalytic theory, linguistics and deconstruction. These theorists seek to appropriate psychoanalysis and deconstruction for a feminist agenda, using them to show how language and the patriarchal order construct meaning through hierarchically organized binary oppositions, such as male/female and active/passive. As well as emphasizing the relationship between language and power, though, French feminist theory also addresses psychic and bodily experience. Cixous, Irigaray and Kristeva all make use of Lacan's distinction between the Imaginary, the pre-Oedipal period when the child is part of the mother, and the Symbolic, the post-Oedipal state ruled by language and the 'Law of the Father', in order to show how women's desire is repressed by the latter. In their different ways, all these critics advocate a kind of 'writing from the body' which originates in pre-Oedipal, pre-linguistic drives, and which attempts to disrupt patriarchy's exclusion of women's experience through a fluid and ambivalent style of writing which is associated with the 'feminine'.

These critics have been accused of either an anatomical or a psychic essentialism in their positing of a specifically female essence as the location of what Cixous calls an *écriture feminine* (feminine writing) (Moi 1985: 126). It is probably fairer to say that there is a fundamental tension at the heart of this kind of theory which stems from its unwillingness to be confined within one area of knowledge. Indebted to Lacan's and Derrida's insights about the linguistic construction of the subject, feminist theory is also always fighting off its entrapment in the realm of language and its status as mere 'theory', and engaging with the actual, bodily experience of women. Kristeva, for example, criticizes Derridean grammatology for 'giv[ing] up on the subject', and having no notion of the bodily or social self that is outside of language (1984: 142). Kristeva and Irigaray see the subject as the product of both physiological and signifying processes which are intimately related, and this demands that areas of knowledge such as psychoanalysis, philosophy, literature and sociology need to be brought together with the sciences. Irigaray argues that many of the problems in understanding the situation of women are founded on an 'insufficiently thought out relation between biology and culture' (1993: 46), and has criticized a lack of dialogue between philosophy and science which impoverishes both areas:

As a philosopher, I am interested in theorizing all domains of reality and knowledge. Only very recently in the history of culture have philosophy and the sciences been separated – the result of method- ological specialization, making them beyond the reach of anyone and everyone. The hypertechnical tendencies of current science lead to the creation of increasingly complex formulae that correspond, so it's believed, to an increasingly truthful truth. Consequently, it's a truth that escapes consideration in the light of wisdom, the scientist's own included.

(Irigaray 1993: 81)

This aim of bringing together the sciences and humanities is most apparent in feminist theory's concern with the body. The recent interest in the body in the humanities and social sciences, and particularly in feminist theory, is partly an attempt to sub- vert the traditional disciplinary division that has conceded this area of study to the sciences, particularly medicine and biology, leaving the supposedly autonomous products of the mind to the non-sciences. Kristeva, in particular, points to the dual status of the body as a product of both biology and language/culture in her notion of the 'chora'. She partly borrows this term from Plato's *Timaeus*, where it is used to refer to a fluid state that serves as a kind of connecting point between mind and body, between the worlds of thought and the senses. However, she also derives it from the biological term, 'chorion', the external membrane of the embryo in birds, reptiles and mammals which forms a link between the mother's body and that of the foetus. In most mammals, the chorion develops blood vessels which become embedded in the lining (or endometrium) of the mother's uterus, and the chorion and endometrium together form the placenta, which allows the mother to provide the unborn baby with its nutritional and other needs.

Kristeva uses the term 'chora' to bring together these philoso- phical and biological meanings. She defines it as a nourishing, womb-like space between mother and child which is both pre- verbal, fluid and outside the patriarchal symbolic order, and the point at which the child begins to separate itself from the mother and become an individual subject (Kristeva 1984: 25–8). More generally, Kristeva argues that pregnancy provides women with an experience that disrupts the established boundaries between self and other and subverts traditional notions of individual identity (1986: 206). It is clear from these arguments that, as Michael Payne points out, 'when Kristeva writes about the body, unlike Lacan and Derrida, she gives it a sense of having bone and flesh and hormones' (1993: 168). At the same time, she suggests that there is an intimate connection between physiology, psychology and language which cannot be understood within traditional disciplinary divisions.

Another problem with the conventional separation between biology and culture is that the body is both a material, biological entity and a cultural product which we can change through, for example, dieting, piercing, tattooing, silicone implants or plastic surgery. For Kristeva, the body's materiality is often denied or devalued in everyday culture, one symptom of this being the fact that women are defined by their bodies (through menstruation and pregnancy, for example) in ways that men are not. In order to take up a position within the symbolic order, she argues, the female subject must repress her material nature by categorizing it as unclean. She uses the term 'abjection' to describe, among other things, the expulsion from the body of menstrual blood, vomit and excrement: the abject is what is excluded, 'ejected beyond the scope of the possible, the tolerable, the thinkable' (Kristeva 1982: 1). Kristeva's work thus draws attention to the materiality of the body, particularly of the female body, while also arguing that the body, as we have access to and understand it, is often a dematerialized product of culture and representation, produced through the 'abjection' of those aspects that cannot be written about or represented.

QUEERING THE DISCIPLINES

Queer theory feeds into and extends the interdisciplinary concerns of feminism, by developing feminist theory's concern with gender codes and differences into an exploration of the cultural construction of sexuality. The text that it has drawn on most productively in this regard is the first volume of Michel Foucault's

History of Sexuality (1976), which examines how language and culture construct 'dominant' and 'deviant' forms of sexuality. Foucault argues that sexuality became prominent in the modern era precisely 'because relations of power had established it as a possible object', and that the 'discursive explosion' about sex over the last few centuries has involved 'the very production of sexuality' itself (1981: 35, 17, 105). This notion of sexuality as a cultural construct bound up with questions of power and knowledge, rather than as a natural given, is what makes queer theory interdisciplinary. If it were solely concerned with the study of homosexuality, the representation and self-representation of gay people and the questioning of heterosexist laws and attitudes, it would be a specialism with fairly definite concerns. In fact, queer theory draws on poststructuralist and psychoanalytic theory to problematize the construction of homosexuality as a unified, foundational category of individual and collective identity. It is therefore far more broadly concerned with the range of discourses and knowledges that organize sexuality as a whole, and with the cultural work that is undertaken to police or subvert these sexual boundaries.

This also means that, like many forms of theory, queer theory is concerned with the disciplining of knowledge, and the way that this determines our understanding of sexual identities, desires and norms. For example, Foucault suggests that from the late nineteenth century onwards, the homosexual became a named category or species, whereas previously same-sex love had just been an activity undertaken by a wide variety of people. This explicit naming of the homosexual was recognized in legal statutes and in medical, biological and psychiatric discourses, coming together in the new discipline of 'sexology' (Foucault 1981: 43), which sought to bring the 'objective' authority of the sciences to bear on what was clearly a cultural project, the outlawing and demonizing of homosexuality. At around the same time, Freudian psychoanalysis was rooting sexuality in biological differences and viewing sexual behaviour based on procreation and the nuclear family as the norm. Queer theory often takes as its object of study these aetiological accounts of sexuality – aetiology being an inquiry into origins or causes – from early sexological theories to more recent attempts to place and define homosexuality 'scientifically'.

In 1991, for example, an American neuroscientist claimed to have found a link between the structure of the brain's hypothalamus and homosexuality, and in 1993 there was the much-publicized discovery of a supposed 'gay gene', a length of the X chromosome that influences sexual orientation in men (LeVay 1994; Hamer and Copeland 1995). Although there have been lengthy debates amongst queer theorists about the significance of these findings, most are concerned that they will be used to pathologize and essentialize homosexuality, defining it solely in the terms of the established scientific disciplines such as biology, neurology or genetics. As Michael Warner puts it, the need for queer theory stems from the fact that 'contested issues of sexuality involve problems not captured by the languages designed to name them' (1993: xv).

Queer theorists tend to point instead to the unstable, imitative and performative nature of sexual identities, and the ways in which cross-dressing, camp attitudes, transsexual bodies and gay readings of 'straight' texts can subvert dualistic notions of male and female, gay and straight. More recently, the queer and feminist theorist Judith Butler, probably the other major influence on queer theory after Foucault, has sought to question the conventional notion of the body as the ultimate determinant of sexuality. Butler seeks to go beyond the sex/gender divide which presents the former as natural and the latter as a cultural construct, which she sees as constraining much feminist criticism and theory. She argues that 'there is no recourse to a body that has not always already been interpreted by cultural meanings ... Indeed, sex, by definition, will be shown to have been gender all along' (Butler 1990: 8). So Butler attempts a similar move to Kristeva's, critiquing the attempt by the sciences to cordon off the biological body as an area of neutral concern, and reclaiming it for textual and theoretical analysis.

The more materialist interdisciplinary work of reclamation undertaken by the queer theorist Alan Sinfield aims to show how dissident forms of sexuality are always breaking into dominant forms, despite attempts to constrain and silence them. Sinfield's work has been consistently concerned with the ways in which the historical equation of homosexuality with the sphere of art, literature and culture has functioned as a kind of 'open secret', making same-sex love acceptable as long as it remains tacit, socially marginal and does not attempt to extend beyond the boundaries of 'culture' (1994a: 64). For example, he looks at the importance of Oscar Wilde and the events leading up to his imprisonment in 1895 as a definitive moment in both the creation of the 'homosexual' as a specific social type and the emergence of a twentieth-century gay sensibility based around notions of 'camp'. Tracing a cultural history of the effeminate man from the seventeenth-century fop to the Wildean dandy, he argues that, up until the Wilde trials, effeminacy or 'campness' was not synonymous with homosexuality; it was a highly contested concept which associated conspicuous idleness, decadence and general debauchery with art and the leisure class. This cultural formation was partly the product of a certain kind of middle-class dissidence mimicking aristocratic, aesthetic values as a way of challenging the manly, bourgeois ones espousing the work ethic, empire and commerce (Sinfield 1994b: 98).

In Sinfield's argument, homosexuality and its cultural representation become inextricably entangled in much wider issues of sexuality, masculinity, capitalism and national identity and so turn out to be far more pivotal to mainstream culture than the latter is prepared to acknowledge. Queer theory begins by working in the margins of the existing disciplines, looking for ways of thinking that they have ignored or devalued; but once these new ways of thinking have been consolidated, we can see that they infiltrate more established areas of knowledge and alter our understanding of them. Queer theorists have thus shown that traditional attempts to categorize and delimit sexuality within disciplines such as biology and psychiatry need to be subjected to rigorous cultural analysis; but they have also expanded the disciplinary reach of literary and cultural criticism by demonstrating that even apparently 'straight' texts can be opened up to readings that draw on sociological, historical and psychoanalytic accounts of homosexuality.

THEORY AS METADISCIPLINE

I began this chapter with the contention that the very different ideas that have been grouped together as 'theory' find a common basis in their efforts to challenge the priorities, assumptions and limitations of the traditional disciplines. As I argued in my discussion of cultural studies in the previous chapter, though, there is a certain inevitability to disciplinary development: interdisciplinary movements will tend to acquire the institutional and intellectual characteristics of disciplines as they become recognized and accepted. One of the particular problems with 'theory' in this context is that it is often forbiddingly difficult and complex, which means that it can seem to non-initiates as jargon-laden and exclusive as any discipline.

Stanley Fish makes this point in an essay entitled 'Being Interdisciplinary Is So Very Hard to Do', which argues that interdisciplinary developments within literary studies such as deconstruction, post-structuralism and feminist theory have only succeeded in creating 'metadisciplines' with their own inward-looking codes and practices (Fish 1994). In his later work, he has expanded and developed this argument to incorporate other forms of interdisciplinarity. Fish argues that interdisciplinarity is impossible because the disciplines are incommensurable; they are all engaged in such different activities that any attempt to bring them together will either involve one of them parasitically drawing on the status and terminology of another or being appropriated by it completely (1995: 83). He suggests that the blurring of disciplinary boundaries simply results in the development of new hierarchies and divisions which are only different from the old ones in that they do not perceive or present themselves as such (Fish 1994: 237). Fish responds to this threat of metadisciplinarity by falling back on a pragmatic belief in the professionalism and disciplinary competence of a more modestly defined literary studies, on the importance of 'our being able to have a share of a franchise to which no one else can lay a plausible claim' (1996: 162). He argues that we need to maintain the boundaries between literary studies and other disciplines in the name of institutional politics and a more secure self-identity, since 'independently of the potent social fact of disciplinary organization we would have nothing to say' (Fish 1996: 165).

Fish accepts the argument, common to many of the theoretical positions analysed above, that a discipline is a social construction, 'a grab-bag of disparate elements held together by the conceptual equivalent of chicken-wire' (1995: 74). Influenced by Derrida's work, he suggests that all objects and phenomena are inextricably bound up with language and discourse, and that disciplines are rhetorical structures which have a discrete identity only as a result of their differential relationship with other disciplines: in other words, what they are is defined by what they are not (Fish 1995: 16). But just because there is no stable entity called 'literary studies', independent of its own circular, self-validating operations, this does not mean that we should dispense with it. On the contrary, it is precisely because it is such a provisional, self-generating activity that we need to preserve it. If the academic divisions of knowledge were naturally evolving boundaries they would still continue to exist regardless of the strength of our commitment to them; in reality, however, a discipline such as literary studies 'lives and dies by the zeal with which we ask its questions and care about the answers' (Fish 1995: 70). In a sense, Fish uses theory to counter theory, arguing for an extreme form of linguistic constructivism which suggests that our attempts to reflect critically on the nature of disciplines will always end up being recontained by them, simply because we cannot think or act outside of textual frameworks.

These points are worth making, in that they remind us that no intellectual system can escape being disciplined to some degree, and that the success of theory as a prestigious, intellectually challenging and ambitious field makes it particularly susceptible to disciplinary recuperation. The problem with Fish's argument is that he does not really provide an *intellectual* justification for the maintenance of traditional disciplinary distinctions, other than to suggest that they are necessary to justify what literary critics have always done, and that if they question this then the whole precarious edifice of their discipline will come tumbling down. This seems to preclude the possibility of *any* kind of critical self-consciousness in relation to the established disciplines. I hope to have shown in this chapter, though, that these various theoretical interventions emerge out of a real engagement with what these disciplines overlook or exclude. There is no doubt that this makes it harder to set limits on and justify conventional forms of intellectual activity, but from the point of view of 'theory', it is better to be self-questioning than to carry on doing what we have always done for reasons of institutional practicality or intellectual inertia.

4

TEXTS IN HISTORY

Ever since their emergence as academic disciplines, literary studies
and history have had a close but problematic relationship. As I
pointed out in Chapter 1, the two subjects were sometimes taught
together in early degrees at dissenting colleges in the nineteenth
century, and they developed as fully fledged academic subjects at
around the same time. Each of these disciplines contains elements
of the other: literary studies often draws on historical material,
while everything, including literature, could be said to have a
history. The obvious connections between the subjects, however,
have not always encouraged co-operation; they have often led to
greater territoriality, as each subject has sought to consolidate its
own separateness and uniqueness. It might be helpful to trace a
brief history of the attempts within the disciplines to cordon
themselves off from each other, before looking at more recent,
interdisciplinary efforts to work across these divisions.

LITERATURE AND HISTORY

One of the differences between humanities subjects such as literature, art and classics and more scientific branches of learning is

that the former tend to be historically organized. In the sciences, knowledge is seen as essentially cumulative: courses tend to focus on the most up-to-date scholarship, with the assumption that the history of the discipline is merely a long prelude to a contemporary state of enlightenment. Even today, though, when issue- or theme-based modules are increasingly prevalent on English degrees, most courses organize themselves in terms of periods and make some attempt at chronological coverage. However, literary studies as a discipline has traditionally emphasized chronological development within a specifically literary frame rather than historical contextualization. This emphasis can be seen in the guides to national literatures that were produced as the discipline matured and took stock of itself: for example, the *Cambridge History of English Literature* (14 vols, 1907–16), Macmillan's *Literary History of the United States* (3 vols, 1948) and the *Pelican Guide to English Literature* (7 vols, 1954–61). These books, and their many rivals and successors, assumed that literature developed chronologically within closed national boundaries. Although there was room for historical context in this arrangement of the material, there was also a sense in which literature was seen as being detached from history, following a specific rationale of its own. Robert Spiller, the editor of *Literary History of the United States*, encapsulated this notion when he argued that 'the true literary historian, however far he may wander, is always on his way, by a circuitous route, back to the literary work as a primary object' (Klein 1996: 151). Within this paradigm, literary genres, techniques and movements could be seen to develop organically from earlier, embryonic forms, before achieving full maturity. This is the conventional narrative of 'the rise of the novel' from the early eighteenth century onwards: it emerged out of earlier literary forms such as romance and epic, and gradually became more developed and sophisticated as the full potential of the genre was realized.

René Wellek and Austin Warren provide a theoretical justification for this self-contained notion of literary history in their *Theory of Literature*. They criticize the tendency of literary historians to appropriate unquestioningly the divisions of historians and argue that 'the accepted periods of English literature are an indefensible jumble of political, literary and artistic labels' (Wellek and Warren 1949: 277), deriving from such disparate fields as ecclesiastical history (the Reformation), art history (the Renaissance) and political history (the Restoration). This argument gestures towards a historicism which accepts that literary periods are always a construction, often invented after the event and having a retrospective meaning not shared by those living and writing at the time. But Wellek and Warren's response to this problem is to turn literary history away from history proper, and to argue that 'the literary period should be established by purely literary criteria' and seen as 'a subsection of the universal development' (1949: 277). Rather like the notion of an organic literary tradition put forward by both Leavis and Eliot, Wellek and Warren's argument is that literature must be conceived 'as a whole system of works which is, with the accretion of new ones, constantly changing its relationships, growing as a changing whole' (Wellek and Warren 1949: 266–7).

It is no coincidence that this conception of literary history emerged at the same time as the new criticism and other contemporaneous critical movements were attempting to establish clearly defined boundaries for the discipline. For Wellek and Warren, history is mere 'background' or 'context', informing the literary work but not interfering with the chronological line of literary development. This enclosed model of literary history, which retains the notion of the literary text as the primary object of study within the discipline, has proved quite persistent over the years. Harold Bloom offers a reworking of it, for example, in his theory of the 'anxiety of influence'. Bloom argues that authors are engaged in a kind of psychic struggle with the great authors of past generations, attempting either to 'complete', creatively misread or unsuccessfully purge themselves of the influence of their predecessors' work. While re-theorizing it with reference to the Oedipal conflicts identified by Freudian psychoanalysis and the Nietzschean 'Will to Power', Bloom essentially preserves the same notion of a literary tradition developing independently of social, cultural and historical determinants (Bloom 1975).

The emergence of history as a professional discipline was also marked by an attempt to distinguish it from literature and literary criticism, in this case by claiming it as a branch of the sciences. History is only a little older than English as an academic subject, which meant that the two subjects were competing for similar institutional space and legitimacy from the beginning. Although the practice of history dates back to the ancient Greeks, it only came to be seen as a systematic, 'objective' science with its professional incarnation in European and North American universities from the mid-nineteenth century onwards. Although there had been attempts to make it more rigorous and methodical before this, it was far more likely to be seen as a branch of literature, on a par with novels and essays, as in the work of popular nineteenth-century British historians like Thomas Macaulay and Thomas Carlyle.

Perhaps because of its origins in *belles-lettres*, history was viewed as an arriviste discipline when it entered the university. A contemporary newspaper attacked the inauguration of history at Oxford in 1850 in much the same way that the new subject of English was criticized a generation or two later:

> Is the subject suitable for Education? Is it an exercise of the mind? Is it not better left till Education is completed? Is it not sufficiently attractive to ensure a voluntary attention to it? Is it a convenient subject for Examination? ... Will it not supersede those subjects where a severer discipline is required?
>
> (Marwick 1970: 46)

As with English, one way in which history attempted to get round this questioning of its intellectual clout was by professing broad humanistic and nationalistic aims. Like English, history was seen as a cultivated activity for gentlemen because it offered the possibility of a non-specialist, humane education and had a mediating relationship with the other disciplines, since everything could in theory form part of historical inquiry. Leopold Ranke, who instituted history as a university discipline from the 1830s onwards along with his colleagues at the University of Berlin, also pointed to these generalist aims, and linked them to an explicitly nationalistic project through which students would come to know their own country's history and culture: 'For history is not simply an academic subject: the knowledge of the history of mankind should be a common property of humanity and should above all benefit our nation, without which our work could not have been accomplished' (Marwick 1970: 38).

However, these humanistic aims existed alongside, and occasionally came into conflict with, the attempt to position history as a scientific activity, by providing it with a clear methodology and rationale and narrowing its focus to certain specified materials. Ranke was largely responsible for establishing the authority of this new scientific approach to history and marking it out clearly from the then dominant humane discipline of philosophy. For Ranke, history emphasized the need for substantiating evidence, principally from archival and other primary sources, the careful analysis of these sources and the meticulous presentation of the facts. In advocating this new approach, he actually set aside some of the broader aims of history in favour of the more modest aspirations of a discipline: 'To history has been assigned the office of judging the past, of instructing the present for the benefit of future ages. To such high offices this work does not aspire: it wants only to show what actually happened' (Marwick 1970: 35).

This central emphasis on the 'facts' distinguished history from the interpretative model of literary criticism, and the creative transformations of literature itself. As J.B. Bury, Regius Professor of Modern History at Oxford, declared in 1903:

> History is a science, no less and no more ... History is not a branch of literature. The facts of history, like the facts of geology or astronomy, can supply material for literary art ... but to clothe the story of human society in a literary dress is no more the part of a historian as a historian, than it is the part of an astronomer to present in an artistic shape the story of the stars.
>
> (Evans 1997: 23)

However, the need to make such statements so forcefully indicates that the process of disciplinary consolidation did not go uncontested, and that there were critics of the scientific approach to history from the beginning. In his never finished *Introduction to the Human Sciences* (Vol. I, 1883), the German historian and philosopher Wilhelm Dilthey argued that the human sciences (*Geisteswissenschaften*), which he defined as the sciences of man and society, should not try to imitate the positivist methods of the natural sciences (*Naturwissenschaften*). For Dilthey, the world could never be known objectively and finally, but could only be interpreted; there was no such thing as a pure reason or absolute knowledge outside of human experience. However, we could know the human world better than the natural world because we had more direct experience of it and had made it ourselves. The natural sciences could only provide causal explanations (*Erklären*) of nature through necessarily vague hypothetical generalizations; the human sciences, however, could intuitively understand (*Verstehen*) lived experience in all its specificity.

These ideas about the special status of the human sciences were taken up by historians in several countries in the first half of the twentieth century. Drawing on the work of Dilthey and earlier thinkers like Vico, the Italian Benedetto Croce argued that history was a necessarily inexact and subjective area of knowledge. He suggested that all history 'has the character of "contemporary history" because, however remote in time events there recounted may seem to be, the history in reality refers to present needs and present situations wherein those events vibrate' (Croce [1941] 1970: 19). British historians such as R.G. Collingwood and George Trevelyan also claimed that history could never be wholly scientific or objective. Trevelyan attacked the 'Germanizing hierarchy' that presented history as a mere 'chronicle of bare facts arranged on scientific principles', suggesting that it was actually a much more broadly conceived activity which combined 'the scientific (research), the imaginative or speculative (interpretation) and the literary (presentation)' (Evans 1997: 24–6).

This attack on an unreflective positivism was later popularized in E.H. Carr's widely read *What Is History?* which claims that history, rather than being a neutral excavation of events, is 'a continuous process of interaction between the historian and his facts, an unending dialogue between the present and the past' (Carr [1961] 1964: 30). Carr's book was a controversial one within the discipline, however, and met with a sustained refutation in G.R. Elton's *The Practice of History*. Elton's book aims to distinguish history clearly from its more modern competitors in the social sciences such as sociology, economics and anthropology. In Rankean fashion, he argues that history is unique in the importance it places on rigorous scholarship and attentiveness to primary sources; he suggests that 'the quality of an historian's work must ... be judged purely by intellectual standards.{...} *Omnia veritas* [Truth is all]' (Elton [1967] 1984: 69). He even makes an audacious attempt to claim the mantle of positivism from the sciences, arguing that while the scientist's experiment is a construct, the historian 'cannot invent his experiment ... the matter he investigates has a dead reality independent of the enquiry' (Elton [1967] 1984: 73). There are similarities here with Leavis's justification for literary studies as a discipline. Just as Leavis argues that the literary text is simply 'there' on the page and does not require theory or philosophy to make sense of it, Elton claims that the past is irreducible to theory and is 'there' in the unfolding of discrete events, which can be discovered by the historian in the relevant documents.

These controversies remain resilient ones within the discipline. Indeed, the current and fiercely contested debates about the 'postmodern' or linguistic turn in history, which essentially amounts to a critique of history's claims to scientific objectivity by stressing that it can only deal with texts and narratives rather than 'reality', can partly be seen as a continuation of controversies that have preoccupied the discipline since its inception (Jenkins 1997). However, it is broadly true that, in recent years, history has become increasingly reflexive about its own theoretical justifications and practices. Historians are now more likely to believe that the facts do not simply 'speak for themselves' and that their work incorporates the literary-critical skills of textual interpretation as well as scientific research.

Aside from these developments, there has been a further shift in emphasis away from merely diplomatic and constitutional history and towards more inclusive forms of history which make use of sources also employed in other disciplines. Ranke championed the former approach with his emphasis on the 'great men' of political history, and his contention that 'general tendencies do not decide alone; great personalities are always necessary to make them effective' (Marwick 1970: 244). Indeed, the scientific, source-based approach suited such an emphasis, because the surviving and readily available primary documents tended to be those of politicians, monarchs and diplomats. Even in the nineteenth century, though, this view was being challenged by works such as J.R. Green's *A Short History of the English People* (1874) and F.W. Maitland's *The Domesday Book and Beyond* (1897), which began to interpret English history through more than its political events. Green consciously turned away from what he called 'drum and trumpet history' and towards social trends and literary and cultural texts, aiming to devote 'more space to Chaucer than to Cressy, to Caxton than to the petty strife of Yorkist and Lancastrian, to the Poor Law of Elizabeth than to her victory at Cadiz, to the Methodist revival than to the escape of the Young Pretender' (Green [1874] 1915: vii).

In France, the work of the influential Annales School, formed in 1929 (with a journal of the same name) by historians such as Fernand Braudel, Lucien Febvre and Marc Bloch, also sought to move the discipline away from a narrow emphasis on the significant individuals of political or constitutional history. Their 'total history' embraced a wide variety of social, economic, cultural and geographical factors, as well as the collective psychology of a people, or 'the history of mentalities'. As Febvre pointed out, this meant that different areas of knowledge could no longer be separated from each other: 'Man cannot be carved into slices. He is a whole. One must not divide all of history – here the events, there the beliefs' (Appleby *et al.* 1994: 82). Their aim was to interpret a wide range of material rather than merely document past events 'scientifically' – or, as Febvre put it succinctly: 'A mere collector of supposed facts is as useful as a collector of matchboxes' (Marwick 1970: 246). The Annalistes' work could thus be seen as an attack on disciplinary hubris: history was not directly available to the historian as the natural world was to the scientist, since the 'truth' about the past lay buried in unexpected places, as well as in the intersection with other disciplines.

The Annalistes' approach was mirrored in Britain by the development of a 'history from below' school, which particularly gathered momentum from the 1960s onwards. In *The Making of the English Working Class*, for example, E.P. Thompson proposes a history that, rather than emphasizing the 'great' men and women of monarchies and governments, will instead 'rescue the poor stockinger, the Luddite cropper, the "obsolete" hand-loom weaver, the "utopian" artisan ... from the enormous condescension of posterity' (Thompson [1963] 1980: 12). For Thompson and others, the traditional historian's emphasis on official documentation only ends up reflecting the vested interests of the rich and powerful; historical evidence, rather than being neutrally and scientifically 'discovered', has to be interpreted actively by the historian in terms of the power relationships it embodies and the narratives it excludes. Historians from below are thus more likely to emphasize social and cultural rather than political history, drawing on 'soft' sources such as literary texts, autobiographies, myths and visual representations as well as 'hard' sources such as official government documents, state papers and statistical data. In other words, their research is likely to be situated on a continuum with that of textual critics and literary historians, rather than being rigidly separated from it.

It will be clear from this discussion that history's status as a science, and its relationship to historical 'truth', has been a perennially problematic one. Moreover, the attempt to draw clear lines of demarcation around the discipline by emphasizing the distinctive nature of its sources, rather like the restrictive emphasis on the canon within literary studies, has been increasingly questioned. Indeed, one can see that many of the debates within the discipline of history about its scope, terms of reference and internal coherence are similar to those conducted within literary studies. Interdisciplinary approaches that attempt to question the boundaries between these two disciplines have often drawn on these long-standing controversies.

MARXISM AND CULTURE

One of the most influential frameworks for thinking about the relationship between literature and history has been Marxism, a necessarily interdisciplinary system of thought in that it believes that historical processes shape the production of art, culture and ideas. Above all, Marxism stresses the interconnectedness of ideas and material forms, and argues that these interconnections are constantly shifting because of the dialectical development of society and culture, the process by which they enact and eventually resolve their internal contradictions. In the twentieth century, Marxist philosophers turned increasingly to a consideration of the way in which historical developments were mediated, transformed and articulated in literary and cultural texts. This cultural turn was partly the result of a series of historical disappointments which all meant that political and economic revolution seemed less imminent: the rise of Stalinist totalitarianism in the Soviet Union, the anti-democratic nature of other communist regimes around the world, and the survival and apparent resilience of the capitalist economies.

In classical Marxism, the historical forces of capitalism have a determining effect on literature, art and culture. Marx argued in his preface to *A Contribution to the Critique of Political Economy* (1859) that a society's 'superstructure', which is made up of both its legal, political and religious institutions and its cultural and intellectual forms, is wholly determined by its economic infrastructure or 'base', which is itself a product of the historical mode of production (such as feudalism or capitalism). As it has developed over the course of the twentieth century, Marxist cultural criticism has gradually moved away from this reductive, 'top-down' model, but it has then been faced with the problem of defining the precise relationship between historical change and cultural forms. It has also debated the status of Marxism as knowledge: is it a discipline, with its own internal criteria for establishing its particular forms of truth? Is it a form of interdisciplinary knowledge, which can be used to bring together and make sense of the existing disciplines? Or is it simply one competing knowledge system amongst many? I want to explore some of these issues with reference to three principal theorists – Theodor Adorno, Louis Althusser and Fredric Jameson – because they have been particularly concerned with the link between culture and history and with the relationship of Marxism to disciplinary knowledge.

The research undertaken by the Frankfurt School, which first emerged in the Institute for Social Research in that city in the late 1920s and which comprised critics such as Adorno, Max Horkheimer and Herbert Marcuse, was specifically interdisciplinary. It aimed to produce a 'critical theory' that would link philosophy with some of the new social sciences, in line with Marx's plea for philosophers to combine their work with socio-political critique. However, Adorno and his colleagues rejected orthodox Marxism as too simplistic to explain the workings of complex capitalist societies. They held out little hope for a proletarian revolution, believing that the working classes had lost the capacity for revolutionary change because they had become so incorporated into mass capitalist society. The task of critical theory was to explain why revolution had not occurred, and its answer was that capitalism had tightened its ideological grip over the oppressed.

Given this concern with ideology, much of Adorno's critique is conducted at the level of culture and is particularly concerned with the differences between avant-garde and mass culture. While mass cultural products such as cinema, jazz and popular literature are tied to the economic and ideological imperatives of the 'culture industry', the sphere of high culture, particularly the non-representational art forms of the modernist avant-garde, remains one of the few areas that can function as a part-escape from a wholly administered, totalitarian society. The uncompromising, atonal music of Arnold Schoenberg, for example, provides an internal critique of its own conditions of production, and its relationship to the history of music and to broader economic and historical forces (Adorno 1981: 149–72). As Adorno makes clear in these comments on music, the most politically useful forms of art complicatedly refract their social situation:

> Music will be better, the more deeply it is able to express – in the antinomies of its own formal language – the exigency of the social situation and to call for change through the coded language of suffering. It is not for music to stare in helpless horror at society. It fulfils its social function more precisely when it presents social problems through its own material and according to its own formal laws.
>
> (Adorno 1978: 131)

Adorno's work has been accused of elitism in assuming that only certain types of culture can escape the surveillance strategies of capitalist society. The advantage of his work from an inter-disciplinary perspective, however, is that it suggests that these cultural forms are not merely passive enactors of historical pro-cesses but can critically reflect on and interact with their own historicity, albeit in a displaced form.

Adorno's work does not seek to institute Marxism as a scientific discipline or metadiscipline but instead provides a critical reflec-tion on the historical contingency and social production of dif-ferent forms of 'truth', arguing that 'the very intelligentsia that pretends to float freely is fundamentally rooted in the very being that must be changed and which it merely pretends to criticize' (Adorno 1981: 48). In *Dialectic of Enlightenment* (1947), Adorno and Horkheimer criticize the notion that knowledge, and parti-cularly science, can somehow step outside of the object of its inquiry. They suggest that the Enlightenment emerged as an open-minded, self-critical project, but that these principles have been dissipated as it has become increasingly doctrinal and dog-matic, asserting its control over the mind, the body and the natural world (Adorno and Horkheimer [1972] 1997: 3–6). In contrast to the 'identity thinking' of post-Enlightenment society, which homogenizes the disparate phenomena of the world, Adorno's work emphasizes the multiplicity of thought. It aims to combine the 'transcendent' critique of Marxism, which seeks a privileged perspective on the huge social and political forces of capitalism, with a form of 'immanent' critique which understands ideas and phenomena from within. Adorno shifts between a *cri-tical* theory which analyses the injustices of capitalism and a *self-critical* theory which is aware that no system of thought can escape the fetishization of reason and rationality in capitalist society.

The work of the French thinker, Louis Althusser, continues to explore some of these tensions between historical processes and cultural forms, while theorizing a different relationship between Marxism and the scientific disciplines. Althusser traces an 'epis-temological break' in Marx's work occurring in the mid-1840s, in which the pre-scientific humanism that had characterized Marx's early career was replaced by a true science of history, historical materialism. He compares this seismic shift to the transformation of the natural sciences in the scientific revolution of the sixteenth and seventeenth centuries. Indeed, Marx's major work, *Das Kapital*, represents 'the founding moment of a new discipline ... the absolute beginning of the history of a science' (Althusser and Balibar 1970: 15). This science has none of the traditional historian's concern with establishing the 'truth' about the past through the sifting of evidence and the study of cause and effect within a chronological framework; rather, it points to 'the absolute necessity of liberating the theory of history from any compromise with "empirical" temporality' (Althusser and Balibar 1970: 105).

Historical materialism thus attempts to purge history of anthropocentric and teleological notions which present it as having an origin, design and ultimate goal determined by human agency. For Althusser, history is *'a process without a subject'*, in the same way that scientific knowledge is 'the historical result of a process which has no real subject or goal(s)' (1976: 56). Althusser's attempt to grasp the true significance of Marx's work could be compared to Lacan's 'return to Freud', but, whereas Lacan questions the scientific ambitions of psychoanalysis, Althusser refashions Marxism as a hard, impersonal science. He argues that Marxism's importance to the humanities and social sciences is that it '"opens up" to scientific knowledge the "continent" in which they work, in which they have so far only produced a few preliminary knowledges ... or a few elements or rudiments of knowledge ... or illusions, pure and simple, illegitimately called knowledges' (Althusser 1971: 72). Althusser's interdisciplinarity could therefore be seen as an argument for the dominance of the sciences: it is based on developing an overarching, superior form of knowledge, the science of historical materialism, which will be able to colonize the non-sciences and bring them to scientific maturity.

This reconfiguring of Marxism as a science allows Althusser to claim that historical proof is only significant to the extent that it supports the theory of historical materialism. This means, for example, that knowledge about Stalin's reign of terror in the

Soviet Union need not necessarily lead us to question the validity of Stalinism. Marxist theory has no need to call on external evidence as long as it is internally consistent:

> *Theoretical practice* is indeed its own criterion, and contains in itself definite protocols with which to *validate* the quality of its product ... This is exactly what happens in the real practice of the sciences: once they are truly constituted and developed they have no need for verification from *external* practices to declare the knowledges they produce to be 'true', i.e. to be *knowledges*. No mathematician in the world waits until physics has *verified* a theorem to declare it proved ... the truth of his theorem is a hundred per cent provided by criteria purely *internal* to the practice of mathematical proof ... We can say the same for the results of every science.
>
> (Althusser and Balibar 1970: 59)

In fact, this is quite a specific notion of science as mathematics, an area of knowledge that proceeds by reducing spatial and numerical relationships to abstract formulae, rather than by generating hypotheses and testing them through empirical observation. Mathematical concepts, such as algebra, calculus and logarithms, are human constructions which are valid within the specific terms they set themselves. By contrast, sciences such as physics, biology and chemistry clearly rely on external proof from the natural world as the basis for their scientific discoveries.

Althusser's attempt to separate theory from practice, and to deny the reality of history except insofar as it supports a Marxist science, has been attacked by many historians. This is hardly surprising, perhaps, given that it questions the whole *raison d'être* of their discipline. E.P. Thompson, for example, accuses Althusser of appropriating his notion of 'theory' from mathematics or analytical philosophy. Like these areas of knowledge, Althusser's work is 'wholly self-confirming. It moves within the circle not only of its own problematic but of its own self-perpetuating and self-elaborating procedures' (Thompson 1978: 204). Thompson links this development of closed theoretical systems to the growing specialization in universities, arguing that today's theorists are 'segregated more than ever before from practice; they work within institutions, which are complexly structured, according to "schedules" and programmes ... their knowledge of the world is composed, increasingly, within their heads or their theories by non-observational means' (Thompson 1978: 300–1).

Thompson's argument is one we have come across already in different forms: it is about the insularity of the disciplines and their refusal to reflect critically on their own operations. He claims that Althusser's Marxism is no more than a sterile academic discipline, less concerned with class struggle or social injustice than with the production of empty theories engaged only in reproducing themselves. Thompson's position is the complete antithesis of Althusser's: whereas Althusser suggests that 'history' is a theoretical construct to be used in the service of science, Thompson argues that the 'real' history that goes on 'outside the academic procedures' can function as a corrective to scholarly divisions of knowledge (1978: 200). There are certainly links between Althusser's position and other arguments discussed in this book in favour of the development of disciplines, particularly the notion that there can be a neutral path to scientific understanding, a 'knowledge effect' which exists independently of cultural or historical factors and which produces an absolute truth within its own frame of reference.

Althusser's work is undeniably valuable from an interdisciplinary perspective, however, because, like Adorno's work, it reinterprets classical Marxism to argue that the sphere of language, culture and representation is inextricably connected to economic and historical processes, principally by proposing an inclusive notion of 'ideology'. In Marx's writings, ideology tends to be seen as 'false consciousness', the illusory beliefs of individuals about their real social conditions. But for Althusser, ideology does not conceal some underlying reality, but forms part of our whole way of making sense of the world, and constructs us as individual subjectivities. The central importance given to ideology in Althusser's work means that the cultural superstructure is seen as 'relatively autonomous' from the economic base (Althusser 1971: 130). Among other things, this suggests that cultural texts are not merely reflective of historical processes, but interact with and help to produce them, so that 'history' and 'text' both become part of a network of interconnected discursive practices. The all-pervasiveness of discourse also means that all forms of knowledge are produced within what Althusser calls a 'problematic': a discursive framework that, rather like a discipline, foregrounds certain modes of thought and excludes others (1977: 32). However, for reasons that are not always made clear, Althusser seems to believe that science, and specifically a Marxist science, can bypass this ideological entrapment.

The work of the foremost contemporary Marxist cultural critic, Fredric Jameson, is founded on an Althusserian tension between a belief that we should 'always historicize' (Jameson 1981: 9), and an awareness that this endeavour is problematized by the mediation of history through texts and theories. In *The Political Unconscious*, his most detailed exploration of his position, Jameson asserts the importance of history as 'the ultimate ground as well as untranscendable limit of our understanding' (Jameson 1981: 100). He goes on to critique what he calls the 'structuralist' turn in cultural criticism since the 1960s, by which he means not merely structuralism but a whole range of theories emphasizing the primacy of language which have transformed the humanities and social sciences. He argues that this shift has 'drive[n] the wedge of the concept of a "text" into the traditional disciplines by extrapolating the notion of "discourse" or "writing" onto objects previously thought to be "realities" or objects in the real world' (Jameson 1981: 297). He questions this tendency to see history as only one narrative code among others, arguing that 'history is what hurts ... we may be sure that its alienating necessities will not forget us, however much we might prefer to ignore them' (Jameson 1981: 102).

At the same time, Jameson acknowledges Althusser's point that history can never be known prior to its textual representation. While 'history is *not* a text', it is 'inaccessible to us except in textual form, and ... our approach to it and to the Real itself necessarily passes through its prior textualisation, its narrativisation in the political unconscious.' History, like the unconscious in Freudian psychoanalysis, can only ever be made available through narrative forms which intermittently reveal their 'absent cause' (Jameson 1981: 35). Jameson thus proposes an interdisciplinary model of Marxist criticism that attempts 'to restructure the problematic of ideology, of the unconscious and of desire, of representation, of history, and of cultural production, around the all-informing process of *narrative*' (1981: 13). This means that a Marxist analysis of history needs to exist alongside the close reading skills learned in subjects such as literary studies, since it is only by carefully interpreting the narrative 'symptoms' of texts that the workings of the political unconscious can be revealed.

Jameson's other distinctive contribution is to point to the 'utopian' elements of texts, retaining the orthodox Marxist belief in the possibility of radical societal transformation. He suggests that what makes literary and cultural texts interesting for Marxist analysis is that they feed into this utopian impulse: although they are always embedded in the ideologies of the period, they are also driven by a desire to imagine a better world, by producing alternatives to contemporary social arrangements and envisaging a future era of class harmony and cultural unity. He argues that the weaknesses of a reductive Marxist analysis of literature and culture (which presents them as simply the effect of historical or economic forces) are avoided or transcended in 'the Utopian perspective'. This perspective looks forward to a classless society in which the historical tensions and contradictions of class society have dissolved, so that the distinction between base and superstructure, or historical processes and cultural forms, no longer exists (Jameson 1981: 293). One might make a comparison here: whereas Leavis's model of the organic society is retrospectively interdisciplinary, imagining an organic society of the past in which culture and society were conjoined, Jameson's is prospectively interdisciplinary, envisaging a future society in which the division between culture and history has withered away.

Jameson's interdisciplinary project is clearly founded on a belief in the possibility of an ultimate, all-inclusive knowledge which he locates in Marxism. While conceding that total knowledge is impossible, because 'totality is not available for representation, any more than it is accessible in the form of some ultimate truth' (1981: 55), he does argue that the *search* for a totalizing perspective should at least be a methodological aim of intellectual work. Marxism provides this sort of perspective in the way that it 'subsumes other interpretive modes or systems; or, to put it in methodological terms ... the limits of the latter can always be overcome, and their more positive findings retained, by a radical historicizing of their mental operations' (Jameson 1981: 47). Broadly speaking, then, we might say that the potential for interdisciplinarity within Marxist cultural criticism has developed in two main directions. First, it has been marked by the progressively more nuanced and complex way in which it has raised questions about the relationship between literature, culture and history. Second, it has sometimes been characterized by a belief that the different disciplines can be brought together in a synthesizing project administered by Marxism, which is seen as a privileged, scientific form of knowledge in its own right, what Jameson calls 'the absolute horizon of all reading and all interpretation' (1981: 17).

KNOWLEDGE AND POWER

Michel Foucault's work, although directly opposed to this quest for synthesis, has also been hugely influential in helping both cultural historians and literary critics to think through the complex relationship between texts and their histories. His work is very hard to place within any one discipline, since it combines a historian's commitment to delving into recondite archive material with philosophical sophistication and an eclectic choice of subject matter. Foucault was elected to the Collège de France in 1970 with a specially created chair in the 'History of Systems of Thought', and this seems a fairly accurate description of his work: much of it is concerned with the intellectual and institutional structures that make certain forms of knowledge possible, and so it obviously deals with the nature of disciplines and the potential for interdisciplinary work. At the beginning of his book, *The Order of Things*, Foucault recalls laughing at a story by Jorge Luis Borges, in which the Argentinian writer describes a Chinese encyclopaedia that divides animals into a series of apparently arbitrary categories, such as 'belonging to the Emperor', 'drawn with a very fine camelhair brush', 'having just broken the water pitcher' and 'that from a long way off look like flies' (1970: xv). For Foucault, the randomness of these groupings suggests that intellectual divisions that we regard as natural might also seem absurd from another perspective.

One of Foucault's main aims is to produce an 'archaeology of knowledge', by uncovering the systems of thought that remain unconscious to scientists, scholars and other people but that still succeed in framing and limiting what they do. He argues that in the modern era, knowledge has become gradually more organized and specialized. In the Renaissance period, thought was organized by the 'principle of mobility' and the world was a 'vast open book' in which 'words glittered in the universal resemblance of things' (Foucault 1970: 23, 27, 49). In the classical age, from the mid-seventeenth to the late eighteenth centuries, discontinuities were established and a process of ordering and classification begun, but within the overall framework of a universal system. With the birth of the modern age from around 1800 onwards, however, 'knowledge closed in upon itself', and the sciences, philosophy and other disciplines began to divide up 'the chaotic monotony of space' (Foucault 1970: 89, 113).

Foucault relates this disciplining of knowledge to the overall development of an increasingly disciplinary society. Indeed, as Keith Hoskin points out, his writing has frequently played on the dual meaning of 'discipline' as a way of organizing knowledge and as an operation of power (Hoskin 1990: 30). Foucault argues that, in the 'post-Enlightenment' society which has developed since the end of the eighteenth century, public and physical forms of punishment such as hanging, flogging and torture have been replaced by more subtle forms of surveillance and self-surveillance. These forms place limitations on what can be said, written and known within society, and so help to create and constrain individual subjectivities. Foucault points out that schools and universities, where the academic disciplines are taught, are also disciplinary environments. They are organized by hierarchical relationships between teachers and students and a system of timetables and examinations, producing 'a surveillance that makes it possible to qualify, to classify and to punish' (Foucault 1979: 184).

In *The Order of Things*, Foucault deals specifically with the 'human sciences', which emerged in the nineteenth century and which attempted to create a science of human behaviour. For Foucault, the principal human sciences are economics, philology and biology, the latter of which is more usually defined as one of the natural sciences, but which he seems to include here because of the biological roots of the sciences of the mind. From these three subjects, there emerged a wide variety of disciplines focusing on human society (for example, sociology, anthropology, criminology, political science and economics), culture (literary criticism, the study of art and mythology) and mental processes (psychology, psychiatry and psychoanalysis). For Foucault, the human sciences actually created a sense of what it meant to be human, since they appeared 'when man constituted himself in Western culture as both that which must be conceived of and that which is to be known' (Foucault 1970: 345). He argues that one of the ways in which modern Western societies control and discipline people is by delegating to the human sciences the authority to decide what constitute the universal 'norms' of human behaviour, a process that also defines what it means to be 'deviant'. The formation of these academic disciplines thus demonstrates one of the most basic insights in Foucault's work: the intimate relationship between knowledge and power.

Foucault's notion of historical development is also organized around this fundamental insight about the interrelatedness of knowledge and power. He argues that power, in order to be established and constituted, requires the production of a discourse in order to make sense of and justify it. For Foucault, a *discourse* refers to a historically constituted form of 'truth', or what specific power arrangements will allow to be said, written and thought within a society. He argues that history proceeds not through the chronological unfolding of historical events but through discursive breaks, shifts in ways of structuring and limiting knowledge. He uses the term, *epistême*, to define a system of thought within a particular period that determines the circumstances under which 'ideas could appear, sciences be established, experience be reflected in philosophies, rationalities be formed, only, perhaps, to dissolve and vanish soon afterwards' (Foucault 1970: xxii).

Since our knowledge of reality itself is a construction of 'discourse', any investigation of reality needs to be based on the study of texts, and these texts cannot be closed off from each other by disciplines or critical approaches that foreground particular forms of writing. As Foucault suggests, if one always 'remains within the dimension of discourse', this questions any notion of an 'interior' and an 'exterior', which one finds in the traditional distinction between text and context in literary studies (1972: 76). It also challenges the disciplinary exclusions of history: Foucault argues that the academic practice of history is too concerned with finding a vantage point from which to reduce the multiplicity of past events to a single, authoritative version. He suggests that the traditional activities of 'history' should be countered with a 'genealogy', which would focus on 'the singularity of events outside any monotonous finality', seeking them 'in the most unpromising places, in what we tend to feel is without history' (Foucault 1977: 139). 'Genealogy' is a term particularly associated with Foucault's later work, and its aim of uncovering the illegitimate knowledges that challenge official accounts is less sweeping than his earlier, 'archaeological' analyses of the powerful discourses that support dominant power structures. While more conventional histories might seek to identify origins, causes and overall trends, genealogies therefore tend to concentrate on specific practices and apparently insignificant details. This suppressed knowledge is likely to be found in the kinds of sources that have been less highly regarded within the discipline of history and more commonly used in other areas of the humanities: novels, stories, narratives, myths, letters, diaries and testimonies, for example.

TEXTUAL HISTORICITIES

The new historicist school of literary and cultural criticism, which emerged in the USA from the early 1980s onwards, has been greatly influenced by Foucault's use of the category of 'discourse' to question the conventional distinctions between different areas of knowledge. New historicists aim to focus on both literature and history in a way in which neither term is privileged over the other, producing a sense of what Louis Montrose calls 'the historicity of texts' and 'the textuality of history':

> By *the historicity of texts*, I mean to suggest the cultural specificity, the social embedment, of all modes of writing. ... By *the textuality of history*, I mean to suggest ... that we can have no access to a full and authentic past, a lived material existence, unmediated by the surviving textual traces of the society in question.
>
> (Montrose 1989: 20)

New historicism thus straddles the divide between history and literary criticism and, perhaps as a consequence, has been criticized by scholars working within both disciplines.

In the essay that first introduced the term, Stephen Greenblatt argues that new historicism is a response to two particular critical assumptions which limit literary studies as a discipline. First, it challenges the new criticism's emphasis on 'the verbal icon', the literary text as a self-contained, formal and thematic unity. Second, it rejects the traditional approach to literary history, with its assumption that the historical material is merely secondary, a useful 'background' to the main business of elucidating the text, and that this background can be understood as unified and consistent, 'a stable point of reference, beyond contingency, to which literary interpretation can securely refer' (Greenblatt 1982: 4–5). New historicism's response to these exclusions has been an 'intensified willingness to read all of the textual traces of the past with the attention traditionally conferred only on literary texts' (Greenblatt 1990: 14), so it tends to deal with both conventional literary sources and non-fictional forms such as autobiographies, travel writing, political documents and economic treatises, as well as visual art, material culture, rituals and other everyday cultural practices.

At the same time, new historicism challenges the social-scientific aspirations of history as a discipline. The postmodern historian Hayden White, whose work has been much cited amongst new-historicist critics, has suggested that every discipline is 'constituted by what it *forbids* its practitioners to do. Every discipline is made up of a set of restrictions on thought and imagination, and none is more hedged about with taboos than professional historiography' (White 1978: 126). White argues that history should not be seen as a science, because it uses figurative rather than technical language, employs narrative techniques similar to those used in literary texts, and relies more on unstated assumptions than controlled experimental methods or theoretical justifications (1995: 243). And yet as a discipline it tends to conceal its narrativity by being unreflective about its own practices; it substitutes a fetishization of the 'facts' and a supposedly scientific methodology for any real critical relationship to the textual traces of the past. One of the ways in which new historicists aim to challenge this scientific model is by being less concerned than traditional historians with cause and effect: how and why events happen, and lead on to other events. They tend to view history synchronically rather than diachronically, which means that they prefer to take a cross-section of one period, examining the range of texts produced within it, rather than seeing how these texts 'progress' into other cultural forms over time. If they see history as process at all, it is in relation to the Foucauldian concern with the epistemological breaks that transform our means of knowing and representing the world.

In this respect, new historicism has much in common with the new cultural anthropology practised by theorists such as Clifford Geertz. Geertz argues that the concept of culture is 'essentially a semiotic one', and that anthropology is therefore 'not an experimental science in search of law but an interpretive one in search of meaning' (1973: 5). In order to show that cultures are full of complex signs and codes which cannot be understood easily from outside, Geertz borrows the example of a wink from the British philosopher Gilbert Ryle: this can be interpreted as a facial twitch, a conspiratorial gesture or an act of mimicry, depending on the context within which it is produced and interpreted. Employing Ryle's terms, Geertz argues that a 'thin description' would see these movements as identical contractions of the eyelid, whereas a 'thick description' would view them as part of the 'stratified hierarchy of meaningful structures' (1973: 7) which constitute the signs and symbols of everyday life.

This emphasis on thick description signifies a more general shift within anthropology away from the sciences: rather than investigating 'primitive' cultures to discover the basic, universal elements of human culture, it is now more inclined to see these cultures as complex systems in their own right which can only be interpreted, rather than scientifically discovered, by the ethnographer. For Geertz, this is part of a more general 'interpretive turn' in the social sciences, through which scholars have 'freed themselves from dreams of social physics' by increasingly using analogies from the humanities (1983: 23). Given that thick description involves picking through ever-more-complex layers of human experience, 'cultural analysis is intrinsically incomplete', and amounts to 'guessing at meanings, assessing the guesses, and drawing explanatory conclusions from the better guesses, not discovering the Continent of Meaning and mapping out its bodiless landscape' (Geertz 1973: 29, 20).

New historicist criticism could be seen as a kind of Geertzian ethnography of past societies, interpreting their strangeness and specificity through their textual remains. Like Geertz, new historicists tend to reject overarching schema or pretensions to disciplinary coverage in favour of what he calls 'local knowledge'. They will often trace or extrapolate broader patterns from a relatively small number of disparate texts, using an anecdotal, patchwork approach which might be compared to the literary trope of synecdoche, in which a part stands for the whole concept. For example, a new historicist specializing in modernism and modernity might take an economic thesis such as F.W. Taylor's *Principles of Scientific Management* (1911), which sought to increase industrial efficiency by controlling the pace of work through assembly-line production and time-and-motion studies; Ezra Pound and R.S. Flint's manifesto for imagist poetry (1913), which presents the imagist poem as 'an intellectual and emotional complex in an instant of time' (Kolocotroni *et al.* 1998: 374); and a new kind of advertisement that emerged in the first few decades of the twentieth century urging housewives to make use of those 'might-have-been hours' through time-saving innovations such as ready-prepared food or laundries. These texts might then be juxtaposed to explore new ways of thinking about temporality and ephemerality in modern culture and society, in an age of the increasing regulation of both work and leisure time.

Scholars working within history departments have sometimes been critical of this deliberately piecemeal approach. Dominick LaCapra, for example, first praises new historicism for its inter-disciplinary ambitions, suggesting that its appeal across the humanities disciplines lies in 'the manifest desire to find connec-tions between levels of culture that are often left in splendid iso-lation'. But he argues that the attempt to make such connections often results in a 'facile associationism' which links together a wide variety of texts without critically considering the real connections or differences between them. New historicist analyses

> take the more or less routinized form of finely crafted, decorous sty-listic assemblages in which there is little attempt to pause and puzzle over difficult or dubious steps in an argument. The commendable but demanding and problematic ideal of intertextual and cross-cultural analysis thus receives too easy and contemplative a solution – what might be called the pseudosolution of weak montage or, if you prefer, cut-and-paste bricolage.
>
> (LaCapra 1989: 193)

From a historian's point of view, LaCapra suggests, we need to ask questions about the status and discreteness of these wide-ranging sources, and examine how representative or useful they are as evidence for the particular historical inquiry we are under-taking. What is also missing in new historicist criticism, he argues, is a sense of the interactions between the various levels of society and culture – between highbrow, lowbrow and middle-brow culture, for example, or between different social groups and classes – which a traditional historian or social scientist might bring to bear on the same material. As LaCapra points out, this concern with the power relationships in society has formed the agenda of much radical history, but new historicists tend to associate it with 'totalizing theory or terroristic metanarrative' (LaCapra 1989: 194). He links this assumption to the political pessimism of new historicism, its notion that dominant forces always ultimately recuperate any politically subversive potential that texts may have, or, as Greenblatt puts it, that the 'apparent production of subversion is ... the very condition of power'

(1985: 45). For critics like LaCapra, this emphasis on the pervasiveness of dominant discourses can too easily degenerate into a kind of homogeneous textual formalism which, for all the professed interdisciplinary ambitions of the new historicists, represents a denial of history as 'what hurts'.

SHAKESPEARE AND ENGLIT

Some of these criticisms of new historicism have been made most vigorously within a roughly contemporaneous but largely British critical movement, cultural materialism. Cultural materialism shares many of the same features of the new historicism: a concern with the complex negotiations between texts and histories, the link between knowledge formations and the power arrangements of society, and the inability of the conventional academic divisions of labour to address these issues. In fact, the differences between the two movements can be exaggerated: neither are unified bodies of thought, and they often undertake quite similar work. Moreover, the critical relationship of these movements to the established disciplines means that they are both characterized by an unwillingness to define themselves and their activities too programmatically. But there are still important differences of critical approach and subject matter which relate to our discussion of interdisciplinarity.

One of the most significant disagreements between the new historicists and the cultural materialists is that the latter tend to regard themselves as more politically engaged than the former, which accounts in part for their hostility to disciplinary and institutional structures. The cultural materialist Alan Sinfield, for example, suggests that academics should form alliances with subcultures outside academia, such as women's-rights campaigners, eco-protestors or gay-rights activists, rather than 'getting sucked into professional Englit – hiding in universities, using long words, and getting to be big fish in a small pond' (Sinfield 1994a: 76). He argues that new historicism's concern with the entrapment of all forms of discourse within dominant power structures allows it to fudge these questions about its relationship to the outside world, and is 'tellingly homologous with its own professional entrapment' (Sinfield 1992: 290).

Sinfield therefore damns the new historicists with faint praise when acknowledging their professionalism: their high standards of literary and historical research and the 'subtlety and rigour of [their] textual analysis' (Sinfield 1992: 7). He argues that these skills are used simply to textualize history, through the sole innovation of applying close reading techniques to a broader range of texts than is common in literary criticism (Sinfield 1992: 285). Sinfield argues that this disciplinary agenda is not enough for cultural materialists, who are 'beset by the question of what it is all for' and 'call for modes of knowledge that literary criticism scarcely possesses or even knows how to discover', located in history and the social sciences (1992: 8, 49–50). He suggests that, because the supposed interdisciplinarity of the new historicism is not informed by a radical political agenda, it is always likely to slip back into a professionalism that serves its own ends and reproduces the traditional frameworks of the discipline.

This difference in emphasis means that cultural materialists are more inclined to use the study of texts from other historical periods as a way of addressing contemporary political issues. By contrast, new historicists tend to focus exclusively on historical material and to emphasize the differentness of the past, being wary of what historians term 'anachronism', the failure to appreciate the unique social, cultural and intellectual frameworks of previous eras. In this sense, both movements tap into long-standing controversies within the discipline of history, about whether it is the historian's task to put aside contemporary prejudices and appreciate the specific social structures, everyday practices and mindsets of other historical periods, or whether, as Croce suggested, all history is contemporary history. In order to point to the usefulness of historical texts as a way of addressing contemporary problems, cultural materialists often seek to identify the ideological tensions and contradictions within them rather than their perpetual entrapment within dominant power formations. Sinfield focuses on what he calls 'fault-line' stories, which cluster around the problematic, unsettling issues in society, since 'the stories that require most attention – most assiduous and

continuous reworking – are the awkward, unresolved ones'
(1989: 37).

In this and other aspects of its work, cultural materialism
draws on the writings of Raymond Williams, who first originated
the term, and in particular his important distinction between the
'residual', 'dominant' and 'emergent' forms that co-exist in a
culture at any one time (Williams 1977: 121–7). This distinction suggests that the dominant culture is heterogeneous and
dynamic, always having to contend with new, oppositional cultures and historical survivals from previous eras. As the mutual
reliance on the work of Williams demonstrates, there are clearly
affinities between cultural materialism and the political and
intellectual project of British cultural studies. But there is a significant difference: whereas cultural studies has challenged disciplinary categories by largely supplanting the study of literature
with an investigation of other forms of culture, cultural materialism has mounted a similar challenge by subverting the discipline from within, taking on its most revered objects from an
interdisciplinary perspective.

As Sinfield points out, cultural materialists tend to concentrate
on literature because, while it is only one of many forms of cultural production, it has considerable authority and prestige. They
have been particularly interested in Shakespeare because he is 'a
powerful cultural token. He is already where meaning is
produced, and people therefore want to get him on their side'
(Sinfield 1994a: 4). Their readings of Shakespeare focus on his
centrality as a figure in British culture, as a source of both commercial exploitation and cultural authority, and, within the discipline of English, as 'the keystone which guarantees the ultimate
stability and rightness of the category "Literature"' (Sinfield 1985:
135). This notion clearly extends to schools and colleges as well as
universities: in Britain, for example, all secondary-school pupils
are required to study Shakespeare, and he is also a compulsory
element on Advanced Level (for pupils aged sixteen to eighteen)
English syllabuses. A cultural materialist reading might examine
how the pivotal role of Shakespeare in most people's school
education plays a part in the reproduction of social and cultural
distinctions, disadvantaging people from less privileged

backgrounds who do not 'get' him or understand the 'universal' truths his work is supposed to convey. It might also explore how Shakespeare's construction as 'the great National Poet whose plays embody universal truths' (Sinfield 1985: 135) allows him to be used in the service of conservative political meanings which stress the importance of maintaining the status quo, in a way that undermines the radical potential of the plays for dealing with such issues as gender, race, class and sexuality.

As part of his ongoing critique of interdisciplinarity, Stanley Fish has attacked cultural materialism, and Alan Sinfield's work in particular. In his book, *Professional Correctness*, Fish claims that he is not against interdisciplinary work per se so much as the whole project of 'interdisciplinarity', an endeavour carried out with religious fervour by leftist intellectuals as a way of challenging the perceived insularity of academic life. In particular, he links this project to a historicized and politicized criticism, which he labels 'new historicist' as an umbrella term also incorporating cultural materialist approaches, and which aims at transforming literary studies into a way of dealing with issues such as racism, patriarchy, homophobia and imperialism (Fish 1995: 1). For Fish, this is a category mistake: literary studies cannot deal with issues like this which are outside its frame of reference because, as soon as it does so, it will stop being literary studies.

Fish argues that the current vogue for historicized and politicized criticism is driven by an unsatisfiable desire for a total knowledge which will unite the disciplines, breaking up their professional coteries and forging links with the broader social and political world. But the disciplines each developed independently for specific historical reasons and serve to constitute knowledge itself, so there is no possibility of them being brought together into a unified field:

> Different forms of disciplinary work, rather than being co-partners in a single teleological and utopian task, are engaged in performing the particular tasks that would pass away from the earth were they to lose themselves in the name of some grand synthesis, be it the discipline of all disciplines or the truth of all lesser and partial truths.
>
> (Fish 1995: 73)

The impossibility of total knowledge means that interdisciplinary study is no more inclusive than other forms of study; it merely substitutes one type of task for another. Fish provides the analogy of a map produced by an automobile association which displays the distance between cities, so that 'the cities themselves become mere nodes, junctures in a relay, while all the attention is focused on what goes on between them'. Similarly, critical approaches that seek interdisciplinary affiliations end up focusing on the affiliations themselves rather than anything specific to the individual disciplines, simply because of the necessary incompleteness of any attempt to organize knowledge. By doing its job, an interdisciplinary map 'necessarily fails to do others; in doing justice to the relationships *between* disciplines it slights the immanent intelligibility of disciplines' (Fish 1995: 80).

Fish argues that interdisciplinary approaches that attempt to link literary studies to a radical political project have far more in common than they would like to admit with the traditional, Leavisite notion of literary studies as the guardian of a cultural heritage. In both cases, he identifies 'the familiar desire of the academic, and especially of the humanist academic, to be something other than what he or she is'. This persistent strain of anti-professionalism within literary studies is sustained by the belief that 'if we get the right account – that is, the account sufficiently responsive to the society's larger needs – the society will hearken to us, and our parents will finally understand why we made this apparently quixotic career choice' (Fish 1995: 140). Fish's response is that it is not that easy to change the world from within an academic discipline, because disciplines are inherently inward-looking and self-reproducing. He therefore advocates a 'professional correctness' in which the disciplinarity of literary studies is accepted and even embraced as an inevitable effect of its professionalization.

Fish's arguments can be countered in two ways. First, a discipline is not as coherent an entity as he supposes: he assumes that there is a recognized phenomenon called 'literary studies' with certain approved procedures and principles, which everyone within that discipline is following until they decide to be interdisciplinary. As I have tried to show so far in this book, literary studies is rarely this internally consistent or homogeneous. Inter-disciplinarity is not a recent development which has taken over the humanities disciplines from the outside over the past few years; it is built into the complicated nature and history of the disciplines themselves, particularly a diverse field such as literary studies. Second, Fish's definition of interdisciplinarity as synonymous with the quest for an ultimate synthesis of knowledge seems an oversimplification. Although cultural materialist and new historicist approaches may regard the cultural text as more inclusive than the literary text, this does not necessarily mean that their work is informed by a synthesizing impulse. In fact, their fundamental concern with the relationship between knowledge and power means that it is more likely to generate intellectual uncertainty, by denaturalizing disciplinary divisions, challenging intellectual orthodoxies and raising problems and issues not addressed in the traditional disciplines.

5

SCIENCE, SPACE AND NATURE

Many of the forms of interdisciplinarity I have examined so far in this book have sought to question the traditional hierarchy that subordinates the humanities to the more narrowly defined concerns of the sciences. The long-standing division between the humanities and the sciences remains a resilient obstacle to interdisciplinary study, but it is still capable of being challenged. This chapter explores some of the connections that have been made in recent years between literary studies and the sciences – and between literary studies and geography, a social science that deals fundamentally with the relationship between the natural and social world – in relation to new understandings of space, nature and the physical world. It goes on to discuss ecocriticism as a field that merges those of literary and cultural criticism, geography and the natural sciences, with its fundamental premise that human culture is inextricably connected to nature. Finally, it investigates the efforts of some scientists to use evolutionary theory and developments in neuroscience to interpret literary and cultural texts.

The most widely discussed attempt to question the divide between the sciences and humanities is C.P. Snow's 'The Two

Cultures and the Scientific Revolution', a lecture delivered at Cambridge in 1959 which was almost immediately published and provoked intense debate in several countries. Snow bemoaned the 'gulf of mutual incomprehension' that existed between the sciences and humanities, arguing that the British education system exacerbated the situation by forcing pupils to specialize too early (Snow [1959] 1993: 4). As I pointed out in Chapter 1, F.R. Leavis was the most outspoken critic of Snow's thesis, perhaps because of the latter's barely concealed animosity towards the 'literary intellectuals' whom he regarded as the dominant force in the humanities. However, although Snow accused these literary intellectuals of being 'natural Luddites' and of 'the most imbecile expressions of anti-social feeling' ([1959] 1993: 22, 8), he also expressed deep reservations about the insularity and narrow-mindedness of much of the scientific profession. His main aim was clearly to show that both fields were impoverished by their ignorance of each other, so that 'in our society ... we have lost even the pretence of a common culture. Persons educated with the greatest intensity we know can no longer communicate with each other on the plane of their major intellectual concern' (Snow [1959] 1993: 60).

In fact, Snow's anxieties about specialization had considerable affinities with Leavis's, since he conceded that there was 'no complete solution' to the problem and that 'in the conditions of our age ... Renaissance man is not possible' ([1959] 1993: 61). Like Leavis, he suggested that the best opportunities for improving the situation were provided by education, and particularly interdisciplinary studies. Unlike Leavis, though, he did not propose any one subject as a meeting point for all the others, suggesting that productive connections needed to be made across the science–humanities divide:

> The clashing point of two subjects, two disciplines, two cultures – of two galaxies, so far as that goes – ought to produce creative chances. In the history of mental activity that has been where some of the break-throughs came. The chances are there now. But they are there, as it were, in a vacuum, because those in the two cultures don't talk to each other.
>
> (Snow [1959] 1993: 16)

Snow's lecture sketched out the fundamental nature of the disagreement between the sciences and humanities, in a way that remains topical. Those in the sciences still tend to criticize humanities scholars for disregarding empirical methods and relying on subjective interpretations; those in the humanities attack scientists, in turn, for a misguided faith in the possibility of absolute objectivity, a narrow conception of useful knowledge and an unwillingness to interrogate the broader social, political and cultural implications of their work. Many of these disagreements can be traced not only to the different scope and subject matter of the sciences and humanities but their contrasting assumptions about how knowledge should actually be accumulated. I want to begin this chapter by tracing the origins of this division in the belief that the sciences have a special claim to 'truth', rooted in the empirical method, which represents a powerful argument for the separation of the disciplines. I then want to look at recent challenges to this unquestioned empiricism from within the sciences themselves, which have paved the way for more productive connections to be made with non-scientific disciplines.

THE CHALLENGE TO EMPIRICISM

The traditional distinction between the humanities and the sciences rests on an assertion of the importance of empirical proof which was first made by philosophers of knowledge in the early seventeenth century and has only recently been seriously challenged. Francis Bacon is often credited with formulating the conventional model of scientific discovery, which he saw as a way of steering a middle path between complete scepticism and arbitrary, dogmatic belief. Bacon attacked the orthodoxy of classical learning and argued instead that human beings and nature should be studied in themselves, without fixed preconceptions. To this end, in *Novum organum scientiarum* (*New Organ of Learning*, 1620), he proposed a model of inductive reasoning: reasoning from specific cases to general conclusions, in gradually increasing levels of generality. In practice, this meant carefully collecting information about instances from the natural world and extrapolating common properties from this information. In *Discourse on Method* (1637) and other works, René Descartes further consolidated the scientific method by developing and refining the process of deduction: inferring conclusions logically from a premise. Descartes's method is sometimes referred to as 'Cartesian doubt', which involves the elimination of all illogical assumptions until the only possible conclusion, which cannot be doubted, remains. The other basic component of Descartes's method is reductionism: breaking up nature, including the human body, into its component parts and considering them separately, a kind of mechanization of the world which sees it as a well-oiled machine. This kind of reductionism partly explains the proliferation of disciplines in the scientific revolution of the sixteenth and seventeenth centuries, as different subjects were given responsibility for exploring separate aspects of nature.

Most people, even if they are not trained scientists, will be familiar with the scientific method inherited from Baconian inductivism and Cartesian reductionism, from writing up laboratory experiments at school. This method is based on empirical observation to discover the fundamental laws of cause and effect: 'The litmus paper turned blue when placed in the alkaline liquid.' As I argued in the introduction, many of the non-scientific disciplines developed in the nineteenth century along this scientific model, but there still remained a powerful sense that science had a privileged access to truth: it was seen as self-evident, accumulated knowledge about general laws which, unlike the humanities, existed independently of interpretation or belief. Science's self-confidence has traditionally stemmed from its self-limitations, its refusal to deal with those metaphysical or subjective concerns on which there are grounds for scepticism, confining itself to aspects of the biological or mechanical world that can be known 'objectively' and 'neutrally'. As Jean-François Lyotard argues, one of the main justifications for the division between the natural sciences and the human sciences is that nature is envisioned as 'an indifferent, not deceptive, opponent', so that in the natural sciences '"nature" is the referent – mute, but as predictable as a die thrown a great number of times', whereas in the human sciences 'the referent (man) is a participant in the game, one that speaks and develops a strategy ... to counter that of the scientist' (Lyotard 1984: 57).

This model was not seriously challenged within the sciences themselves until Karl Popper formulated his notion of 'falsifiability' in *The Logic of Scientific Discovery* (1934). For Popper, scientific discovery proceeds not through careful processes of induction and deduction but through the creative generation of falsifiable hypotheses. No scientific theory can ever be completely substantiated through inference from empirical observation: it is always possible to find exceptions to the rule at some future date. We cannot say for sure that 'all swans are white' because, although we might have seen a million white swans, the next swan we see might be black: indeed, to emphasize the point, black swans were recently discovered in Australia. Popper's work thus suggests that scientific knowledge advances through trial and error, rather than a systematic and methodical pursuit of the 'facts':

> The empirical basis of objective science has thus nothing 'absolute' about it. Science does not rest upon solid bedrock. The bold structure of its theories rises, as it were, above a swamp. It is like a building erected on piles. The piles are driven down from above into the swamp, but not down to any natural or 'given' base; and if we stop driving the piles deeper, it is not because we have reached firm ground. We simply stop when we are satisfied that the piles are firm enough to carry the structure, at least for the time being.
>
> (Popper [1959] 1972: 111)

At the same time, Popper does not completely abandon science to relativism, because he suggests that, if theories are *disprovable*, they can be tentatively accepted until they are falsified. This allows him to describe certain fields of learning as 'pseudo-scientific', not because they cannot lay claim to absolute truth, but because their theories are unfalsifiable. For Popper, the two great 'pseudosciences' are psychoanalysis and Marxism, because they rely on necessarily speculative theories about the unconscious mind or about the historical inevitability of communist revolution. Although he does not discuss the subject directly, it is clear that literary studies is a pseudoscience as he defines one, because it relies fundamentally on textual interpretation rather than the accumulation of falsifiable evidence. Despite his questioning of the traditional scientific method, then, Popper still believes in the possibility of objective knowledge, which he locates in the sciences as opposed to the humanities or social sciences, and which he defines as '*knowledge without a knower* ... *knowledge without a knowing subject*' (Popper 1973: 109).

A more radical challenge to the self-confident empiricism of the sciences, and the most well known and cited across the disciplines, is made by Thomas Kuhn in *The Structure of Scientific Revolutions* (1962). Kuhn argues that scientific knowledge does not emerge in a vacuum, but takes place within particular 'paradigms'. Kuhn's concept of the 'paradigm' could be seen as a more narrowly defined and institutionally oriented version of Foucault's *epistême*, in that only certain kinds of knowledge production are possible within it. In the 'normal science' that is conducted within particular paradigms, inconvenient discoveries which challenge dominant ways of thinking tend to be disregarded or devalued. Scientific revolutions thus depend upon 'paradigm shifts', in which one paradigm is substituted for another – for example, the shift from the Ptolemaic paradigm, which sees the earth as the centre of the universe, to a Copernican one which positions the earth as one of many planets orbiting the sun.

Kuhn's scientific constructivism can be interpreted in two, competing ways. On the one hand, it can be seen as a radical awareness of science as the product of institutional politics and cultural contexts, in which 'there is no standard higher than the assent of the relevant community'. In this formulation, theories produced within discrete paradigms, such as Newtonian and Einsteinian physics, are completely incommensurable because they are each engaged in affirming the truth-value of their own paradigm, and 'cannot be made logically or even probabilistically compelling for those who refuse to step into the circle' (Kuhn 1970: 94). On the other hand, Kuhn's theories can be viewed as a more moderate acceptance of paradigms as a necessary condition for scientific development. Rather like Popper, he differentiates between paradigmatic sciences, 'preparadigmatic' sciences which are not ruled by a single paradigm, and non-sciences which do not have one at all, and which thus suffer from a debilitating lack of agreement about the most basic questions of method and procedure (Kuhn 1970: viii). When his thesis was first disseminated in the 1960s, many literary critics were initially influenced by this aspect of his work, believing that their own subject needed to develop a clear paradigm in order to consider itself a proper discipline (Sosnoski 1995: 36).

The work of Paul Feyerabend, a former student of Popper's at the London School of Economics, takes Kuhn's ideas a stage further. Feyerabend proposes an almost wholly relativistic 'epistemological anarchism' which challenges the post-Enlightenment rejection of magic, religion and myth in favour of respectable science. He argues that scientific orthodoxy propagates views of the natural and physical world that are convenient to the social and political status quo, disguising its origins in 'aesthetic judgements, judgements of taste, metaphysical prejudices, religious desires' (Feyerabend 1975: 285). Science is the modern religion, with no greater claim to ultimate authority than voodoo or witchcraft. But while freedom to practise any religion, or to be an agnostic or atheist, is enshrined in most modern constitutions, there is no freedom to dissent from scientific knowledge, since it is taught and disseminated as a universal truth in schools, universities and elsewhere. Feyerabend therefore argues that we must 'free society from the strangling hold of an ideologically petrified science just as our ancestors freed *us* from the strangling hold of the One True Religion!' Science should be taught in schools, but only as a historical phenomenon alongside other 'fairytales', such as the myths of so-called 'primitive' societies which also seek to explain the natural and physical world (Feyerabend 1975: 307–8).

It is fair to say that Feyerabend's views have not been universally accepted by scientists. But the wide circulation and discussion of his work, and that of Kuhn and other scientific constructivists, suggests that scientists have come a long way from a simple faith in empiricism. Science is now increasingly seen not as a neutral account of phenomena based on the pursuit of pure knowledge, but as a way of making sense of the world, one influenced by the contexts within which scientific problems are framed, discussed and 'solved'. This recognition of the interpretative nature of science offers the potential for questioning the division between the sciences and humanities, which has been partly based on a policing of the distinction between objective 'facts' and subjective 'interpretations'.

SCIENCE AS CULTURE

It is also worth noting that, in many areas of current science, natural phenomena are seen to be governed by uncertainty and flux and cannot always be readily determined through experimentation. To give only a few examples of this new science: relativity theory, which is concerned with how objects behave at very high and normally immeasurable speeds, suggests that areas of the external world that we tend to regard as fixed, such as time, are in fact relative; quantum theory argues that subatomic particles do not behave according to classical laws, and that this indeterminacy limits the accuracy of measurement; 'chaos theory' suggests that complex systems, which are governed by deterministic laws and should therefore be predictable, are in fact chaotic because their sensitivity to initial conditions produces a huge range of variables (so that, for example, a butterfly flapping its wings in Milton Keynes can cause a tornado in Guadeloupe); fractal geometry aims to show that complex objects such as snowflakes, trees and coastlines have an infinite, and thus immeasurable number of fractional dimensions; and developments in mathematics, such as Gödel's theorem and fuzzy logic, argue that certain mathematical formulae are neither provable nor disprovable, and that we have to deal instead with a continuum of possible propositions. Science has not abandoned its search for deterministic laws or total knowledge: indeed, with the increasing sophistication of computers, many scientists working in the above fields still hold out the possibility of discovering 'deep order', the powerful rules governing even complex systems. Physicists, for example, still tend to believe in the possibility of a 'theory of everything', or, at least, a theory that will ultimately explain the origins of the universe and the fundamental particles that constitute it. Such a theory will allow us, in the famous words of Stephen Hawking, to 'know the mind of God' (1988: 193). However, it is still true that contemporary scientists do not always subscribe to the Baconian ideal of dealing only with concrete, observable evidence; they are much more likely to use intuition, interpretation, guesswork and 'thought experiments' alongside empirical observation.

Many of these scientific developments have been taken on board by literary and cultural critics (sometimes to the chagrin of more traditionally empiricist scientists) to develop inter-disciplinary approaches. For these critics, the new forms of science have not merely changed the way we understand the natural and physical world, they form part of a much broader philosophical questioning of the nature of reality itself, in a 'postmodern' culture governed by indeterminacy, open-endedness and fragmenta-tion. Lyotard, in his analysis of 'the postmodern condition', argues that these forms of science contribute to a general scepticism about what can be known and believed in contemporary culture:

> Postmodern science – by concerning itself with things such as un-decidables, the limits of precise control, conflicts characterized by incomplete information, '*fracta*', catastrophes, and pragmatic para-doxes – is theorizing its own evolution as discontinuous, cata-strophic, nonrectifiable, and paradoxical. It is changing the meaning of the word *knowledge*, while expressing how such a change can take place. It is producing not the known, but the unknown.
>
> (Lyotard 1984: 60)

Some of the most audacious links between postmodern cultural criticism and the new science have been made by the French philosopher, Jean Baudrillard. In *The Illusion of the End*, for example, he makes a series of suggestive connections between different areas of science and a postmodern sense of the 'vanishing of history', a decline of any narrative of historical progress in a world driven by instantaneity and ephemerality. Drawing an analogy with the 'escape velocity a body requires to free itself from the gravitational field of a star or planet', he argues that 'the acceleration of modernity, of technology, events and media, of all exchanges – economic, political and sexual – has propelled us to "escape velocity," with the result that we have flown free of the referential sphere of the real and of history' (Baudrillard 1994: 1). Just like the universe, history will 'come to a stop and be extinguished like light and time in the vicinity of an infinitely dense mass' (Baudrillard 1994: 4). It is not so much that history has ended, but that it has turned back on itself: 'Once the apogee of time, the summit of the curve of evolution, the solstice of history had been passed, the downward slope of events began and things began to run in reverse. It seems that, like cosmic space, historical space–time is also curved' (Baudrillard 1994: 10). Baudrillard introduces many different concepts here from distinct areas of theoretical physics, such as gravitational fields, escape velocity, critical mass and space–time, in order to convey a general sense of fluidity and uncertainty in contemporary culture.

Some of these theoretical interventions have produced a counter-response from scientists who resent their disciplines being appropriated in this way, the most notorious recent example being the much publicized 'Sokal Affair'. In summer 1996, a professor of physics, Alan Sokal, published an article in an American cultural studies journal claiming to argue that science had no special claim to truth but was instead the product of dominant ideologies (Sokal 1996a). Soon after the article appeared, Sokal revealed that it was a hoax, full of nonsense and cut-and-pasted together from quotes by leading philosophers of science, who he now attacked for undermining 'the normative conception of scientific inquiry as a search for truths or approximate truths about the world' (Sokal and Bricmont 1998: 5). Anyone who believed that the laws of physics were open to interpretation, he claimed, was welcome to interpret them by jumping out of his twenty-first-floor apartment window (Sokal 1996b: 62).

In a book written in response to the subsequent controversy, Sokal and his co-writer, Jean Bricmont, extend their remit to criticize the use of scientific theories and concepts in postmodern cultural theory. They argue that French thinkers such as Lyotard and Baudrillard, along with others such as Jacques Lacan, Julia Kristeva, Luce Irigaray and Gilles Deleuze, have appropriated ideas from the fields of mathematics and physics, name-dropping concepts and theorists without really understanding them or the huge conceptual distinctions that exist between different special-isms (Sokal and Bricmont 1998: 178). They claim that they are not against greater interaction between the sciences and the human sciences but want to establish the 'preconditions' for such a dialogue, one of which must be a recognition that 'the natural sciences are not a mere reservoir of metaphors ready to be used in the human sciences' (Sokal and Bricmont 1998: 174, 177). The question seems to be *how* scientific ideas are employed by these postmodern critics. Lyotard uses the new science as the basis for a series of reflections on the provisional nature of knowledge in contemporary culture; Baudrillard, on the other hand, seems to make more direct use of the intellectual authority of the scientific concepts themselves, linking them by analogy to other concepts in cultural theory. It is not always clear how these abstruse, highly technical scientific ideas, which are not widely known in the culture at large, feed into a broader postmodern sense of indeterminacy and undecidability.

A more productive interdisciplinary space might be constructed by examining the ways in which scientific ideas extend beyond the area of specialist inquiry and form part of culture: how they are informed by the dominant philosophies, preoccupations and representations of society, and how they interact with 'non-science' when they are widely disseminated. In a follow-up essay to the 'Two Cultures' lecture, Snow suggests that biology might provide the best model for interdisciplinary work across the sciences and humanities, because it can be understood without mathematical training, and it fundamentally affects the way that people think about themselves, asking big questions about the origins of life, our relationship to other species and the nature of the self (Snow [1959] 1993: 73–4). Charles Darwin's theory of natural selection, which suggests that the evolutionary develop-ment of species proceeds through the adaptation of those best able to survive and reproduce, is one obvious example of the way in which scientific developments are not confined rigidly within disciplines but are constrained by external factors. For example, Darwin's original formulation of the theory, in *On the Origin of*

Species (1859), excludes direct reference to humans and their relationship to other species, perhaps in deference to the Victorian religious orthodoxy that it implicitly challenged. As Gillian Beer and others have pointed out, the book also fudges the question of agency: while Darwin did not mean to argue that natural selection was driven by some ultimate purpose or benign Creator, the phrase itself still leaves open the possibility of an 'active selector', and the book frequently uses words such as 'selecting' and 'preferring' in relation to nature (Beer 1996a: xxiv). This is not simply a case of Darwin himself being influenced by Victorian society; science is unavoidably connected to other kinds of discourse because it uses language, which is never a pure mediator of reality, but a human construct which incorporates metaphor, narrative pattern and the inflections of society and culture. Although Darwin actually meant to decentre humans from his account of the origin of species by stressing the role of chance and contingency, the language he used to relate his theories implied intention, agency and design.

In the mid-nineteenth century, when Darwin was writing, the connection between scientists and a broader, non-scientific culture was also commonly acknowledged: scientists often tried to speak to an audience of non-specialist peers with non-technical language, and relied on the 'shared stories' of the period as well as literature, the Bible and theology (Beer 1996b: 8). *On the Origin of Species*, for example, draws on Shakespeare, Milton and natural theology, and is particularly influenced by Thomas Malthus's *Essay on the Principle of Population* (the sixth and final edition of which appeared in 1826), an apocalyptic vision of an overpopulated world, driven by famine, disease and the competitive struggle for limited resources, which recommends that the lower and 'inferior' classes should practise sexual abstinence. The openendedness and intertextuality of Darwin's text, its use of different tropes, narrative forms and a wide variety of scientific and nonscientific discourses to construct an argument, is extremely significant. Evolution is not observable within the space of a single human lifetime, so it can only be deduced from incomplete evidence such as fossil records and comparative anatomy and does not strictly conform to the Baconian emphasis on empirical observation. By extending beyond the usual self-limiting framework of a science, Darwin could thus formulate his theories in the absence of a great deal of supporting evidence.

With the rise of the academic disciplines within the professionalized context of the research university, scientists are much more likely to aim their research at specialized readerships, and avoid openly metaphorical language. Despite the enormous success of popular-science writing in recent years, most science still takes place within the confines of disciplines and is often incomprehensible to scientists working in other specialisms, let alone lay people. However, this does not stop science being part of culture: as Richard Rorty points out, professionalized science proceeds through the literalization of metaphors. In other words, scientific ideas begin life as metaphors, but as they become more accepted and familiar they tend to be seen as literal presentations of the 'truth', in a way that obscures the unavoidably metaphorical nature of language (Rorty 1989: 28, 37). Richard Dawkins's neo-Darwinian notion of the 'selfish gene' is one example of such a literalized metaphor. The selfish-gene theory supposes that some genes are concerned solely with replicating themselves: organisms exist as 'survival machines' for these genes, which means that they will behave in ways that maximize their chances of transmitting copies of their genes to succeeding generations (Dawkins 1976). But the word 'selfish' implies agency and even morality: it suggests that genes are actively seeking a particular outcome, when they are clearly not conscious or intentional in this way. This anthropocentric metaphor has been appropriated by some of its popularizers to posit a view of genes, and even individuals and societies, as inherently 'selfish', and in the 1980s the left-leaning Dawkins was wrongly seen as an apologist for a go-getting 'yuppie' culture and the conservative economic policies of the New Right. Dawkins's theory is therefore another example of how the inescapably figurative nature of language contaminates the apparently self-contained scientific disciplines with extra-disciplinary concerns.

Darwin's ideas also point to the ways in which science can never be constrained within purely scientific discourse. The theory of natural selection, for example, quickly entered wide circulation in the culture as a whole, becoming part of a whole series of interconnecting narratives. Despite Darwin's attempts to avoid discussing humans, the popular incarnations of his theories explicitly related humans to other species on an evolutionary scale. This was particularly apparent in the late-nineteenth-century phenomenon of 'Social Darwinism', a fusion of biology and social thought in which whole populations and classes of people were seen as evolving through a process of natural selection, according to what the British scientist and philosopher Herbert Spencer referred to as 'the survival of the fittest'. These ideas were variously used to justify the colonial domination of 'savage' peoples, the eugenics movement, anti-immigration policies, racial segregation, *laissez-faire* economics and other programmes that left the poor and 'unfit' to fend for themselves. Darwin's theories also influenced many of the literary and cultural texts of the period. The idea of a 'missing link' between monkeys and humans, although a travesty of Darwin's own theoretical position, quickly took hold in journalism, fiction and other media, often demonized as some kind of ogre or racial 'other' (Beer 1996b: 118). More fundamentally, Beer suggests that evolutionary theory had implications at the level of narrative in the nineteenth-century novel, which developed a Darwinian concern for hidden laws, interrelationships and processes, alongside a new interest in chance events and multiple possibilities (Beer 1983: 149 ff.). The efforts to contain science within a discipline or professional group can thus never be complete, because 'the excluded or left-over meanings of words' can be 'brought to the surface and put to use by those outside the accord or professional "contract," as well as by those future readers for whom new historical sequences have intervened' (Beer 1996b: 156).

The sphere of technology provides the most obvious way in which science can break out of this professional 'contract', since it is here that scientific discoveries are transformed into cultural products. The work of Donna Haraway, a trained biologist who moved into cultural studies and the history of science, has been fundamentally concerned with such 'technoculture'. Haraway's notion of the 'cyborg', a contraction of 'cybernetic organism', refers to a combination of human and machine: in contemporary culture, she argues, 'we are all chimeras, theorized and fabricated hybrids of machine and organism; in short, we are cyborgs' (Haraway 1991: 150). It is not difficult to think of examples of this melding of technology with the human: developments in medicine and micro-technology have produced artificial hip joints and limbs, as well as ear and eye implants for the deaf and blind; cosmetic surgery can transform a person's physical appearance; and sex changes can produce transsexual bodies. More mundanely, we could argue that we are being 'cyborgs' whenever we use contact lenses, sit at a computer screen, watch TV, listen to a walkman, or wear trainers designed to improve our athletic performance.

The important point for Haraway, though, is that the cyborg is 'a creature of social reality as well as a creature of fiction ... a condensed image of both imagination and material reality' (1991: 149–50). Technologies are both material objects and narrative devices and have as much to do with imagining and representing a particular vision of society as they do with providing specific solutions to practical problems. Cyborgs have appeared in popular fiction, for example, from Mary Shelley's *Frankenstein* (1818) onwards. In fact, Shelley's text, like the genre of science fiction which it is often seen as inaugurating, clearly lends itself to an interdisciplinary reading in that it draws on scientific research while using narrative and metaphor to imagine the future possibilities and dangers of science. She bases her account of the creation of Frankenstein's monster on developments in dissection and vivisection, Sir Humphrey Davy's innovations in electrochemistry and Luigi Galvani's experiments detailing the twitching movements of dead animals when an electric current is passed through them. The novel thus feeds into a newly confident view of scientists as 'hav[ing] acquired new and almost unlimited powers; they can command the thunders of heaven, mimic the earthquake, and even mock the invisible world with its own shadows' (Shelley [1818] 1994: 30–1). But in its tale of a 'mad scientist' who retreats from the responsibilities and consequences of generating life, the text also foregrounds perennial concerns about the power of science to control and manipulate humans and nature. The often nightmarish visions of unchecked science that one finds in popular representations, such as the recent media controversies about human cloning or genetically modified ('Frankenstein') foods, continue to demonstrate this fusion of technology with the imagination, while at the same time speaking to real anxieties about the power of genetics to control life.

Much of Haraway's work has been aimed at puncturing science's claims to neutrality and objectivity, repositioning it as a form of 'situated knowledge' (Haraway 1997: 3) which uses metaphors to reproduce particular power relations. But she is no technophobe: she argues that the cyborg can be positioned as the 'illegitimate' child of patriarchy, science and capitalism (Haraway 1991: 154), because it usefully subverts conventional class and gender positions and forces us to rethink the whole notion of identity, producing 'a kind of disassembled and reassembled, postmodern collective and personal self'. This androgynous cyborg threatens the 'hierarchical dualisms' that have ruled Western thought since Aristotle: mind and body, animal and human, public and private, nature and culture, man and woman (Haraway 1991: 163). For Haraway, it is technology, as it interacts with culture and takes on an existence separate from 'pure' science, which subverts some of our traditional ways of thinking, particularly the division between the sciences and the humanities. The sphere of technoculture, like the Darwinian study of species differentiation, demonstrates that science is unavoidably interdisciplinary because, although it might claim to be confined within the limiting framework of a discipline, it is always part of other narratives and knowledges.

GEOGRAPHY AS TEXT

The foundational assumptions of the field of geography have also been challenged in recent years by interventions from other disciplines. The main impetus for this has been an interest in interdisciplinary conceptions of space, which conceive it not as a neutral category but as something that is culturally produced, lived and represented in various ways. This new form of cultural geography undermines any tendency to think of the subject as 'a discipline-in-waiting, whose formation is determined not so much by the internal logic of intellectual inquiry as the imperatives of an "external" reality' (Gregory 1994: 8). In other words, since space is never neutral, it is not waiting there patiently to be discovered by the geographer: it is produced by a whole range of different agents and practices and requires the insights of other disciplines to understand and discuss it.

The American scholar Carl O. Sauer is largely credited with initiating the new cultural geography in works such as *Man in Nature* (1939) and *Land and Life* (1963), which sought to show that landscapes were not natural but culturally produced, by forging links between geography and other subjects such as anthropology, sociology, archaeology and history. The more recent work of critics such as Henri Lefebvre, Edward Soja and David Harvey is often concerned with space itself, and 'how space can be made to hide consequences from us, how relations of power and discipline are inscribed into the apparently innocent spatiality of social life' (Soja 1989: 6). Lefebvre, for example, deals specifically with the origins of the 'strictly geometrical meaning' of space in Cartesian logic, which imagines space as an 'empty area', an 'absolute, infinite *res extensa* [extended thing], a divine property which may be grasped in a single act of intuition' (Lefebvre 1991b: 1, 14). He proposes instead a concern with 'the space of social practice, the space occupied by sensory phenomena, including products of the imagination such as projects and projections, symbols and utopias' (Lefebvre 1991b: 11–12).

This new notion of space can usefully be applied, for example, to an understanding of cities. Cities are clearly material entities, products of some of the traditional concerns of geography such as labour, land and capital, but they are also textualized. In a sense, the city can only ever be understood textually, because it is far too complicated and labyrinthine to be encapsulated in its material totality: we only ever have access to a selective interpretation of it. Marshall Berman, focusing on the city in the late nineteenth and early twentieth centuries, has seen it as an explicit manifestation of competing visions of modernity. Many of New York's monuments and skyscrapers, for example, were specifically designed to symbolize the modernity of urban life, creating 'a Baudelairian forest of symbols' which struggle with each other for dominance, 'endlessly fighting each other for sun and light, working to kill each other off, melting each other along with themselves into air' (Berman 1983: 289). This may explain why some of the world's tallest buildings are today in the poorer cities: they are designed to bring modernity into being, to proclaim the city as futuristic and forward-looking. These textual configurations within cities are also bound up with relations of power, producing a kind of symbolic geography which decides who should be able to work, live in or even enter particular spaces. As Sharon Zukin puts it: 'The look and feel of cities reflect decisions about what – and who – should be visible and what should not' (1995: 7). Interdisciplinary approaches to the city thus tend to focus on the textualization of social space within the material reality of the city itself, while relating this to its representation in other kinds of text: novels, poetry, films and other media.

These interdisciplinary notions of space can also be applied fruitfully to the study of colonial and post-colonial discourse. One of the founding texts of post-colonial theory, Edward Said's *Orientalism*, explores the ways in which racial otherness is founded on geographical essentialism, 'the notion that there are geographical spaces with indigenous, radically "different" inhabitants who can be defined on the basis of some religion, culture or racial essence proper to that geographical space' (Said [1978] 1995: 322). The perceived differences between the Orient and the West, for example, are the product of an 'imaginative geography' which 'help[s] the mind to intensify its own sense of itself by dramatising the distance and difference between what is close to it and what is far away' (Said [1978] 1995: 55). This geographical essentialism is clearly evident in terms such as 'Near East', 'Middle East' and 'Far East', which define what is a comparative relation between different regions from a purely Eurocentric perspective.

Among many other factors, Said links the development of Western stereotypes and myths about the Orient, which have the effect of appropriating the East as the 'Other', to the transformation of the discipline of geography at the end of the nineteenth century. As Lord Curzon, former Viceroy of India, told the Royal Geographical Society in 1912, geography had been converted from a 'dull and pedantic' science into 'the most cosmopolitan of all sciences ... the handmaid of history' (Said [1978] 1995: 215). This rise of geography to the higher ranks of the social sciences was directly related to the colonial project, as topographical information became a valued resource, linked to the accumulation of wealth, prestige and power. The geographical societies themselves had a significant role in encouraging politicians and other interested parties to make further imperial conquests; indeed, as one French member put it, such societies were 'formed to break the fatal charm that holds us enchained to our shores' (Said [1978] 1995: 218). Said's post-colonial critique is thus partly aimed at subverting the notion of geography as a 'neutral' science by pointing to its insistently cultural nature, the way in which 'space acquires emotional and even rational sense by a kind of poetic process, whereby the vacant or anonymous reaches of distance are converted into meaning' ([1978] 1995: 55).

A great deal of interesting work in cultural geography has centred on the process of mapping: the way that it abstracts social space, establishing it as a universally measurable and homogeneous concept. The early maps of uncharted territories like South America, Africa and Australia were often works of art and imagination rather than science, with speculative drawings of monsters and pygmies substituting for lack of topographical knowledge. From the Renaissance period, onwards, however, maps came to be valued for their 'objectivity', because accuracy was now politically and economically important. But this did not make the maps neutral; maps are inevitably textual representations because it is impossible to reproduce reality in a reduced form. Certain features are emphasized at the expense of others, symbols and explanatory text are included, and human decisions are made about scale, orientation and projection (the method of representing a spherical surface on a flat one). A map of the world that employs the Mercator projection, for example, which has been widely used since the sixteenth century, distorts the size of the land masses so that Europe and North America appear bigger than they actually are. Most importantly, the huge increase in the number of maps in circulation in the seventeenth and eighteenth centuries was directly related to the colonization of the rest of the world by the European powers. The process of 'discovering' land in colonization was supported by cartography, which became a way of textually appropriating spaces and renaming them, naturalizing politically and culturally created boundaries and power arrangements. Moreover, the blank spaces on undiscovered territories in maps from the colonial period came to signify, as Bill Ashcroft, Gareth Griffiths and Helen Tiffin point out, 'a literal *terra nullius* [no-one's land], an open and inviting (virginal) space into which the European imagination [could] project itself and into which the European (usually male) explorer [could] penetrate' (Ashcroft *et al.* 1998: 32).

Travel writing is a particular genre that could benefit from an interdisciplinary critique drawing on some of these issues in cultural geography. It is an inherently interdisciplinary form because of its cross-generic status, its often unstable intermixing of fiction, autobiography, history, reportage and natural history. Travel writing has also been predominantly produced by European or American travellers exploring the colonial or post-colonial world; as Mary Louise Pratt argues, it is centrally engaged in the metropolis's 'obsessive need to present and re-present its peripheries and its others continually to itself' (Pratt 1992: 6). Travel writing thus also involves a kind of mapping, an imaginative geography which turns the experience of an unfamiliar place into narrative. As Dennis Porter writes:

> From the beginning, writers of travel have more or less unconsciously made it their purpose to take a fix on and thereby fix the world in which they found themselves; they are engaged in a form of cultural cartography that is impelled by an anxiety to map the globe, center it on a certain point, produce explanatory narratives, and assign fixed identities to regions and the races that inhabit them.
>
> (Porter 1991: 20)

In fact, travel writing as a genre has been directly related to other ways of mapping the world. Although travel in the sixteenth and seventeenth centuries was almost exclusively opportunistic and commercial, from the eighteenth century onwards there emerged new kinds of travellers, such as biologists, botanists and geographers, initially sponsored by government or commerce, but then developing an independent momentum of their own. Pratt refers to the various activities undertaken by these travellers as forms of 'anti-conquest', which she defines as the apparently innocent strategy whereby Europeans have sought to secure hegemony over their colonial subjects, supporting the more explicit projects of political and economic imperialism (Pratt 1992: 28). The expeditions of geographers and naturalists provided some of the earliest examples of travel writing, such as Darwin's *The Voyage of the Beagle* (1840), and many travel narratives also draw on the conventions of the 'anti-conquest'. In other words, while often opposed to racism and imperialism, they reinstate colonialist assumptions in their romanticization of exoticism, primitivism and pre-modern 'authenticity'. Ali Behdad suggests that many travel writers are 'belated orientalists' who, in attempting to 'come to terms with the loss of the object of [their] desires – the disappearance of the Orient, its dissolution ... under the weight of European colonialism', exhibit an 'exoticist desire for the disappearing other ... that simultaneously affirms and exposes the ideological discrepancies and political predicaments of colonial hegemony'. (Behdad 1994: 66, 14). Behdad suggests that exoticism is a way of offloading the guilt of imperial expansion while still othering the colonial subject, in the same way that the activities of the cartographers and naturalists were ostensibly detached from the colonial enterprise while in fact being intimately related to it. By reading maps and literary texts that 'map' the world in such a way, we can see that geography's concerns are insistently cultural and interdisciplinary, even though it has sometimes sought to emphasize its neutrality by defining itself as a scientific discipline.

ECOCRITICISM AND SCIENCE

Some of the new insights of cultural geography and the natural sciences come together with the humanities disciplines in the field of ecocriticism. Broadly speaking, ecocriticism explores the relationship between literature and other forms of culture and the natural world, often combining this with a commitment to raising awareness about environmental issues. It has a dual agenda: on the one hand, it deals with 'natural' phenomena that are normally the province of geography and biology and shows them to be the product of cultural and historical forces, inflected with meaning and metaphor; on the other hand, it examines the ways in which culture effects a separation from nature, producing hierarchical distinctions between the human and non-human. As Jonathan Bate points out, this hierarchy is inscribed in the meaning of key words: for example, 'culture', which once had an agricultural slant, but from Matthew Arnold onwards came to mean intellectual, spiritual work as distinct from physical labour; and 'environment', a word that emerged in the nineteenth century to describe the external aspects of nature separate from humanity, literally 'the world around us' (Bate 2000: 5, 138).

One of the founding texts of ecocriticism, Raymond Williams's *The Country and the City*, examines the cultural meanings traditionally attaching to these two geographical entities: while the former represents both 'peace, innocence, and simple virtue' and 'backwardness, ignorance, limitation', the latter stands for both 'learning, communication, light' and 'noise, worldliness and ambition'. In fact, as Williams points out, both the city and the country are extremely varied and mutually interconnected, since the industrial revolution transformed them both and was initiated by the development of agrarian capitalism (Williams 1973: 1–2). He therefore criticizes poets and literary scholars who uncritically celebrate the pastoral tradition for emphasizing the myth of an 'enamelled world' over the harsh reality of agrarian life (Williams 1973: 18). He gives the example of Sir Philip Sidney's romance *Arcadia* (1590), which is seen as a key text in the pastoral tradition, but which was actually composed in a park that had been constructed by enclosing an entire village and expelling all the tenants (Williams 1973: 22). The pastoral myth of the countryside as a retreat from modern civilization is thus a relatively recent invention, based on a desire to rewrite the past in a reaction to industrialization and urbanization. Williams's book, though, also has a strong ecological conscience. While recognizing that pastoralism is a myth, he sees it as the product of real historical anxieties about a world that values 'modes of using and consuming rather than accepting and enjoying people and things' (Williams 1973: 298).

While recognizing that redemptive notions of nature often draw their force from culture, then, ecocriticism also analyses the appropriation of nature by culture. Bate links this usurpation of nature to the predatory project of Enlightenment science, particularly Baconian empiricism and Cartesian dualism. In several of his works, Bacon argued that science would allow people eventually to control the weather, alter the pattern of the seasons and increase crop productivity: one studied nature in order ultimately to take control of it (Bate 2000: 77). Baconian science, according to Adorno and Horkheimer, was based on 'the disenchantment of the world', a 'patriarchal' notion of 'the concordance between the mind of man and the nature of things ... the human mind, which overcomes superstition, is to hold sway over a disenchanted nature' (Adorno and Horkheimer [1972] 1997: 3–4). One example of this 'patriarchal' mastery of nature is the Linnaeus system of nature classification. This system, which was first formulated by Carolus Linnaeus in *Systema naturae* in 1735 and came to dominate the study of nature by the end of the eighteenth century, imposed a human-made order on the natural world through a Latinized system of nomenclature which organized it clearly into species, genera, orders, classes and kingdoms.

Another key element in this subjugation of nature was the dualism between mind and body first established by Descartes in *Meditations* (1642), in which he insists that 'those things which we conceive clearly and distinctly as being diverse substances, as we regard mind and body to be, are really substances essentially distinct one from the other ... the human body may indeed easily enough perish, but the mind ... is owing to its nature immortal' (Descartes 1955: 141). The efforts of Descartes and other scientists and philosophers in the sixteenth and seventeenth centuries to separate out the body, which was seen as mechanically functioning like the rest of nature, from the autonomous human mind, was an extremely significant development in the understanding of nature. It paved the way for more thorough dissections of the human body, and was also used as a justification for vivisection, since animals were seen as having no mind or soul in the way that humans did. This division was also important in separating the sciences from the humanities. The former were given the task of bringing under control the neutral 'other' of nature, which included the human body; the latter were left with the apparently autonomous, human-made products of the mind and culture.

Ecocriticism challenges these divisions between matter and mind, nature and culture, and between natural sciences (such as biology and geology) and humanities subjects (such as literary criticism, cultural studies and cultural history). One way in which it seeks to do this is by showing that science's understanding of nature is always culturally produced. Haraway explores this issue in her study of the science of primatology, the study of primates, which she suggests always involves a 'traffic in meanings', based on interrogating what it means to be 'almost human' (Haraway 1989: 1–2). Although primatologists often believe that they are accessing 'pure' nature, their understandings of primates are inevitably anthropocentric, and are particularly influenced by a Judaeo–Christian concern with 'primal stories, the origin and nature of "man"', and 'reformation stories, the reform and reconstruction of human nature' (Haraway 1989: 9). Borrowing from Said's work, Haraway also suggests that Western primatology is a kind of 'Simian Oriental-ism', which is concerned with 'the construction of the self from the raw material of the other, the appropriation of nature in the production of culture, the ripening of the human from the soil of the animal' (Haraway 1989: 11). In her view, science's attempts to understand nature are often based on taming it and subjecting it to our control, preserving the traditional distinction between the active human and the passive object of nature. As she reminds us, though, 'nature is constructed, constituted historically, not discovered naked in a fossil bed or tropical forest' (Haraway 1991: 106).

Another way in which ecocriticism has sought to bridge the science–humanities divide is by drawing on the recent insights of the sciences, particularly biology, in order to read literary and cultural texts. One example of this is the use by ecocritics of the concepts of 'bioregion' and 'biodiversity', which are associated with the work of Edward O. Wilson and other environmentally conscious biologists. According to Wilson, a bioregion is a self-sustaining area which cannot be contained within the normal political boundaries established by local or national governments, and within which a whole diversity of species coexist and depend upon each other for survival. Biodiversity literally 'holds the world steady' in that the sheer variety of species allows equilibrium to be restored in the event of a natural disaster, although this equilibrium is increasingly being threatened by human interventions (Wilson 1994: 303, 13). The emphasis on biodiversity within ecocriticism inevitably involves a reconsideration of the literary canon, which has traditionally been founded on texts that are defiantly not bioregional. Bate gives the example of modernism, which is a cosmopolitan, mobile, urban movement tied inextricably to multinational monopoly capitalism, in the same way that the nineteenth-century novel was linked to the nation-state and imperialism (Bate 1998a: 63). Within these frameworks, those writers who are associated with particular bioregions have sometimes been dismissed as insignificant and parochial. An ecocritical project, Bate suggests, might entail challenging the conventional chronological history of English literature as the development of a canon of great 'national' writers with a survey of literature according to region (Bate 1998b: 19).

John Clare is one example of a 'bioregional' author who has been extensively re-evaluated in recent ecocriticism, as a poet whose work cannot be understood without reference to both cultural geography and ecology. The process of parliamentary enclosure of open fields and common land in the late eighteenth and early nineteenth centuries – a process accompanied by the production of the first Ordnance Survey maps, since one of its necessary accompaniments was the extensive mapping of the country – is central to an understanding of Clare's life and work. The Enclosure Acts drew on new understandings of space in capitalist societies which can be traced at least as far back as John Locke's notion of property in *Two Treatises of Government* (1689). For Locke, the whole idea of property is bound up with the enclosure of land: people have the right to the products of their labour when they turn untilled soil into enclosed farmland, because 'God, who hath given the World to Men in common, hath also given them reason to make use of it to the best advantage of Life, and convenience' (Locke [1689] 1970: 304). The effect of this, of course, is to privilege entrepreneurial agricultural improvement over other forms of the social organization of space. Clare, who worked as an agricultural labourer in Northamptonshire, was deeply affected by the process of enclosure, which deprived people of livelihoods and transformed the natural world by chopping down trees and damming streams, and he wrote many poems about it:

> Enclosure came, and trampled on the grave
> Of labour's rights, and left the poor a slave ...
> Fence meeting fence in owner's little bounds
> Of field and meadow, large as garden-grounds,
> In little parcels little minds to please,
> With men and flocks imprisoned, ill at ease.
>
> ('Enclosure', Clare 1965: 114–15)

For Clare, the trauma of enclosure stems from the fact that he is a bioregional poet totally tied to place, so that he portrays his own parish as his 'knowledge' and anywhere beyond it as 'outside his knowledge' (Barrell 1988: 118). After his removal in 1832 from his village of Helpston to Northborough, just three miles away, Clare writes that 'the summer like a stranger comes / ... the sun een seems to lose its way / Nor knows the quarter it is in', and that 'Nature herself seems on the flitting' ('The Flitting' and 'Decay', Robinson and Powell 1984: 251, 256). His poetry also tends to have a small focus: not the picturesque landscapes and vistas of much Romantic poetry, but such objects as birds' nests, leaves, twigs and molehills. In Clare's work, there is little of the homocentrism of the Romantic lyric, which abstracts the poet from nature by making the latter the means through which a transcendent, interiorized experience is achieved; he sees himself as fully part of this biodiversity. One of his poems, 'The Lament of Swordy Well', for example, is actually written in the persona of 'a piece of land', which laments the pain of enclosure:

> The gipsey's camp was not affraid
> I made his dwelling free

> Till vile enclosure came and made
> A parish slave of me.
>> (Robinson and Powell 1984: 147)

As John Barrell points out, this may be one of the reasons why Clare's poetry has been undervalued by critics: it does not conform to conventional distinctions between 'nature' and the 'human' that one expects to find in pastoral poetry, particularly in the post-Romantic period. He makes the further point that Clare's poems were originally written unpunctuated, giving the sense of 'a language of the first involuntary motions of the passive mind, unable to differentiate itself from the circumstantial and the contingent, from nature and the impressions of the senses' (Barrell 1988: 130–1). The editing of Clare's poems for punctuation by his London editors therefore attempted to turn the poet into a perceiving subject defined by 'its ability to divide, organise and reflect upon its experiences' and separate itself from nature (Barrell 1988: 134). The interdisciplinarity of ecocriticism is thus as much about questioning the traditional concerns of literary studies as it is about developing new understandings of literature: it aims to show that one of the most significant ways in which literary studies has constituted itself as a discipline has been to exclude the sphere of nature or, more accurately, the non-human.

THEORIES OF EVERYTHING

Ecocriticism's project of bringing the humanities and the natural sciences together finds a parallel in the growing influence of neo-Darwinian thought over the past few decades. This can be seen in the popular success of books such as Edward O. Wilson's *On Human Nature* (1978) and Richard Dawkins's *The Selfish Gene* (1976) and *The Blind Watchmaker* (1985), which see the gene as the basic unit of evolutionary development. Scientists like Wilson and Dawkins are distinct from ecocritics, however, in that they retain a faith in the possibility of ultimate explanation, a 'theory of everything' which will unite the different fields of knowledge. To Hamlet's caution that 'There are more things in heaven and earth, Horatio, / Than are dreamt of in our philosophy', Dawkins's response as a scientist is: 'Yes, but we're working on it' (Dawkins 1999: xiii). In particular, the interdisciplinary project of these writers is founded on a belief that *all* the cultural products of humanity, including literature, have a biological, genetic base.

The most ambitious of these neo-Darwinian projects is Wilson's concept of 'consilience', a term which he borrows from an attempted synthesis of the sciences in 1840 by the Cambridge don, William Whewell. Acknowledging that disciplinary boundaries within the sciences are being undermined and replaced by new configurations such as biochemistry, chemical ecology and physical chemistry, Wilson now calls for greater collaboration 'between scientists and philosophers, especially where they meet in the borderlands between biology, the social sciences, and the humanities' (1999: 10). The subject that will be able to achieve this consilience between the sciences, the social sciences and the humanities is biology, which is, perhaps not coincidentally, Wilson's own specialism. This is because he believes that a link can be found between 'genetic evolution' and 'cultural evolution': the latter is simply a more recent manifestation of the former. Cultural evolution is thus also biologically determined, even if the specific nature of this relationship is yet to be discovered (Wilson 1999: 139). Since we all have biologically similar brains, the mind and its products are ultimately the effect of biological evolution, existing to promote the survival and reproduction of genes, or as Wilson puts it, 'the genes hold culture on a leash' (1978: 167). Once the workings of the human mind are seen to be biologically based, he argues, the disciplines will have to reorganize themselves:

> Let us now consider man in the free spirit of natural history, as though we were zoologists from another planet completing a catalog of social species on earth. In this macroscopic view the humanities and the social sciences shrink to specialized branches of biology; history, biography, and fiction are the protocols of human ethology

[the scientific study of animal behaviour patterns]; and anthropology and sociology together constitute the sociobiology of a single primate species.

(Wilson 1980: 271)

Dawkins also aims to bridge the gap between the 'two cultures' from a specifically scientific perspective. Inverting a quote from W.H. Auden in which the poet refers to his inferiority complex when among scientists, Dawkins complains that contemporary scientists are made to feel 'like shabby curates among literary dukes' (Dawkins 1999: 29). In his book, *Unweaving the Rainbow*, Dawkins takes issue with Keats for accusing Newton of destroying the poetry of the rainbow by explaining it as a product of the refraction of white light. For Dawkins, science enhances, rather than destroys, the beauty of the world, and writers and critics in the humanities would do well to acknowledge this. He criticizes a 'wholly inaccurate' D.H. Lawrence poem about hummingbirds for its bad science, for example, explaining that the author 'lacked only a couple of tutorials in evolution and taxonomy to bring his poem within the pale of accuracy, and it would be no less arresting and thought-provoking as a poem' (Dawkins 1999: 25). One way in which Dawkins attempts to connect biology with culture is through his concept of the 'meme'. A 'meme' is a metaphorical term for the cultural equivalent of a gene, a unit of cultural transmission that replicates in gene-like fashion as a result of cognitive evolution. It refers to such things as ideas, music, rituals and texts which survive, reproduce and are inherited by subsequent generations because they fulfil some kind of useful genetic function (Dawkins 1999: 304). It should be said that these ideas are extremely controversial – one of the main points of contention, in fact, in the bitter 'Darwin wars' of the past few decades. While 'hard' Darwinians like Dawkins and Wilson believe that everything, including culture, can be explained by evolution, 'soft' Darwinians like Stephen Jay Gould and Steven Rose see life as a complex process in which not every product of human consciousness is determined by particular strands of DNA.

A related area of science that also holds out the possibility for a fusion of culture with biology is the field of neuroscience, which deals with the specifically biological roots of memory and consciousness. The Cartesian division between body and mind is increasingly questioned in this field, where debates tend to centre on whether there is any such thing as a non-physical mind, a stable consciousness which constitutes a non-biological 'self', or whether the mind is simply a highly developed computer designed by natural selection to solve various problems. The cognitive scientist Steven Pinker, who subscribes to the latter notion, argues that we can learn about the structure of the mind from the way young children conjugate irregular verbs. Through a process of trial and error, they learn that language is made up of a combination of 'words and rules': while some words follow rules which can be learnt, others simply have to be memorized individually, and these distinct activities are carried out by different areas of the brain (Pinker 2000: 1). This might get us to think about language as a dynamic concept which is constructed, adapted and developed in specific contexts by writers and readers, while still being constrained by basic biological factors. As Pinker puts it: 'Regular and irregular inflection has long been mulled over by novelists and poets, dictionary writers and editors, philologists and linguists. Now this topic straight out of the humanities is being probed with the cutting-edge tools of molecular genetics and imaging of the brain' (Pinker 2000: 299). Discussing some of these scientific developments, Mary Thomas Crane and Alan Richardson suggest that literary critics might 'need to begin to consider the implications of the brain as the material site where culture and biology meet and shape each other' (Crane and Richardson 1999: 131).

These areas of research certainly offer the prospect of using scientific discoveries to provide insights into literary and cultural texts, a form of interdisciplinarity whose possibilities have hardly begun to be explored. However, literary critics have so far been slow to take up this challenge. This may simply be because of their lack of adequate scientific knowledge, but I would suggest another reason: the projects of evolutionary biology, genetics and neuroscience can look suspiciously like intellectual imperialism rather than interdisciplinarity, in that they attempt to understand the concerns of other disciplines solely from the perspective of their own. In fact, this kind of project could be seen as a scientific version of Leavis's vision for English: the call for inter-disciplinarity is presented as a project of intellectual synthesis, but is actually based on the vested interests of one discipline. Above all, there is a failure in these projects to understand the cultural dimensions of science, and to present it instead as a disinterested form of scholarship which can oversee the less developed disciplines.

One example of this lack of reflexiveness about the cultural contexts of science is the way that neo-Darwinian thought has rediscovered Darwin's notion of sexual selection, which deals with the preference of animals for mates that show certain sexually specific characteristics. According to Wilson, 'it pays males to be aggressive, hasty, fickle and undiscriminating ... it is more profit-able for females to be coy, to hold back until they can identify the male with the best genes' (1978: 125). This allows him to compare male and female behaviour in contemporary societies with that of ancient 'hunter–gatherer societies'; in both cases, the women pri-marily stay at home to care for the children while the men go out into the world to provide for their families (Wilson 1978: 133–9). The danger here is that culturally and historically specific practices can be reduced to biology and come to seem natural and inevitable as a consequence. Indeed, the response of the feminist critic, Lynne Segal, to Wilson's argument, is short and sweet: 'Dream on!' (1999: 84) As I have sought to argue, the project of ecocriticism, and the other interdisciplinary developments I have examined in this chapter, are partly based on challenging science's confident self-image: while drawing on many recent developments in the sciences, they use the interpretative model of the humanities to critique their status as 'special' types of knowledge.

CONCLUSION
INTERDISCIPLINARITY TODAY

So far this book has aimed to highlight some of the advantages and opportunities of interdisciplinary approaches: they can challenge ossified, outmoded systems of thought and produce new, innovative theories and methodologies which open up the existing disciplines to new perspectives; and they can help people to think more creatively about the relationship between their own subject and other ways of doing things both within and outside universities. But it has also acknowledged that there might be a problem with assuming that interdisciplinarity has all the answers, and that it can easily transcend the exclusions and limitations of the traditional disciplines. My approach up to now has been largely historical, examining how these ideas about interdisciplinarity have developed in the humanities over the past few decades. In this conclusion I want to discuss some more recent perspectives on interdisciplinarity with particular reference to literary studies. It is certainly true that interdisciplinarity remains, in the postcolonial critic Graham Huggan's words, 'a term that is as fraught as it is fashionable' (2002: 255). But in recent years it is possible to detect a minor backlash in the humanities against 'interdisciplinarity', or at least a desire to examine more precisely its claims to be more intellectually creative and transgressive than conventional disciplinary work. One professor of religious studies, Robert Segal, complains for example that 'the word has become a mantra. The concept has become a human right ... interdisciplinarity ... is being touted as the intellectual equivalent of penicillin' (2009: 24).

THE CRITIQUE OF INTERDISCIPLINARITY

In his 1996 book, *The University in Ruins*, Bill Readings was one of the first to challenge some of the ambitious claims made for interdisciplinarity, and the unquestioned acceptance of them by many people working within the humanities disciplines. Readings's critique of interdisciplinarity is linked to his overarching argument that the contemporary Western university has become 'a transnational bureaucratic corporation', organized by the pursuit of profit and a wholly empty notion of 'excellence' (Readings 1996: 3). He suggests that the nebulous and malleable nature of the term, 'interdisciplinary', means that it can be easily appropriated in pursuit of the market-oriented university's aims: 'We can be interdisciplinary in the name of excellence, because excellence only preserves preexisting disciplinary boundaries insofar as they make no larger claim on the entirety of the system and pose no obstacle to its growth and integration' (Readings 1996: 39).

In other words, Readings suggests that interdisciplinarity has as much to do with universities managing budgets and being flexible to the demands of the marketplace as it does with the admirable aims of intellectual dialogue and co-operation, since merging departments into interdisciplinary programmes can be a form of downsizing and cost-cutting (Readings 1996: 191). Readings taught at the University of Montreal and he was writing in the context of the shrinkage of humanities departments in North American universities. Hal Foster, writing at the same time as Readings from a US perspective, similarly points to the ways in which some university administrators can 'seek to recoup interdisciplinary ventures as cost-effective programs' (1996: 280).

He argues that we need to accept the inevitability of disciplinary knowledge before attempting to move beyond it, or it is likely to produce an intellectual free-for-all rather than groundbreaking forms of scholarship:

> Even two decades ago there were very restrictive disciplinary conventions: nothing but disciplinary cops! This is not the case now. Today so much work that purports to be interdisciplinary seems to be non-disciplinary to me. To be interdisciplinary you need to be disciplinary first – to be grounded in one discipline, preferably two, to know the historicity of these discourses before you test them against each other. Many young people now come to interdisciplinary work before they come to disciplinary work. As a result they often fall into an eclecticism that does little work on any one discipline; it is more entropic than transgressive.

(Foster 1998: 162)

Readings and Foster are not attacking interdisciplinarity per se, so much as the claim that it is radical or innovative in its own right and can transcend the nature of the university as an economic and political institution. As I have sought to argue in this book, there is no such thing as non-disciplinary, unstructured knowledge; both Readings and Foster usefully draw attention to the institutional investments of interdisciplinarity, the way in which it is often implicated in the academic hierarchies it aims to critique.

Both Readings and Foster suggest that interdisciplinary study represents the future of the university. Readings argues that interdisciplinarity's intellectual and institutional battles have already been decisively won, and that 'disciplinary structure is cracking under the pressure of market imperatives'. The immediate future of the university will be 'the development of an increasingly interdisciplinary general humanities department amid a cluster of vocational schools' (Readings 1996: 174). This again is part of Readings's overall argument about the role of the marketplace in the contemporary university in breaking down existing institutional and governmental structures.

Readings's arguments about the collapse of what he calls the 'national' university in an era of global monopoly capitalism may apply more to the American university system than the more nationalized university systems in countries like Britain and Australia, where links with business are still less important than central government funding. But both Readings and Foster point to an important factor which this book has so far tended to skirt around. There is a politics to interdisciplinarity that is not merely intellectual: academic teaching and research do not occur in a political vacuum. Universities are territorial institutions and the academics who work in them often engage in 'turf wars' with colleagues in other departments. There are also often battles between departmental, discipline-oriented academics and the managers who oversee the institutions, and whose agendas are driven by the need to balance budgets and generate income across the whole university.

In this context, Readings's and Foster's anxiety, that university managers promote interdisciplinarity because they consider it both a good way of breaking down entrenched disciplinary hierarchies and of appealing to student 'consumers', is now also being voiced beyond the USA. Graham Huggan, for example, worries that 'increasingly routine calls for interdisciplinarity and cross-departmental affiliation might be the siren-songs university management uses to lure departments and other larger administrative units into its own Machiavellian cost-cutting schemes' (2002: 245). The British critical theorist, Thomas Docherty, also has this new market-led culture in mind when he argues that 'interdisciplinary ... is cant: like "modernisation", it is meaningless, but no less powerful for that'. For Docherty, the constant call to be ever more interdisciplinary can be traced all the way back to the 1960s counterculture, with its belief that disciplinary regimes, like 'discipline' in its most common dictionary sense, were somehow restrictive, punitive or exclusivist. Back then, there was much radical rhetoric about breaking down the barriers between disciplines that hindered creativity and innovative thought. 'Just as the 1960s let it all hang out,' as Docherty puts it, 'so we let our disciplines overflow into each other like anarchic lava lamps.' He argues that this idea came to be, whatever the protestations to the contrary, 'complicit with a marketisation approach that suggests research is about the production of new, commodifiable ideas, and endless novelty: fresh configuration of the lava' (Docherty 2009: 25). For Docherty, the imperative to be interdisciplinary is now really about governments wanting to control the ideas and research produced by academics, to make them marketable and accessible rather than difficult or cliquey.

The principal targets of Docherty's ire are the UK's government-funded research councils, which allocate funding for academic research projects and constantly talk up the virtues of 'interdisciplinarity'. The Arts and Humanities Research Council, for example, allocates its large-scale research grants by inviting bids around a series of interdisciplinary themes such as 'Religion and Society', 'Science and Heritage', 'Diasporas, Migration and Identities' and 'Landscape and Environment'. Within these broad-ranging themes, the value of collaboration and cross-fertilization across disciplines tends to be simply taken as read.

Docherty makes the valid point that the desire to break down academic boundaries is not necessarily liberatory in itself. He is also not alone in arguing that much of the revolutionary rhetoric of the 1960s has been incorporated into modern ideas of the marketplace. Luc Boltanski and Eve Chiapello have similarly claimed that what they call 'the new spirit of capitalism' has accommodated elements of the 'artistic critique' of capitalism emerging in bohemian urban cultures in the nineteenth century and reaching its highpoint in the 1960s counterculture. Their survey of 1990s management literature argues that this new 'connexionist' capitalism, which emphasizes flexible practices and flattened hierarchies, has significant parallels with the libertarian left's philosophy of the late 1960s, which also valued self-expression and self-management over bureaucratic conformity (Boltanski and Chiapello 2005). The model of interdisciplinarity that has found favour with university managers could be said to echo this modern, neo-liberal idea that unregulated markets are fundamentally egalitarian and democratic, helping to sweep away outmoded hierarchies and inefficient bureaucracy. This interdisciplinary model certainly fits the rhetoric of modern business, particularly American human-relations management theory, which emphasizes teamwork and collaboration over rigid rules and hierarchies. In the modern university, just as in modern business, networking, co-operation and 'creative partnerships' are seen as inherently good, even ends in themselves. A current fashion in the British research councils is for 'sandpits', where small groups of researchers from different areas are brought together for several days of discussion around a particular theme and encouraged to form interdisciplinary partnerships which can then bid for funding. The term 'sandpit', which some academics see as overtly infantilizing, suggests that interdisciplinarity will emerge out of playful, creative interaction.

In this new environment, Docherty is right to remind us that there is nothing intrinsically wrong with the notion of 'discipline', either in the narrowly academic or the wider sense of the word. Indeed, discipline is essential to all good writing, research and thought. The danger is that interdisciplinary work, without some clear justification or rationale, will simply produce a vague, bland eclecticism. It is worth recognizing as well that there may be human intellectual limits to interdisciplinarity. Given that most research in the humanities (even research that involves collaboration, such as edited collections) is still undertaken by scholars working on their own, it may be difficult for these people to become conversant in the theories, methods and materials of two or more disciplines, without producing significant gaps in their knowledge. Disciplines may be artificial constructions, but there is a reason for the artifice: no one can know everything.

Some of these concerns were touched on by Marjorie Garber in a 2006 presidential address to the Modern Language Association, the premier professional association for the discipline of literary studies in the USA and the rest of the world. She began her talk with a question: 'Why *is* the "merely" literary so suspect today?' (Garber 2007: 655). Observing that academic jobs in literary studies were now unlikely to go to candidates who had written conventional doctoral dissertations on a single author, Garber noted the number of Ph.Ds instead in which 'the fictions, dramas, or poems in question are taken to be means to an end – they are windows through which we see the world beyond the text, symptoms of cultural desires, drives, anxieties, or prejudices' (2007: 654). However 'interdisciplinary' literary studies might be at the moment, she suggested, there is 'one discipline that is conspicuously absent, and that discipline is what the Greeks called *poetike*, the discipline of poetics'. Often, Garber argued, literary scholars were strangely unwilling to address the *literary* nature of the wide range of texts they were examining, and so 'it would be more accurate to call the predominant activity of contemporary literary scholars *other-disciplinary* rather than interdisciplinary' (2007: 655).

Yet Garber concluded her talk with the optimistic observation that 'a specter is haunting the academy, the specter of literature' (2007: 658). The fundamental core of literary studies could not be so easily dismissed, she suggested, and literary scholars would eventually return to their original discipline of poetics:

> Those of us who teach literature may come to see that we have a lot more expertise than we think we have. It is time to trust the literary instinct that brought us to this field in the first place and to recognize that, instead of lusting after those other disciplines that seem so exotic primarily because we don't really practice them, what we need is more theoretical, historical, and critical training in our own discipline.
>
> (Garber 2007: 662)

In many ways, these sceptical voices offer a reworking of the arguments made by Stanley Fish (discussed at the ends of Chapters 3 and 4), who in a more recent work has reiterated his call for literary critics to teach analytical skills and specialized knowledge rather than set themselves up as 'moralists, therapists, political counsellors, and agents of global change' (2008: 14). The difference now is that the argument is being made by critics who could not, like Fish, be described as politically conservative and whose past work has been indisputably interdisciplinary. Garber, a professor of visual and environmental studies as well as English, has frequently moved out of her specialism in Shakespeare to write about subjects as diverse as cross-dressing, bisexuality and real estate. The Marxist literary critic, Terry Eagleton, whose wide-ranging body of work could also hardly be accused of being inwardly literary, makes a similar move to Garber's at the start of his book, *How to Read a Poem* (the title itself suggesting a back-to-basics approach). 'I first thought of writing this book,' he begins, 'when I realized that hardly any of the students of literature I encountered these days practiced what I myself had been trained to regard as literary criticism. Like thatching or clog dancing, literary criticism seems to be something of a dying art' (Eagleton 2007: 1). Nowadays, according to Eagleton, students tend to produce only 'content analysis' of texts:

> They give accounts of works of literature which describe what is going on in them, perhaps with a few evaluative comments thrown in. To adapt a technical distinction from linguistics, they treat the poem as *language* but not as *discourse* ... it would be hard to figure out, just by reading most of these content analyses, that they were supposed to be about poems or novels rather than about some real-life happening. What gets left out is the *literariness* of the work ... they treat the poem as though its author chose for some eccentric reason to write out his or her views on warfare or sexuality in lines which do not reach to the end of the page. Maybe the computer got stuck.
>
> (Eagleton 2007: 2–3)

It should be said that Eagleton does not blame this state of affairs on interdisciplinarity; like any good Marxist, he blames capitalism. 'It is a specific way of life, not a set of abstract ideas, which is the culprit here,' he argues. 'What threatens to scupper verbal sensitivity is the depthless, commodified, instantly legible world of advanced capitalism, with its unscrupulous way with signs, computerised communication and glossy packaging of "experience"' (Eagleton 2007: 17). But while Eagleton does not mention the word 'interdisciplinary', there are connections here with Docherty's argument. Both suggest that modern market imperatives encourage the creation of a fuzzy, ill-disciplined smorgasbord of knowledge. If commodity capitalism is a world in which 'all that is solid melts into air,' in Karl Marx and Friedrich Engels's famous phrase (Marx and Engels [1848] 2002: 223), then perhaps more than ever we need some hard thinking, some rigour, some discipline.

THE SURVIVAL OF THE DISCIPLINES

But these various critiques of interdisciplinarity, while making valid points, seem to me to go too far; they underestimate the survival of the disciplines within contemporary universities. It is, for example, still quite hard to get a job teaching in a university unless you are firmly located within a discipline, indeed have a recognized specialism within it. Academic jobs tend to be advertised in areas like 'eighteenth-century literature' or 'Victorian studies', although it usually helps if you can chip in with other teaching as well. The survival of disciplines is particularly evident in the UK where there is central control of academic budgets. National bodies such as the Quality Assurance Agency for Higher Education and the Higher Education Funding Council for England, which assess what universities are doing and fund them accordingly, impose institutional constraints on interdisciplinarity. The demands of research assessment exercises and quality reviews of teaching help to reinforce disciplinary boundaries by monitoring standards within measurable units, often with the help of specialist assessors or panels of experts on particular subjects. These exercises produce league tables and other 'performance indicators' which not only guide funding decisions but are also reproduced in newspapers and other media, contributing to the marketing of degrees and departments in relation to recognized disciplines. In particular, the government-initiated Research Assessment Exercise (RAE), and its successor, the Research Excellence Framework (REF), have largely been managed and controlled by individual disciplines. Despite the best efforts of governments to make economic profitability and other forms of 'knowledge transfer' an important element in assessment, the most important factor has been peer review by the so-called 'invisible college' of a particular discipline – the national or international network of scholars working in a particular area which stretches beyond any university or institution.

The need to sell degrees to students in a highly competitive undergraduate marketplace, and to sell degrees to employers in an equally competitive graduate marketplace, also helps to strengthen the disciplines. The current emphasis on 'graduate-ness', the skills and knowledges that students should have acquired and demonstrated by graduation, is often linked to particular subjects. There is a growing emphasis on specialized professional training and expertise, which reinforces conventional intellectual hierarchies by necessitating the identification of skills appropriate to each discipline. Fee-paying students (and their parents, who may be subsidising them) understandably want to know what their degree is worth in the marketplace beyond the university. Disciplines like English thus develop a recognized 'brand name' with an established bank of cultural capital, which can appeal to both prospective students and employers. To give one example, my own department had to change its name from 'Literature, Life and Thought' (which, as I noted in Chapter 2, was also the name of the first English degree at Cambridge) to 'Literature and Cultural History' and then finally to 'English', partly for pragmatic reasons. In order to know about our interdisciplinary English course, prospective students needed to be able to find it in the UCAS (Universities and Colleges Admissions Service) handbook along with all the other 'English' degrees.

Given all these economic and institutional factors, it seems likely that disciplines will remain a powerful force within the contemporary university. To paraphrase Mark Twain, rumours of the death of the disciplines have been exaggerated. Research conducted within English departments now ranges across literature, cultural history, cultural studies, philosophy, psychoanalysis, politics, sociology, art history, linguistics, the philosophy of science and many other areas. There may even be people working within such departments who rarely or never study 'literature' as it is commonly understood. But English as a discipline still exists: it has its discrete organizational units, its specialist journals, its professional bodies and associations, its marketing potential as a name and, most importantly, students who still want to study it. This is partly because disciplines are as much a product of institutional and economic pragmatism as they are of intellectual justification, which means that they will often continue to exist even as their methodological and theoretical assumptions are being challenged. But it is also because interdisciplinary approaches exist alongside more traditional perspectives. Some of the current work undertaken within English departments is not radically different from what literary scholars have always done since the birth of the discipline: source studies, literary biography and history, close textual analysis and the production of authoritative critical texts, for example.

As it stands today, the subject of English brings together a complex mix of disciplinary and interdisciplinary perspectives, and this is reflected in the range and diversity of the university courses that go under its name. Despite this diversity, it is still possible to identify general shifts in the way that many English courses have been taught over the past few decades, which are a response to some of the interdisciplinary developments I have explored in this book. For example, there is now likely to be less emphasis on chronological coverage, from *Beowulf* to Virginia Woolf and beyond, since such disciplinary breadth is often regarded as less important than introducing students to significant issues, debates and research problems across the humanities disciplines. Alongside conventionally periodized or genre modules (such as English Literature 1900–50, or Romantic Poetry), there may be modules based around particular theoretical approaches (feminist, Marxist or psychoanalytical, for example) or themed courses exploring the broad field of representation around a central topic, such as the city, slavery, childhood, war and so on.

Perhaps the most significant development has been the continuous revision and expansion of the literary canon. This is partly related to what in the USA have been called the 'culture wars', the sometimes ill-tempered battles to introduce more racial and gendered diversity into the syllabuses taught on English degrees. But in academic research this expansion of the canon has probably been equally driven by interdisciplinary impulses, particularly the urge to supplement high-cultural creative writing, the traditional staple of literary studies, with other kinds of text like popular fiction, travel writing, children's literature, autobiography and even scientific and medical texts. Often the move away from canonical literary texts into marginal or non-literary texts happens because the canon seems over-researched and overwritten about, and therefore less open to new critical insights.

One of the catalysts for this growing use of marginal kinds of text has been the expanding area of the digital humanities, with its electronic subversion of conventional notions of textuality. A digital archive is no respecter of cultural hierarchies: a simple word search can produce 'hits' across a wide range of texts. As William B. Warner and Clifford Siskin write, 'our new electronic databases have helped break the spell of "Literature" by recovering the true scope of "literature" in its earlier comprehensive sense' (2008: 105). This has particularly been the case with research on nineteenth-century literature, probably because this is a period which witnessed a huge expansion of print culture and which is now largely out of the reach of copyright law. There have been several major projects to digitize Victorian periodicals, for example, and the British Library has digitized many nineteenth-century newspapers, provincial as well as national titles. In the digital era, literature is becoming 'print culture' in its broadest sense.

In interdisciplinary literary studies in recent years there has also been a move away from philosophy and back towards the traditional partner of English, history. In particular there has been a turn away from the 'big theory' I discussed in Chapter 3. Post-structuralist critics like Derrida, Lacan, Foucault and Barthes, whose work was central to the understanding of interdisciplinarity in literary studies at the end of the last century, are not quite as widely cited today. It is also now less common for English courses to have a specific 'theory' module. This is partly because these theories have been so thoroughly integrated into the subject that they no longer need to be flagged so directly; and partly because intellectual fashions change and there has been a desire to return to 'the real', however complicatedly defined, after years of grappling with abstract theory. In anglophone literary studies, high theory has most commonly been superseded by what is sometimes called 'neo-historicism', a conflation of literature into cultural history with numerous applications. I want to conclude by looking briefly at how this new type of interdisciplinarity has played itself out in two areas: Victorian studies and contemporary cultural studies.

VICTORIAN STUDIES/CULTURAL STUDIES

Victorian studies emerged in the 1950s before the advent of theory or the growth of cultural studies had started to shake up the discipline of English. The major interdisciplinary journal, *Victorian Studies*, now one of the most influential in the humanities, was first published in 1957 when there was only a tiny vanguard of scholars preaching the merits of interdisciplinarity. In the 1960s and 1970s the Victorian period became central to interdisciplinary manoeuvres within both literature and history. The growing area of social and urban history, as practised by historians such as Raphael Samuel, Asa Briggs and E.P. Thompson, often centred on this period. In the 1980s and 1990s Victorian studies benefited from the popularity of American new historicist approaches in literary studies and from the linguistic or cultural turn in history (see my discussion in Chapter 4). More recently Victorian studies has been a fertile ground for the growing influence of 'cultural history'. Broadly speaking, cultural history brings together textual criticism, historical scholarship and social anthropology to explore shifts in human subjectivity over time, as manifested in cultural and material practices: the whole history of human meaning-making, in other words. It has some crossover with what French historians call the 'history of mentalities': the study of how the thoughts, feelings and attitudes of entire cultures change throughout history.

For the historian Martin Hewitt, however, Victorian studies is still not interdisciplinary enough. Noting that most Victorian studies journals are populated mainly by literary scholars, albeit historically oriented or otherwise interdisciplinary minded ones, he calls for more genuine dialogue and collaboration between literary critics and historians:

> If Victorian studies is to transcend its current limitations, to thrive as a truly interdisciplinary field based on combination rather than aggregation, it ... must produce for itself a new scholarly integration, the sense of a shared literature, a common focus of enquiry, a set of broadly accepted modes of enquiry and theoretical assumptions, and ultimately a deference of the utility of "Victorian" as a frame of analysis. The walls of disciplinary particularism will not simply crumble – they need to be deliberately and systematically undermined; a sense of interdisciplinary community will not evolve, it must be built.

> (Hewitt 2001: 152)

Hewitt's call for interdisciplinarity through 'a common focus of enquiry' might seem paradoxical; it sounds suspiciously like creating a new discipline. But I agree with Hewitt that often interdisciplinary work needs the security of taking place within a recognized specialism. This is partly because all innovative intellectual activity is personally risky, in the sense that it can be more open-ended than disciplinary work, and its publishing 'outputs' (as university managers like to call them) may be less certain. One way of offsetting this risk is to have a kind of institutional base: a number of likely publishing outlets for your work and a network of conferences and professional associations where you can meet like-minded scholars. Over the past decade or so, Victorian studies, mainly as a conjunction of literature, history and visual culture, has come to seem like more of a discipline in this sense, with the establishing of dedicated journals like the *Journal of Victorian Culture*, and the formation of organizations like the British Association for Victorian Studies, founded in 2000, and the North American Victorian Studies Association, founded in 2002. When this kind of inevitable institutionalization occurs in a growing field there is always a danger of research becoming too cautious, too conventional, too similar; but there is also an opportunity for interdisciplinary work to become more inventive as the relatively safe intellectual haven of a sub-field creates the space for new ideas to be explored.

In contemporary British literary and cultural studies, the situation is less clear. There is no such sub-field that might bring together scholars working in the areas of literature, history, politics and culture to create something like a post-war 'history of mentalities'. This is partly because there has not been as much dialogue between textual critics and historians in this area. Post-war and contemporary historians still tend to be tied to conventional modes of political, economic and diplomatic history. As the historian Stephen Brooke argues, 'our understanding of post-1945 Britain has yet to be entirely loosed from its moorings in Whitehall and Kew', by which he means it is still rooted in central government institutions and the National Archives (2003: 136). Contemporary British history remains relatively untouched by the new cultural history and there is a marked disparity between the ambitious interdisciplinary work on previous centuries – in Victorian studies, for example, or studies of the Renaissance and Romantic eras – and the preponderance in late twentieth-century history of narrowly economic and political accounts.

Another part of the problem, as Richard Johnson has suggested, is the sense of an interrupted dialogue between history and cultural studies. In the mid- to late 1970s, the work of the CCCS in Birmingham was beginning to develop an account of the shifting post-war cultural-political hegemonic order, and the beginnings of the Thatcherite challenge to it, as well as the politicized uses of history in the heritage industry and other contemporary representations of the past (Johnson 2001: 266–7). But more recently, if contemporary history has neglected to pay enough attention to culture, then cultural studies has moved away from historicized accounts of the recent past. Its consolidation as a discipline has led to more purely ethnographic or textual approaches centred around popular consumption, sub-cultural lifestyle and innovative or emergent media and technologies. Cultural studies has largely become the study of popular culture.

If cultural studies is starting to emerge from what Tony Bennett calls its 'disciplinary bashfulness' (see Chapter 2) – not necessarily something to be lamented, Bennett would argue – then its connections with English and history departments have inevitably weakened. As a result there is not really such an entity as 'contemporary studies' which might draw together scholars in literature, history and cognate disciplines in a similar way to Victorian studies. But for interdisciplinary researchers in this area, this lack of an institutional base is potentially a strength as well as a weakness. It is worth remembering that much of the groundbreaking interdisciplinary work I have discussed in this book was undertaken by scholars such as Roland Barthes, Raymond Williams, Stuart Hall and Richard Hoggart, who were working somewhat on the margins of established academia or the recognized disciplines. There are problems in being on the academic margins, but also opportunities.

CONCLUSION

It could be argued that, because they are relatively new and exploratory, interdisciplinary ways of thinking have a tendency to be more disorganized and fragmentary than established forms of knowledge. But if a certain messiness goes with the territory of interdisciplinarity, this is also what makes that territory worth occupying. Interdisciplinarity, as Cathy N. Davidson and Theo Goldberg put it, could be seen as 'a function of the uncontainability of what, in the history of ideas, is called "the real." It derives from the sense that objects (and subjects) of social and cultural life (real life, real conditions, real relations) exist beyond the constraints of analytic singularity and methodological rules' (Davidson and Goldberg 2004: 50). In its constant search for the uncontainable 'real', interdisciplinarity can disrupt the deceptive smoothness and fluency of the disciplines, questioning their status as conveyors of disinterested knowledge by pointing to the problematic nature of all claims to scientific objectivity and neutrality. If, as I have attempted to show in this book, interdisciplinarity has produced some of the most interesting intellectual developments in the humanities over the past few decades, then this may be precisely because its problems and shortcomings are not obscured by established structures or conventions.

In *The University in Ruins*, Readings suggests that, since attempts at interdisciplinary collaboration are always compromised by their institutional contexts, we should try to create a reflexive form of disciplinarity that recognizes its own limits and artificiality, 'not a generalized interdisciplinary space but a certain rhythm of disciplinary attachment and detachment, which is designed so as not to let the question of disciplinarity disappear, sink into routine'. Within this framework, the various disciplines would have to 'answer to the name of Thought, to imagine what kinds of thinking they make possible, and what kinds of thinking they exclude' (Readings 1996: 176). I think Readings is right: we can seek to transform the disciplines, encourage communication between them or use them to create new intellectual configurations or alliances, but we can never entirely dispense with them as means of organizing knowledge. Interdisciplinarity could therefore be seen as a way of living with the disciplines more critically and self-consciously, recognizing that their most basic assumptions can always be challenged or reinvigorated by new ways of thinking from elsewhere. Interdisciplinary study represents, above all, a denaturalization of knowledge: it means that people working within established modes of thought have to be permanently aware of the intellectual and institutional constraints within which they are working, and open to different ways of structuring and representing their understanding of the world.

FURTHER READING

While the bibliography provides a list of all the texts cited in this book, the following sources are a good starting point for those wishing to read further on the debates around interdisciplinarity.

Anderson, Amanda and Valente, Joseph (eds) (2002) *Disciplinarity at the Fin de Siècle*, Princeton, NJ: Princeton University Press. A thought-provoking series of essays which attempt to qualify contemporary celebrations of interdisciplinarity by examining the rise of a number of disciplines, including English, in the late Victorian era. The essays argue that disciplines are not inherently narrow or coercive, and have always been in dialogue with other disciplines.

Beer, Gillian (1996) *Open Fields: Science in Cultural Encounter*, Oxford: Oxford University Press. A ground-breaking series of essays on the relation between literature and science, with particular focus on Charles Darwin and mainly centred on nineteenth-century and early twentieth-century writing. Chapter 6, 'Forging the Missing Link: Interdisciplinary Stories', is particularly enlightening.

Coles, Alex and Defert, Alexia (eds) (1998) *The Anxiety of Interdisciplinarity*, London: BACKless Books. A theoretically engaged, somewhat quirky collection of essays ranging across cultural studies, critical theory and visual culture.

Davidson, Cathy N. and Goldberg, David Theo (2004) 'Engaging the Humanities', *Profession*: 42–62. A call by two American academics for a new interdisciplinary humanities to challenge the hegemony of the sciences and the professions in the contemporary university.

Eaglestone, Robert (2002) 'Interdisciplinary English', in *Doing English: A Guide for Literature Students*, 2nd edn, London: Routledge, pp. 121–8. A brief but useful introduction, aimed at orientating undergraduates into degree-level English and arguing that English as a discipline is 'diffuse, fuzzy and interwoven'.

Fay, Elizabeth (2006) 'Cultural History, Interdisciplinarity and Romanticism', *Literature Compass*, 3 (5): 1065–81. This article examines cultural history as a particular mode of interdisciplinary study in the humanities, with specific reference to histories of the body and gesture in Romantic studies.

Fish, Stanley (1994) 'Being Interdisciplinary Is So Very Hard to Do', in *There's No Such Thing as Free Speech, and It's a Good Thing, Too*, New York: Oxford University Press, pp. 231–42. This is probably the definitive critique of interdisciplinarity and a call for literary critics to return to their specialism.

Garber, Marjorie (2007) 'Presidential Address 2006: It Must Change', *PMLA*, 122 (3): 652–62. This article began as a speech at the Modern Language Association conference and is a plea for literary studies scholars not to overlook the discipline that distinguishes what they do from other fields: poetics.

Hayes Edwards, Brett (2008) 'The Specter of Interdisciplinarity', *PMLA*, 123 (1): 188–94. A response to Garber's article, which argues that the literary 'must not relinquish its unique point of articulation with the social'.

Hewitt, Martin (2001) 'Victorian Studies: Problems and Prospects?', *Journal of Victorian Culture*, 6 (1): 137–61. This article, discussed in my conclusion, is a call for all scholars working on Victorian culture to consolidate their area as a thoroughly interdisciplinary field.

Huggan, Graham (2002) 'Postcolonial Studies and the Anxiety of Interdisciplinarity', *Postcolonial Studies*, 5 (3): 245–75. An article which uses post-colonial studies as a case study for discussing the anxieties and hostilities created by inter-disciplinarity in contemporary universities.

Klein, Julie Thompson (2005) *Humanities, Culture, and Interdisciplinarity: The Changing American Academy*, Albany, NY: State University of New York Press. Klein has written widely on interdisciplinarity in the context of American universities, and this work focuses particularly on the study of culture across the humanities.

Limon, John (1990) *The Place of Fiction in the Time of Science: A Disciplinary History of American Writing*, Cambridge: Cambridge University Press. In attempting to map out an interdisciplinary method for discussing the relations between literature and science, the opening chapter, 'Toward a Disciplinary Intellec-tual History', offers some illuminating reflections on the discipline of literary criticism and the philosophy of science.

Shattock, Joanne (2007) 'Where Next in Victorian Literary Studies? Revising the Canon, Extending Cultural Boundaries, and the Challenge of Inter-disciplinarity', *Literature Compass*, 4 (4): 1280–91. This article, focusing on the interdisciplinary possibilities of Victorian literary studies, has an interest-ing discussion on the impact of the ongoing digitization of archives.

Warner, William B. and Siskin, Clifford (2008) 'Stopping Cultural Studies', *Profession*: 94–107. This article explores the influence of cultural studies in literary stu-dies and the expansion of the category of 'literature' into 'culture' – but, as its title suggests, it ends with a call for literary studies to refocus on its core material: print culture.

Willis, Martin (2006) *Mesmerists, Monsters, and Machines: Science Fiction and the Cultures of Science in the Nineteenth Century*, Kent, OH: Kent State University Press. The first chapter and the conclusion contain a useful synoptic discussion of interdisciplinary criticism with particular reference to science fiction.

BIBLIOGRAPHY

Adorno, Theodor (1978) 'On the Social Situation of Music', *Telos: A Quarterly Journal of Radical Thought*, 35: 129–64.
—— (1981) *Prisms*, Cambridge, MA: MIT Press.
Adorno, Theodor and Horkheimer, Max ([1972] 1997) *Dialectic of Enlightenment*, trans. John Cumming, London: Verso.
Alasuutari, Pertti (1995) *Researching Culture: Qualitative Method and Cultural Studies*, London: Sage.
Althusser, Louis (1971) *Lenin and Philosophy and Other Essays*, trans. Ben Brewster, London: New Left Books.
—— (1976) *Essays in Self-Criticism*, trans. Grahame Lock, London: New Left Books.
—— (1977) *For Marx*, trans. Ben Brewster, London: New Left Books.
—— and Balibar, Étienne (1970) *Reading Capital*, trans. Ben Brewster, London: New Left Books.
Appleby, Joyce, Hunt, Lynn and Jacob, Margaret (1994) *Telling the Truth about History*, New York: Norton.
Aristotle (1947) *Metaphysics*, trans. Hugh Tredennick, 2 vols, London: Heinemann.
—— (1961) *Politics*, trans. Ernest Barker, Oxford: Clarendon Press.
Arnold, Matthew ([1869] 1993) *Culture and Anarchy and Other Writings*, ed. by Stefan Collini, Cambridge: Cambridge University Press.
Ashcroft, Bill, Griffiths, Gareth and Tiffin, Helen (1998) *Key Concepts in Post-Colonial Studies*, London: Routledge.
Bacon, Francis ([1620] 1980) *The Great Instauration and New Atlantis*, ed. J. Weinberger, Arlington Heights, IL: Harlan Davidson.
Barrell, John (1988) *Poetry, Language and Politics*, Manchester: Manchester University Press.
Barthes, Roland (1973) *Mythologies*, selected and trans. Annette Lavers, London: Paladin.
—— (1975) *S/Z*, London: Jonathan Cape.
—— (1977) *Image-Music-Text*, trans. Stephen Heath, London: Fontana.
—— (1986) *The Rustle of Language*, trans. Richard Howard, Oxford: Basil Blackwell.
Bate, Jonathan (1998a) 'Poetry and Diversity', in Richard Kerridge and Neil Sammells (eds), *Writing the Environment: Ecocriticism and Literature*, London: Zed Books, pp. 53–70.
—— (1998b) 'The Climates of Literary History: Past, Present, Future', *The European English Messenger*, 7 (2): 12–20.
—— (2000) *The Song of the Earth*, London: Picador.
Baudrillard, Jean (1994) *The Illusion of the End*, trans. Chris Turner, Cambridge: Polity Press.

Becher, Tony (1989) *Academic Tribes and Territories: Intellectual Enquiry and the Cultures of Disciplines,* Milton Keynes: Open University Press.

Beer, Gillian (1983) *Darwin's Plots: Evolutionary Narrative in Darwin, George Eliot and Nineteenth-Century Fiction,* London: Routledge & Kegan Paul.

—— (1996a) 'Introduction', in G. Beer (ed.), *Charles Darwin, The Origin of Species,* Oxford: Oxford University Press, pp. vii–xxviii.

—— (1996b) *Open Fields: Science in Cultural Encounter,* Oxford: Clarendon Press.

Behdad, Ali (1994) *Belated Travelers: Orientalism in the Age of Colonial Dissolution,* Durham, NC: Duke University Press.

Bennett, Tony (1979) *Formalism and Marxism,* London: Methuen.

—— (1998) *Culture: A Reformer's Science,* London: Sage.

Bennington, Geoffrey (1999) 'Inter', in Martin McQuillan, Graeme MacDonald, Robin Purves and Stephen Thomson (eds), *Post-Theory: New Directions in Criticism,* Edinburgh: Edinburgh University Press, pp. 103–19.

Bentham, Jeremy ([1789] 1982) *An Introduction to the Principles of Morals and Legislation,* ed. J.H. Burns and H.L.A. Hart, London: Methuen.

Bergonzi, Bernard (1990) *Exploding English: Criticism, Theory, Culture,* Oxford: Clarendon Press.

Berman, Marshall (1983) *All that Is Solid Melts into Air,* London: Verso.

Bloom, Harold (1975) *The Anxiety of Influence: A Theory of Poetry,* Oxford: Oxford University Press.

Board of Education (1921) *The Teaching of English in England* (The Newbolt Report), London: HMSO.

Boltanski, Luc and Chiapello, Eve (2005) *The New Spirit of Capitalism,* trans. Gregory Elliot, London: Verso.

Bourdieu, Pierre (1971) 'Intellectual Field and Creative Project', in Michael F.D. Young (ed.), *Knowledge and Control: New Directions for the Sociology of Education,* London: Collier-Macmillan, pp. 161–88.

—— (1984) *Distinction: A Social Critique of the Judgement of Taste,* trans. Richard Nice, London: Routledge & Kegan Paul.

—— (1988) *Homo Academicus,* trans. Peter Collier, Cambridge: Polity.

—— (1990) *In Other Words: Essays towards a Reflexive Sociology,* trans. Matthew Adamson, Cambridge: Polity.

—— (1991) *Language and Symbolic Power,* ed. John B. Thompson, trans. Gino Raymond and Matthew Adamson, Cambridge: Polity.

—— (1993) *The Field of Cultural Production: Essays on Art and Literature,* ed. Randal Johnson, New York: Columbia University Press.

—— (1996a) *On Television and Journalism,* trans. Priscilla Parkhurst Ferguson, London: Pluto.

—— (1996b) *The Rules of Art: Genesis and Structure of the Literary Field,* trans. Susan Emanuel, Cambridge: Polity.

Brantlinger, Patrick (1990) *Crusoe's Footprints: Cultural Studies in Britain and America,* New York: Routledge.

Brooke, Stephen (2003) 'Moments of Modernity', *Journal of British Studies,* 42 (1): 132–9.

Butler, Judith (1990) *Gender Trouble: Feminism and the Subversion of Identity*, New York: Routledge.

Carr, E.H. ([1961] 1964) *What Is History?*, Harmondsworth: Penguin.

Cassirer, Ernst (1950) *The Problem of Knowledge*, trans. William H. Woglom and Charles W. Hendel, New Haven, CT: Yale University Press.

Clare, John (1965) *Selected Poems*, ed. J.W. Tibble and Anne Tibble, London: Dent.

—— Hall, Stuart, Jefferson, Tony and Roberts, Brian (1976) 'Subcultures, Cultures and Class', in S. Hall and T. Jefferson (eds), *Resistance through Rituals: Youth Subcultures in Postwar Britain*, London: Hutchinson, pp. 9–74.

Comte, Auguste ([1830–42] 1974) *The Essential Comte*, ed. Stanislav Andreski, trans. Margaret Clarke, London: Croom Helm.

Crane, Mary Thomas and Richardson, Alan (1999) 'Literary Studies and Cognitive Science: Toward a New Interdisciplinarity', *Mosaic*, 32 (2): 123–40.

Crane, R.S. (1957) 'Preface', in R.S. Crane (ed.), *Critics and Criticism*, Chicago, IL: University of Chicago Press, abridged edn, pp. iii–vi.

Croce, Benedetto ([1941] 1970) *History as the Story of Liberty*, trans. Sylvia Sprigge, Chicago, IL: Henry Regnery.

Culler, Jonathan (1983) *On Deconstruction: Theory and Criticism after Structuralism*, London: Routledge & Kegan Paul.

Davidson, Cathy N. and Goldberg, David Theo (2004) 'Engaging the Humanities', *Profession*: 42–62.

Dawkins, Richard (1976) *The Selfish Gene*, Oxford: Oxford University Press.

—— (1999) *Unweaving the Rainbow: Science, Delusion and the Appetite for Wonder*, London: Penguin.

de Beauvoir, Simone ([1953] 1997) *The Second Sex*, ed. and trans. H.M. Parshley, London: Vintage.

de Certeau, Michel (1984) *The Practice of Everyday Life*, trans. Steven F. Rendall, Berkeley, CA: University of California Press.

de Man, Paul (1979) *Allegories of Reading: Figural Language in Rousseau, Nietzsche, Rilke and Proust*, New Haven, CT: Yale University Press.

—— (1986) *The Resistance to Theory*, Manchester: Manchester University Press.

Dennis, Norman, Henriques, Fernando and Slaughter, Clifford (1956) *Coal is Our Life: An Analysis of a Yorkshire Mining Community*, London: Tavistock.

Derrida, Jacques (1976) *Of Grammatology*, trans. Gayatri Chakravorty Spivak, Baltimore, MD: Johns Hopkins University Press.

—— (1978) *Writing and Difference*, trans. Alan Bass, London: Routledge & Kegan Paul.

—— (1981) *Positions*, trans. Alan Bass, London: Athlone.

—— (1982) *Margins of Philosophy*, trans. Alan Bass, Brighton: Harvester.

—— (1992a) *Acts of Literature*, ed. by Derek Attridge, New York: Routledge.

—— (1992b) 'Mochlos; or, The Conflict of the Faculties', in Richard Rand (ed.), *Logomachia: The Conflict of the Faculties*, Lincoln, NB: University of Nebraska Press, pp. 3–34.

—— (1995) *Points ... Interviews, 1974–1994*, ed. Elizabeth Weber, trans. Peggy Kamuf, Palo Alto, CA: Stanford University Press.

Descartes, René (1955) *Philosophical Works*, vol. I, trans. Elizabeth S. Haldane and G.R.T. Ross, New York: Dover.

Docherty, Thomas (2009) 'Our Cowed Leaders Must Stand Up for Academic Freedom', *Times Higher Education*, 9 April: 24–5.

Durkheim, Émile ([1895] 1964) *The Rules of Sociological Method*, ed. George E.G. Catlin, trans. Sarah A. Solovay and John H. Mueller, New York: Free Press.

Eagleton, Terry (1996) *Literary Theory: An Introduction*, 2nd edn, Oxford: Blackwell.

—— (2007) *How to Read a Poem*, Oxford, Blackwell.

Easthope, Anthony (1991) *Literary into Cultural Studies*, London: Routledge.

Eichenbaum, Boris (1965) 'The Theory of the "Formal Method"', in Lee T. Lemon and Marion J. Reis (eds and trans.), *Russian Formalist Criticism*, Lincoln, NB: University of Nebraska Press, pp. 3–24.

Elam, Diane (1994) *Feminism and Deconstruction: Ms. en Abyme*, London: Routledge.

Eliot, T.S. (1948) *Notes towards a Definition of Culture*, London: Faber and Faber.

—— (1951) *Selected Essays*, London: Faber and Faber.

Elton, G.R. ([1967] 1984) *The Practice of History*, London: Flamingo.

Evans, Richard (1997) *In Defence of History*, London: Granta.

Felman, Shoshana (1982) 'To Open the Question', in S. Felman (ed.), *Literature and Psychoanalysis: The Question of Reading: Otherwise*, Baltimore, MD: Johns Hopkins University Press, pp. 5–10.

Feyerabend, Paul (1975) *Against Method: Outline of an Anarchistic Theory of Knowledge*, London: New Left Books.

Fish, Stanley (1994) 'Being Interdisciplinary Is So Very Hard to Do', in *There's No Such Thing as Free Speech, and It's a Good Thing, Too*, New York: Oxford University Press, pp. 231–42.

—— (1995) *Professional Correctness: Literary Studies and Political Change*, Cambridge, MA: Harvard University Press.

—— (1996) 'Them We Burn: Violence and Conviction in the English Department', in James C. Raymond (ed.), *English as a Discipline; or, Is There a Plot in This Play?*, Tuscaloosa, AL: University of Alabama Press, pp. 160–73.

—— (2008) *Save the World on Your Own Time*, New York: Oxford University Press.

Fiske, John (1989) *Understanding Popular Culture*, Boston, MA: Unwin Hyman.

'Forum: Defining Interdisciplinarity' (1996) *PMLA*, 111 (2): 271–311.

Foster, Hal (1996) *The Return of the Real: The Avant-Garde at the End of the Century*, Cambridge, MA: MIT Press.

—— (1998) 'Trauma Studies and the Interdisciplinary: An Overview', in Alex Coles and Alexia Defert (eds), *The Anxiety of Interdisciplinarity*, London: BACKless Books, pp. 157–68.

Foucault, Michel (1970) *The Order of Things: An Archaeology of the Human Sciences*, London: Tavistock.

—— (1972) *The Archaeology of Knowledge*, trans. A.M. Sheridan Smith, London: Tavistock.

—— (1977) *Language, Counter-Memory, Practice: Selected Essays and Interviews*, ed. Donald F. Bouchard, trans. Donald F. Bouchard and Sherry Simon, Ithaca, NY: Cornell University Press.

Foucault, Michel (1979) *Discipline and Punish: The Birth of the Prison*, trans. Alan Sheridan, Harmondsworth: Penguin.

—— (1981) *The Will to Knowledge: The History of Sexuality, Volume 1*, trans. Robert Hurley, Harmondsworth: Penguin.

Frank, Roberta (1988) '"Interdisciplinarity": The First Half Century', in E.G. Stanley and T.F. Hoad (eds), *Words: For Robert Burchfield's Sixty-Fifth Birthday*, Cambridge: D.S. Brewer, pp. 91–101.

Freud, Sigmund ([1915] 1973) 'Introduction', in James Strachey and Angela Richards (eds), *Introductory Lectures on Psychoanalysis*, trans. James Strachey, Harmondsworth: Penguin, pp. 39–49.

—— ([1925] 1986) 'The Resistances to Psychoanalysis', in Albert Dickson (ed.), *Historical and Expository Works on Psychoanalysis*, Harmondsworth: Penguin, pp. 263–73.

Friedan, Betty ([1963] 1992) *The Feminine Mystique*, Harmondsworth: Penguin.

Frow, John (1988) 'Discipline and Discipleship', *Textual Practice*, 2 (3): 307–23.

—— (1995) *Cultural Studies and Cultural Value*, Oxford: Clarendon Press.

Gaddis, William (1976) *JR*, London: Jonathan Cape.

Garber, Marjorie (2007) 'Presidential Address 2006: It Must Change', *PMLA*, 122 (3): 652–62.

Geertz, Clifford (1973) *The Interpretation of Cultures: Selected Essays*, New York: Basic Books.

—— (1983) *Local Knowledge: Further Essays on Interpretive Anthropology*, New York: Basic Books.

Genette, Gérard (1982) *Figures of Literary Discourse*, trans. Alan Sheridan, Oxford: Blackwell.

Graff, Gerald (1989) *Professing Literature: An Institutional History*, Chicago, IL: University of Chicago Press.

—— (1996) 'Is There a Conversation in This Curriculum? Or, Coherence Without Disciplinarity', in James C. Raymond (ed.), *English as a Discipline; or, Is There a Plot in This Play?*, Tuscaloosa, AL: University of Alabama Press, pp. 11–28.

Green, John Richard ([1874] 1915) *A Short History of the English People, Volume One*, London: Dent.

Greenblatt, Stephen (1982) 'Introduction', in S. Greenblatt (ed.), *The Power of Forms in the English Renaissance*, Norman, OK: Pilgrim Books, pp. 3–6.

—— (1985) 'Invisible Bullets: Renaissance Authority and its Subversion', in Jonathan Dollimore and Alan Sinfield (eds), *Political Shakespeare: New Essays in Cultural Materialism*, Manchester: Manchester University Press, pp. 18–47.

—— (1990) *Learning to Curse: Essays in Early Modern Culture*, New York: Routledge.

Gregory, Derek (1994) *Geographical Imaginations*, Oxford: Blackwell.

Hall, Stuart (1980a) 'Cultural Studies and the Centre: Some Problematics and Problems', in Stuart Hall, Dorothy Hobson, Andrew Lowe and Paul Willis (eds), *Culture, Media, Language*, London: Hutchinson, pp. 15–47.

—— (1980b) 'Encoding/Decoding', in Stuart Hall, Dorothy Hobson, Andrew Lowe and Paul Willis (eds), *Culture, Media, Language*, London: Hutchinson, pp. 128–38.

—— (1992) 'Cultural Studies and its Theoretical Legacies', in Lawrence Grossberg, Cary Nelson and Paula Treichler (eds), *Cultural Studies*, New York: Routledge, pp. 277–94.

—— Critcher, Chas, Jefferson, Tony, Clarke, Tony and Roberts, Brian ([1978] 1987) *Policing the Crisis: Mugging, the State, and Law and Order*, Basingstoke: Macmillan.

Hamer, Dean and Copeland, Peter (1995) *The Science of Desire: The Search for the Gay Gene and the Biology of Behaviour*, New York: Simon & Schuster.

Haraway, Donna (1989) *Primate Visions: Gender, Race, and Nature in the World of Modern Science*, New York: Routledge.

—— (1991) *Simians, Cyborgs, and Women: The Reinvention of Nature*, London: Free Association Books.

—— (1997) *Modest_Witness@Second_Millennium.FemaleMan©_Meets_Onco-Mouse™: Feminism and TechnoScience*, New York: Routledge.

Hawking, Stephen (1988) *A Brief History of Time: From the Big Bang to Black Holes*, London: Bantam.

Hewitt, Martin (2001) 'Victorian Studies: Problems and Prospects?', *Journal of Victorian Culture*, 6 (1): 137–61.

Hoggart, Richard ([1957] 1958) *The Uses of Literacy*, Harmondsworth: Penguin.

—— (1970) *Speaking to Each Other, Volume 2: About Literature*, London: Chatto & Windus.

—— (1982) *An English Temper: Essays on Education, Culture and Communications*, London: Chatto & Windus.

—— (1991) *A Sort of Clowning: Life and Times, 1940–1959*, Oxford: Oxford University Press.

Hoskin, Keith (1990) 'Foucault under Examination: The Crypto-Educationalist Unmasked', in Stephen J. Ball (ed.), *Foucault and Education: Disciplines and Knowledge*, London: Routledge, pp. 29–53.

Hough, Graham (1964) 'Crisis in Literary Education', in J.H. Plumb (ed.), *The Crisis in the Humanities*, Harmondsworth: Penguin, pp. 96–109.

Huggan, Graham (2002) 'Postcolonial Studies and the Anxiety of Interdisciplinarity', *Postcolonial Studies*, 5 (3): 245–75.

Irigaray, Luce (1993) *Je, Tu, Nous: Toward a Culture of Difference*, trans. Alison Martin, New York: Routledge.

Jameson, Fredric (1981) *The Political Unconscious: Narrative as a Socially Symbolic Act*, London: Methuen.

Jenkins, Keith (ed.) (1997) *The Postmodern History Reader*, London: Routledge.

Johnson, Richard (1996) 'What Is Cultural Studies Anyway?', in John Storey (ed.), *What Is Cultural Studies? A Reader*, London: Arnold, pp. 75–114.

—— (2001) 'Historical Returns: Transdisciplinarity, Cultural Studies and History', *European Journal of Cultural Studies*, 4 (3): 261–88.

Kant, Immanuel ([1790] 1928) *Critique of Teleological Judgment*, trans. James Creed Meredith, Oxford: Clarendon Press.

—— ([1798] 1992) *The Conflict of the Faculties*, trans. Mary J. Gregor, Lincoln, NB: University of Nebraska Press.

Kerr, Madeline (1958) *The People of Ship Street*, London: Routledge.

Klein, Julie Thompson (1990) *Interdisciplinarity: History, Theory and Practice*, Detroit, MI: Wayne State University Press.

—— (1996) *Crossing Boundaries: Knowledge, Disciplinarities and Interdisciplinarities*, Charlottesville, VA: University Press of Virginia.

Kolocotroni, Vassiliki, Goldman, Jane, and Taxidou, Olga (eds) (1998) *Modernism: An Anthology of Sources and Documents*, Edinburgh: Edinburgh University Press.

Kristeva, Julia (1982) *Powers of Horror: An Essay on Abjection*, trans. Leon S. Roudiez, New York: Columbia University Press.

—— (1984) *Revolution in Poetic Language*, trans. Margaret Waller, New York: Columbia University Press.

—— (1986) 'Women's Time', in Toril Moi (ed.), *The Kristeva Reader*, Oxford: Blackwell, pp. 187–213.

Kuhn, Thomas S. (1970) *The Structure of Scientific Revolutions*, 2nd edn, Chicago, IL: University of Chicago Press.

Lacan, Jacques (1977a) *Écrits: A Selection*, trans. Alan Sheridan, London: Tavistock.

—— (1977b) *The Four Fundamental Concepts of Psycho-Analysis*, ed. by Jacques-Alain Miller, trans. Alan Sheridan, London: Hogarth Press.

LaCapra, Dominick (1989) *Soundings in Critical Theory*, Ithaca, NY: Cornell University Press.

Leavis, F.R. (1948) *Education and the University: A Sketch for an 'English School'*, 2nd edn, London: Chatto & Windus.

—— (1962) *Two Cultures? The Significance of C.P. Snow*, London: Chatto & Windus.

—— (1969) *English Literature in Our Time and the University: The Clark Lectures 1967*, London: Chatto & Windus.

—— (1972) *The Common Pursuit*, Harmondsworth: Penguin.

—— (1975) *The Living Principle: 'English' as a Discipline of Thought*, London: Chatto & Windus.

—— (1982) *The Critic as Anti-Philosopher*, ed. G. Singh, London: Chatto & Windus.

Leavis, F.R. and Thompson, Denys (1933) *Culture and Environment: The Training of Critical Awareness*, London: Chatto & Windus.

Lefebvre, Henri (1991a) *Critique of Everyday Life, Volume 1: Introduction*, trans. John Moore, London: Verso.

—— (1991b) *The Production of Space*, trans. David Nicholson-Smith, Oxford: Blackwell.

Lentricchia, Frank (1980) *After the New Criticism*, London: Athlone.

LeVay, Simon (1994) *The Sexual Brain*, Cambridge, MA: MIT Press.

Liu, Alan (1989) 'The Power of Formalism: The New Historicism', *ELH: English Literary History*, 56 (4): 721–71.

Locke, John ([1689] 1970) *Two Treatises of Government*, Cambridge: Cambridge University Press.

Lyotard, Jean-François (1984) *The Postmodern Condition: A Report on Knowledge*, trans. Geoff Bennington and Brian Massumi, Manchester: Manchester University Press.

MacKillop, Ian (1997) *F.R. Leavis: A Life in Criticism*, London: Penguin.

Marx, Karl, and Engels, Friedrich ([1848] 2002) *The Communist Manifesto*, trans. Samuel Moore, ed. Gareth Stedman Jones, London: Penguin.

Marwick, Arthur (1970) *The Nature of History*, London: Macmillan.

Milner, Andrew (1996) *Literature, Culture and Society*, London: UCL Press.

Moi, Toril (1985) *Sexual/Textual Politics: Feminist Literary Theory*, London: Methuen.

Montrose, Louis (1989) 'Professing the Renaissance: The Poetics and Politics of Culture', in H. Aram Veeser (ed.), *The New Historicism*, New York: Routledge, pp. 15–36.

Moretti, Franco (1988) *Signs Taken for Wonders*, 2nd edn, London: Verso.

Mulhern, Francis (1981) *The Moment of 'Scrutiny'*, London: Verso.

Nietzsche, Friedrich ([1886] 1990) 'We Scholars', in *Beyond Good and Evil: Prelude to a Philosophy of the Future*, trans. R.J. Hollingdale, Harmondsworth: Penguin, pp. 129–46.

Ohmann, Richard (1976) *English in America: A Radical View of the Profession*, New York: Oxford University Press.

Olson, Elder (1952) 'An Outline of Poetic Theory', in R.S. Crane (ed.), *Critics and Criticism: Ancient and Modern*, Chicago, IL: University of Chicago Press, pp. 546–66.

Ortega y Gasset, José ([1932] 1957) *The Revolt of the Masses*, New York: Norton.

Palmer, D.J. (1965) *The Rise of English Studies: An Account of the Study of English Literature from its Origins to the Making of the Oxford English School*, London: Oxford University Press.

Payne, Michael (1993) *Reading Theory: An Introduction to Lacan, Derrida, and Kristeva*, Cambridge, MA: Blackwell.

Pinker, Steven (2000) *Words and Rules: The Ingredients of Language*, London: Phoenix.

Popper, Karl ([1959] 1972) *The Logic of Scientific Discovery*, London: Hutchinson.

—— (1973) *Objective Knowledge: An Evolutionary Approach*, Oxford: Clarendon Press.

Porter, Dennis (1991) *Haunted Journeys: Desire and Transgression in European Travel Writing*, Princeton, NJ: Princeton University Press.

Porter, Roy (1997) *The Greatest Benefit to Mankind: A Medical History of Humanity*, New York: Norton.

Pratt, Mary Louise (1992) *Imperial Eyes: Travel Writing and Transculturation*, New York: Routledge.

Ransom, John Crowe (1938) 'Criticism, Inc.', in *The World's Body*, New York: Scribner's, pp. 327–50.

Readings, Bill (1996) *The University in Ruins*, Cambridge, MA: Harvard University Press.

Reichenbach, Hans (1951) *The Rise of Scientific Philosophy*, Berkeley, CA: University of California Press.

Richards, I.A. (1926) *Principles of Literary Criticism*, 2nd edn, London: Routledge & Kegan Paul.

—— (1935) *Science and Poetry*, 2nd edn, London: Kegan Paul, Trench, Trubner & Co.

Robinson, Eric and Powell, David (eds) (1984) *Oxford Authors: John Clare*, Oxford: Oxford University Press.

Rorty, Richard (1989) *Contingency, Irony and Solidarity*, Cambridge: Cambridge University Press.

—— (1991) *Consequences of Pragmatism: Essays, 1972–80*, Brighton: Harvester.

Rosen, Harold (1981) *Neither Bleak House nor Liberty Hall: English in the Curriculum*, London: Institute of Education.

Said, Edward ([1978] 1995) *Orientalism*, Harmondsworth: Penguin.

Saussure, Ferdinand de ([1916] 1966) *Course in General Linguistics*, ed. by Charles Bally, Albert Sechehaye and Albert Riedlinger, trans. Wade Biskin, New York: McGraw-Hill.

Segal, Lynne (1999) *Why Feminism?*, Cambridge: Polity Press.

Segal, Robert A. (2009) 'Crossing Borders Can Lead to Gold – But So Can Digging Deep', *Times Higher Education*, 18 June: 24–5.

Shelley, Mary ([1818] 1994) *Frankenstein; or, The Modern Prometheus*, ed. by Marilyn Butler, Oxford: Oxford University Press.

Sinfield, Alan (1985) 'Give an Account of Shakespeare and Education', in Jonathan Dollimore and Alan Sinfield (eds), *Political Shakespeare: New Essays in Cultural Materialism*, Manchester: Manchester University Press, pp. 134–57.

—— (1989) *Literature, Politics and Culture in Postwar Britain*, Oxford: Blackwell.

—— (1992) *Faultlines: Cultural Materialism and the Politics of Dissident Reading*, Oxford: Clarendon Press.

—— (1994a) *Cultural Politics – Queer Reading*, London: Routledge.

—— (1994b) *The Wilde Century*, London: Cassell.

Snow, C.P. ([1959] 1993) *The Two Cultures*, Cambridge: Cambridge University Press.

Soja, Edward W. (1989) *Postmodern Geographies: The Reassertion of Space in Critical Social Theory*, London: Verso.

Sokal, Alan (1996a) 'Transgressing the Boundaries: Toward a Transformative Hermeneutics of Quantum Gravity', *Social Text*, 46/47: 217–52.

—— (1996b) 'A Physicist Experiments with Cultural Studies', *Lingua Franca*, (May/June): 62–4.

—— and Bricmont, Jean (1998) *Intellectual Impostures: Postmodern Philosophers' Abuse of Science*, London: Profile.

Sosnoski, James J. (1995) *Modern Skeletons in Postmodern Closets: A Cultural Studies Alternative*, Charlottesville, VA: University Press of Virginia.

Steele, Tom (1997) *The Emergence of Cultural Studies, 1945–1965: Cultural Politics, Adult Education and the English Question*, London: Lawrence & Wishart.

Swartz, David (1997) *Culture and Power: The Sociology of Pierre Bourdieu*, Chicago, IL: University of Chicago Press.

Thompson, E.P ([1963] 1980) *The Making of the English Working Class*, Harmondsworth: Penguin.

—— (1978) *The Poverty of Theory and Other Essays*, London: Merlin Press.

Toulmin, Stephen (1972) *Human Understanding, Volume 1: General Introduction and Part 1*, Oxford: Clarendon Press.

Vico, Giambattista ([1709] 1965) *On the Study Methods of Our Time*, trans. Elio Gianturco, Indianapolis, IN: Bobbs-Merrill.

Warner, Michael (1993) 'Introduction', in M. Warner (ed.), *Fear of a Queer Planet: Queer Politics and Social Theory*, Minneapolis, MN: University of Minnesota Press, pp. vii–xxxi.

Warner, William B. and Siskin, Clifford (2008) 'Stopping Cultural Studies', *Profession*: 94–107.

Wellek, René and Warren, Austin (1949) *Theory of Literature*, London: Jonathan Cape.

White, Hayden (1978) *Tropics of Discourse: Essays in Cultural Criticism*, Baltimore, MD: Johns Hopkins University Press.

—— (1995) 'Response to Arthur Marwick', *Journal of Contemporary History*, 30 (2): 233–46.

Williams, Raymond ([1958] 1961) *Culture and Society, 1780–1950*, Harmondsworth: Penguin.

—— ([1961] 1965) *The Long Revolution*, Harmondsworth: Penguin.

—— (1973) *The Country and the City*, London: Chatto & Windus.

—— ([1976] 1988) *Keywords: A Vocabulary of Culture and Society*, London: Fontana.

—— (1977) *Marxism and Literature*, Oxford: Oxford University Press.

—— (1989) *Resources of Hope: Culture, Democracy, Socialism*, London: Verso.

Willis, Paul (1977) *Learning to Labour: How Working Class Kids Get Working Class Jobs*, London: Saxon House.

Wilson, Edward O. (1978) *On Human Nature*, Cambridge, MA: Harvard University Press.

—— (1980) *Sociobiology: The Abridged Edition*, Cambridge, MA: Harvard University Press.

—— (1994) *The Diversity of Life*, Harmondsworth: Penguin.

—— (1999) *Consilience: The Unity of Knowledge*, London: Abacus.

Wimsatt, W.K. Jr. ([1954] 1970) *The Verbal Icon: Studies in the Meaning of Poetry*, London: Methuen.

Young, Michael and Wilmott, Peter (1957) *Family and Kinship in East London*, London: Routledge.

Zukin, Sharon (1995) *The Cultures of Cities*, Cambridge, MA: Blackwell.

Index

Also available from Routledge

The Routledge Dictionary of Literary Terms

Peter Childs and Roger Fowler

The Routledge Dictionary of Literary Terms is a twenty-first century update of Roger Fowler's seminal *Dictionary of Modern Critical Terms*. Bringing together original entries written by such celebrated theorists as Terry Eagleton and Malcolm Bradbury with new definitions of current terms and controversies, this is the essential reference book for students of literature at all levels. This book includes:

- New definitions of contemporary critical issues such as 'Cyber-criticism' and 'Globalization'.
- An exhaustive range of entries, covering numerous aspects to such topics as genre, form, cultural theory and literary technique.
- Complete coverage of traditional and radical approaches to the study and production of literature.
- Thorough account of critical terminology and analyses of key academic debates.
- Full cross-referencing throughout and suggestions for further reading.

978-0-415-36117-0 (Hbk)
978-0-415-34017-5 (Pbk)
978-0-203-46291-1 (Ebook)

Available at all good bookshops
For ordering and further information please visit:
www.routledge.com

Related titles from Routledge

The Handbook to Literary Research
Second Edition

Edited by Delia da Sousa Correa and W.R. Owens

The Handbook to Literary Research is a practical guide for students embarking on postgraduate work in Literary Studies. It introduces and explains research techniques, methodologies and approaches to information resources, paying careful attention to the differences between countries and institutions, and providing a range of key examples.

This fully updated second edition is divided into five sections which cover:

- tools of the trade – a brand new chapter outlining how to make the most of literary resources
- textual scholarship and book history – explains key concepts and variations in editing, publishing and bibliography
- issues and approaches in literary research – presents a critical overview of theoretical approaches essential to literary studies
- the dissertation – demonstrates how to approach, plan and write this important research exercise
- glossary – provides comprehensive explanations of key terms, and a checklist of resources.

Packed with useful tips and exercises and written by scholars with extensive experience as teachers and researchers in the field, this volume is the ideal handbook for those beginning postgraduate research in literature.

ISBN13: 978-0-415-49732-9 (hbk)
ISBN13: 978-0-415-48500-5 (pbk)
ISBN13: 978-0-203-87333-5 (ebk)

Related titles from Routledge

Doing English
A Guide for Literature Students

Robert Eaglestone

Doing English does English proud.... This is essential reading for
students intending to study English to degree level – and for all
those preparing for the challenges of new AS/A2. – *Adrian Beard,
Gosforth High School*

A valuable, original book. I know of no other that prepares students for
higher education in this way. – *Peter Childs, University of Gloucestershire*

Aimed at students of English Literature in their final year of secondary
education or beginning degrees, this immensely readable book is the ideal
introduction to studying English Literature.

Doing English presents the ideas and debates that shape how we 'do'
English today, covering arguments about the value of literature, the canon,
Shakespeare, theory, politics and the future of the subject.

In his lucid and engaging style, Robert Eaglestone:

- orientates you, examining what it is to 'do English'
- equips you for future study, explaining key ideas and trends in
  English Studies in context
- enables you, bridging the gap between 'traditional' and 'theoretical' approaches to literature.

Practical and provocative, the new third edition of this classic guide is
fully updated, including new material on English assessment objectives
and a new chapter on creative writing.

ISBN13: 978-0-415-49673-5 (hbk)
ISBN13: 978-0-415-49674-2 (pbk)
ISBN13: 978-0-203-09185-2 (ebk)

Available at all good bookshops
For ordering and further information please visit:
www.routledgeliterature.com

Related titles from Routledge

The Cultural Studies Reader
Third Edition

Edited by Simon During

The Cultural Studies Reader is the ideal introduction for students to this exciting discipline. A revised introduction explaining the history and key concerns of cultural studies brings together important articles by leading thinkers to provide an essential guide to the development, key issues and future directions of cultural studies.

This fully updated third edition includes:

- 36 essays including 21 new articles
- an editor's preface succinctly introducing each article with suggestions for further reading
- comprehensive coverage of every major cultural studies method and theory
- an updated account of recent developments in the field
- articles on new areas such as culture and nature and the cultures of globalization
- new key thinkers such as CLR James, Gilles Deleuze, Antonio Negri and Edward Said, included for the first time
- a global appeal – *The Cultural Studies Reader* is designed to be read around the world and deals with issues relevant to each continent.

Essays by:

Theodor Adorno, Benedict Anderson, Arjun Appadurai, Roland Barthes, Simone de Beauvoir, Walter Benjamin, Tony Bennett, Pierre Bourdieu, Judith Butler, Michel de Certeau, Jodi Dean, Gilles Deleuze, Michel Foucault, Nancy Fraser, Paul Gilroy, Antonio Gramsci, Stuart Hall, Donna Haraway, Michael Hardt, Dick Hebdige, Max Horkheimer, C.L.R. James, Fridrich A. Kittler, Eve Kosofsky Sedgwick, Bruno Latour, Teresa de Lauretis, Henri Lefebvre, Justin Lewis, Hau Ling Cheng, Eric Ma, Meaghan Morris, Antonio Negri, Claire Parnet, Russell A. Potter, Janice A. Radway, Edward Said, Gayatri Spivak, Peter Stallybrass, Allon White, Raymond Williams.

ISBN13: 978-0-415-37412-5 (hbk)
ISBN13: 978-0-415-37413-2 (pbk)

Available at all good bookshops
For ordering and further information please visit:
www.routledge.com

Cultural Studies: A Critical Introduction

Simon During

Cultural Studies: A Critical Introduction is a wide-ranging and stimulating introduction to the history and theory of cultural studies from Leavisism, through the era of the Centre for Contemporary Cultural Studies, to the global nature of contemporary cultural studies.

Cultural Studies: A Critical Introduction begins with an introduction to the field and its theoretical history and then presents a series of short essays on key areas of cultural studies, designed to provoke discussion and raise questions. Each thematic section examines and explains a key topic within cultural studies.

Sections include:

- the discipline
- time
- space
- media and the public sphere
- identity
- sexuality and gender
- value.

Cultural Studies: A Critical Introduction will be very useful in classrooms but will also appeal to anyone with an interest in keeping up or familiarising themselves with cultural studies in its contemporary forms.

ISBN13: 978-0-415-24656-9 (hbk)
ISBN13: 978-0-415-24657-6 (pbk)
ISBN13: 978-0-203-01758-6 (ebk)

Related titles from Routledge

Critical Theory Today
Second Edition

Lois Tyson

This new edition of the classic guide offers a thorough and accessible introduction to contemporary critical theory. It provides in-depth coverage of the most common approaches to literary analysis today: feminism, psychoanalysis, Marxism, reader-response theory, new criticism, structuralism and semiotics, deconstruction, new historicism, cultural criticism, lesbian/gay/queer theory, African-American criticism, and postcolonial criticism. The chapters provide an extended explanation of each theory, using examples from everyday life, popular culture, and literary texts; a list of specific questions critics who use that theory ask about literary texts; an interpretation of F. Scott Fitzgerald's *The Great Gatsby* through the lens of each theory; a list of questions for further practice to guide readers in applying each theory to different literary works; and a bibliography of primary and secondary works for further reading.

This book can be used as the only text in a course or as a precursor to the study of primary theoretical works. It motivates readers by showing them what critical theory can offer in terms of their practical understanding of literary texts and in terms of their personal understanding of themselves and the world in which they live. Both engaging and rigorous, it is a 'how-to' book for undergraduate and graduate students new to critical theory and for college professors who want to broaden their repertoire of critical approaches to literature.

ISBN 13: 978-0-415-97409-7 (hbk)
ISBN 13: 978-0-415-97410-3 (pbk)

Available at all good bookshops
For ordering and further information please visit:
www.routledgeliterature.com

Related titles from Routledge

Routledge Critical Thinkers
Series Editor: Robert Eaglestone, Royal Holloway, University of London

Routledge Critical Thinkers is designed for students who need an accessible introduction to the key figures in contemporary critical thought. The books provide crucial orientation for further study and equip readers to engage with each theorist's original texts.

The volumes in the Routledge Critical Thinkers series place each key theorist in his or her historical and intellectual contexts and explain:

- why he or she is important
- what motivated his/her work
- what his/her key ideas were
- who and what influenced the thinker

- who and what the thinker has influenced
- what to read next and why.

Featuring extensively annotated guides to further reading, Routledge Critical Thinkers is the first point of reference for any student wishing to investigate the work of a specific theorist.

'These little books are certainly helpful study guides. They are clear, concise and complete. They are ideal for undergraduates studying for exams or writing essays and for lifelong learners wanting to expand their knowledge of a given author or idea.' – Beth Lord, *THES*

'This series demystifies the demigods of theory.' – Susan Bennett, University of Calgary

Available in this series:

Available at all good bookshops
For further information on individual books in the series, visit:
www.routledge.com/literature/rct/